A VOYAGE TO THE SEA

A VOYAGE
TO THE SEA

Denis Gorman

Matador
9 Priory Business Park,
Wistow Road, Kibworth Beauchamp,
Leicestershire. LE8 0RX
Tel: 0116 279 2299
Email: books@troubador.co.uk
Web: www.troubador.co.uk/matador
Twitter: @matadorbooks

ISBN 9781785899744

British Library Cataloguing in Publication Data.
A catalogue record for this book is available from the British Library.

Typeset in 11pt Aldine by Troubador Publishing Ltd, Leicester, UK
Printed in the UK by TJ International, Padstow, Cornwall

Matador is an imprint of Troubador Publishing Ltd

For Dad and his Grandchildren.

The following story is true.

The names of the characters behind Jessica Jane Pember and her parents Lionel and Ann have been changed. This is purely for purposes of anonymity.

Contents

One   First Light   1

Two   The South Atlantic   33

Three   Tides of Fortune   105

Four   The Azores   133

Five   Newport Rhode Island   187

Appendices
Finisher results   277
The remaining challengers   286
Some accounts from our first gale   288

Acknowledgements

It is said that, in order to write a good book, a prospective author needs to surround himself with good people. It was only in completing my first draft of '*A Voyage to the Sea*' that I understood the true meaning of this. I am indebted to my fellow JC, Roger Taylor, author of '*Voyages of a Simple Sailor*', for his constructive advice and editorial assistance of the original manuscript. This proved invaluable.

I also needed to test the manuscript and I'm indebted to my kind friends who read it at various stages of its pre-edited finish. From this, I was able to better determine the definition and shape of the finished article and to decide on the level of technical description that, for instance, a non-sailor might stand. I'm indebted to Cavan Durney, Grantham Burgess, Bente Beining, Tony Banks, Ellen Morton, Simon Jamieson and especially, Diana Moon. Their patience, encouragement and unsentimental feedback, caused me many sleepless nights but disciplined me sufficiently to rework and reconstruct the many inadequacies of the original text.

To the same Tony Banks I am also indebted for his photographic work which included the reconstruction of many old pictures.

I reserve a special mention to my dear friend Stan Snape. It was his former boat that took me across the Atlantic, and it was he who helped me, to prepare the boat, and to set myself up psychologically for the coming voyage. I doubt that I could have done it without him....The same is true of this book.

As I look upon this finished product I realise that family, adventure and friendships are what makes life worth living... what makes it all worth the candle. You are born to a family and have little choice in what you're dealt. But if you should ever undertake to fulfil a dream or an adventure of your own, then I hope, like me, you will be as blessed as I have been, with such good friends.

Denis Gorman

ONE

First Light

1

Exercise caution in your business affairs; for the world is full of trickery. But let this not blind you to what virtue there is; many persons strive for high ideals; and everywhere life is full of heroism.

Max Ehrmann 1927

My story starts in Glasgow in the early 1960's. My earliest memories are of my mother, Olga, the terror of my life, flying into a chaotic rage and lashing into us with a wooden spoon, attacking our father and being restrained on our living room floor until she calmed down. My father, John, was the hero; he always saved us.

The fact that I was ever born at all was due to the stubborn Catholic determination ingrained in my parents to make their impossible marriage work.

I was the youngest of three children, born within the first hour of April Fool's day, 1st April 1961. My sister, Maureen, was my elder by five years and my brother, Edward, by three. Whilst I was still an infant, my mother returned to her hometown of Naples in her native Italy, ostensibly to attend her father's funeral. She stayed there for six months, leaving Dad to look after the three of us. Whilst he was out at work, Maureen and Eddie became latchkey kids, taken in by kindly neighbours and I was looked after by our Gran.

Olga made out that her mother was on the cusp of life

and death and her presence was ever needed at her side. Dad repeatedly begged her to return home but Olga continually resisted his pleadings. Only when he himself flew out to Italy, was he able to persuade her to come back to Glasgow, to her marriage and her kids. It was a mistake.

It must have been clear to all but Dad that his marriage to Olga would never fly. The relationship was doomed to disaster and, sure enough, before too long she was on her way again and Dad was left with the three of us.

It would later be discovered that Olga's mother had died three months before her father's funeral. The whole cock-and-bull story was concocted to cover up an affair with an American serviceman. Olga had only returned because she'd been dumped by the Yank and was effectively out of cash.

Our father had excellent grounds to sue for divorce and custody of his children but he believed that, first, he had to do the right thing by his faith. He asked the church for an annulment to his marriage, citing amongst other things, his wife's infidelity with the American. The church listened sympathetically to the pleadings of this sincere Catholic man and agreed, without reservation, that he should be granted the annulment he wanted.

The terms of the annulment were spelled-out... 'It is a marriage that never was'... because...' The true Christian spirit was not entered into by the offending party'... They decreed... 'You will be free to marry again'... 'In Catholic faith and in a Catholic Church'... 'Your character is unblemished.'

The fly in the ointment was the declaration that it was, 'A marriage that never was'. This would mean that in the eyes of the church, Maureen, Eddie and I would be illegitimate, bastards no less.

Dad could not accept this. Whatever happened to him, he had to ensure that his children would have the chance of remaining within the kingdom of God and respected by the society that we were born into. He now turned to the courts and sued for a legal separation and custody. But these things take time and, left with three children and no wife, Dad found it impossible to cope. He had a job to hold down and our Gran was too unwell to look after us. It was an agonising decision but he had to hand us into Smilum, a Catholic orphanage in Falkirk.

We lived there for six months and I remember much of this as clear as day. Because of my young age, I was placed into a girl's ward. I can picture the blond haired girl who slept in the adjacent bed. She was pretty, but always looked so sad. The nuns, who were cheerful and kind, seemed to have a purpose and goodness flowing from them that you could see and almost feel.

It was here in Smilum that I had my first ever adventure; I went searching for Maureen and Eddie and, after negotiating two security doors and a long colonnade that separated the senior and junior parts of the complex, I found them playing together in a hall full of older kids. They recognised me and we sat for a while not quite knowing what to do. My presence was causing a bit of a stir. Other children gathered round. Some were laughing. I knew it wouldn't last and, sure enough, a kindly flustered nun tracked me down and with the gentlest chastisement, picked me up and took me back to where I belonged.

I don't ever remember Mother coming to visit, although I later found out that she did so once. Within minutes, for some reason, she slapped my brother across the face and was subsequently thrown out by the nuns.

Unbeknown to me, behind the scenes, a legal battle was well underway and firmly in the media spotlight. My mother was suing for maintenance and custody of the children she had abandoned. Father was trying to keep us, for our own safety, with him.

A psychiatrist gave evidence and said that they did not know whether my mother was mad, bad or misunderstood. The judge concluded that, from his perspective, he could not believe a word that came out of her mouth; he did, however, find my father to be an honourable man and described him as a, 'highly credible witness'.

When Lord Leechman awarded in favour of our father, it was an extremely rare occurrence, one, in fact, that made Scottish legal history. The Scottish newspapers carried it as a leading story. Father, however, would need to pay maintenance to his estranged wife whilst carrying the sole financial burden of his children. It would be tough but John now had a clear track to take his children home.

Occasionally, Dad visited us at Smilum. He always brought presents and he was always kind. We would hug him and ask, 'When can we leave... when can we visit Gran...?

Please don't let Olga come and get us...'

I was favoured, because I was the youngest, so my father occasionally took me home to Gran for the weekend and short breaks. Gran was Dad's mum. Visiting her was the greatest joy of my life. With her was my Granddad (Edward senior) and my Uncle Edward (Dad's brother) who was crippled from birth and had never left home.

I can remember them spoiling me and making such a fuss whenever I came to stay. At the end of these visits, Dad and I took the long multiple bus journeys back to Smilum and, on these journeys, I would ask the question, 'Dad, when can we go and live with Gran forever?' to which he assured me, 'Someday son, try to be patient...'

I held his hand and said no more.

During this time further stresses would play on my family. Granddad, who had been disabled and in poor health for much of his life, passed away in his sleep, and Gran went on to suffer a short-term nervous breakdown. All this in the midst of Dad's troubles.

In the meantime, Smilum and its dutiful nuns continued to look after us.

Then one day, I remember, it was a grey cold day, the kind of day that captures your breath and turns it into mist that nips your ears and fingers, we were on our way to Gran's house again, just me and Dad. He seemed tense. There was no jubilation or joy, just a purposeful man holding the hand of a very small boy whilst we waited for the bus. I fidgeted and then asked the question, the same question that I always asked, 'Dad, are we going to visit Gran today?' to which he replied. 'Yes, that's right son.'

After a few moments I went on to the next predictable question, 'Are we going for a little while or can we stay there forever?'

He turned, and looking at me without any expression, he simply said. 'This time we are going to stay forever.'

He looked straight ahead again and, so did, I but I could hardly believe what I had heard. It must be true. Dad always told the truth. It was a sin to tell a lie.

My heart soared with joy but I couldn't speak. I felt butterflies in my stomach and a swelling in my chest and a flush of heat rush to my cheeks but, still, I couldn't speak. I wanted to run and jump and shout but I didn't, somehow Dad's expression forbade it. I was too afraid to move or to ask the question again in case I got a different answer.

I stood there facing forward with a trembling throat and my eyes bloated with moisture. I felt Dad's hand. I pressed it firmly and a reassuring pressure came back. We stood there silently facing forward together, waiting for the bus.

I remember this, as the happiest moment of my life.

2

We moved into Gran's tenement flat at Ravenscraig Drive and, shortly after that, to a newly built property at 29 Priesthill Road where Maureen and Eddie were able to join us. Our new home was in a block of six flats with another identical block attached, so that the whole block housed 12 families with two independent entrances. Our flat had two bedrooms, a hallway, a bathroom, kitchenette and the living room. We also had a small veranda which is typical of so many Glasgow tenement buildings.

Now, together again and released from Smilum, we had a new home and we three children loved it.

Six of us lived here. Gran and Maureen shared one room and Uncle Eddie and I, with Dad and Brother Ed, shared the other. The boys' room had two parallel sets of bunk beds. I had the top bunk and Uncle Ed had the one under me. Dad slept on the top one opposite and Brother Ed slept under him. In the corner of our room, stood a small table with a small vice attached. There were small boxes of hooks, threads of coloured wool, glue and feathers on the table. Here, Uncle Eddie would spend a couple of hours each day whipping and turning bare hooks into colourful and intricate flies for fly-fishing. When sufficient numbers had been gathered, he would sell them to a wholesaler in the city.

Uncle Ed was the most unusual and entertaining of us all.

He was 4'10", pigeon chested, crippled from birth and afflicted with brittle bones. He needed metal callipers with kneepads and special boots to be drawn up around his legs in order for him to walk and this he did with the aid of a stick. Uncle Ed could walk for a short distance but he had never been able to run or swim, and never would. Of all the people that I have ever known, my Uncle Eddie remains the most inspiring. With disabilities that would make many people baulk, he always found the practicality and optimism to achieve things. He never felt sorry for himself and had a great sense of fun and humour.

He excelled at Chess and was an avid book reader and storyteller. He presided over the Monopoly board on Saturday mornings when all the kids from our block dropped in for a game. He was notorious for his practical jokes. Water pistols, stink bombs and funny gorilla masks. A big kid at heart. He tormented my poor Gran who would scold him as being 'Worse than all the kids put together.'

That being said, Gran was fun too. She was good in company and people always seemed to enjoy coming to our house. My enduring memories of Gran are of her happily singing along with her favourite Patsy Cline or Jim Reeves records whilst pottering around the house. She was house proud and was often cleaning and cooking, but never too busy to tell us stories, or what the words of her favourite songs meant.

Dad was solid and content although he spent a lot of time at work. He was a telephone engineer. He was proud of his work and sounded so important whenever he talked about his job. Dad was also very practical and could turn his hand to anything, especially if it meant saving money. He decorated our house from top to bottom and fitted the carpets. When our old sofa collapsed, he made a new one from an old mattress, plywood and a bolt of orange vinyl material that he got from a factory which was closing down. The instructions came from a library book. It turned out to be an excellent, albeit a rather garish, piece of furniture.

After that he made a new fireplace - with glowing orange lights and plate-glass tiles. Our living room looked like an orange palace! Dad was also a keen cook and would make us exotic food such as Pizza and Spaghetti Bolognaise, cuisine that, in the mid 1960's, other kids had never heard of.

Some time after we moved to Priesthill Road there came a great event. The Government gave our Uncle Ed a car. A car, no less! It was a three wheel mobility car, light blue and made from glass fibre. It was quite unlike any car that I had ever seen before. It was steered with a motorbike-type bar which had a clutch lever and twist throttle on one end and a hinge, which led into a steering box, at the other. Here, at the box end, you could select and work through four gears which wound the car to a top speed of 40mph.

The vehicle was for one person only and therefore had only one seat for the driver, but the Gorman family had other ideas - 'To hell with the rules.' In no time at all, we fitted a little stool beside the driver's seat and Uncle Ed would frequently take one of us out for a run. Try as we might, we found it impossible to fit in two passengers. But we did succeed in squeezing in our dog, a great beast, half Labrador and half black Alsatian. A great result.

I can honestly say that the years between Smilum when I was four, until I was 10 were among the happiest of my whole life. It was here that my early character was formed, somewhat intense, definite in the rules of right and wrong, down to earth working class with an almost neurotic affection for my family.

We three children prospered. Maureen became really pretty and never held back in voicing her opinions, as young girls often do. Gran would say... 'When Maureen is happy, the whole world is happy and when she is sad, the whole world knows about it.'

My brother Eddie did well at school. That being said, he was a bullish lad who'd rather go through a problem than around it. He was easily the most academic of all of us three.

As for myself, I never had a care in the world. I was blissfully happy. I was, without doubt, the most adventurous of us all. I loved to wander and take off for long bike rides. I would dream of visiting the wilderness, to live amongst the wild animals and to explore. Uncle Eddie and I would talk about this for hours and together we would trundle down to the library in his peculiar little car for books to fuel our fantasy.

There was, however, one thing that interested me more than any other. On Saturday mornings, in eager anticipation, we would tune in to episodes of 'Jacques Cousteau and the Silent World', a television documentary that followed Capt. Jacques, his crew, all Frenchmen, and their ship, 'Calypso'as they risked their lives to develop sub- aqua diving techniques and to explore the underwater world. I was mesmerised. They made the World look exciting and wonderful. They wore little red woolly hats as a sign of their camaraderie. They dived on wrecks, flooded caves, ancient cities that had sunk beneath the sea. They even found treasure! They ate food I had never heard of, like squid and lobsters. They swam with sharks and whales. They did everything that I ever wanted to do. One Saturday morning, after a particularly good episode, I stood up in front of the whole family and announced, 'When I grow up, I'm going to be a diver.'

They looked at me and then burst into laughter. We lived in Priesthill. We were poor and working class. We didn't have any money and 'you', they said, were never likely to earn enough to live that kind of life.

To my young mind, it all seemed so simple and the rebuttal, however humorous, hurt my pride and feelings.

When the laughter settled down and I had subsided miserably, Gran took me to one side. She cupped her hand on my face, raised my head and while looking into my eyes said, 'You hold onto your dream, son, and always remember... you can be anything you want to be if you put your mind to it'. With these simple words my Gran sowed the seeds of a philosophy in me; things didn't have to stay the same forever - a strong heart, a touch of courage and a dream, really could change my life. I came to realise that the first and most important thing was to have a dream. And the second was that I must never let anyone take it from me.

3

The World, as seen through a child's eyes, is very different from the adult world. Sooner or later, the strain and pressure of three adults and three growing children sharing a tiny flat, were bound to tell. The fact that we had six happy years living together in these cramped quarters is, to my mind, a remarkable thing.

Gran's health began to deteriorate. Sometimes she would be ordered to bed for days on end and was taken to hospital for what Dad called 'A woman's operation'. I noticed Dr Cowen coming and going and packets of pills being left. Unbeknown to me, she had suffered a heart attack. Also, her having been a lifetime smoker, emphysema was taking its toll on her lungs and in time, her excursions from the house would become less and less frequent.

Dad's time was divided between work and home. He had no hobbies that I knew of and if he did, he had neither the time nor money to pursue them. He was a modest drinker, never visited the pub and had no girlfriends until, when I was 10, he met Margaret. She was the daughter of one of Gran's friends, herself divorced with four children, all older than Maureen, Eddie and I. Dad was nothing if not romantic and, I suppose, in Margaret he saw the possibility of a new partner in life.

He began to spend more and more time around Margaret's house while leaving the burdens of our own home to fall increasingly upon our ill Gran and Uncle Ed. We children became aware of low-voiced disagreements taking place behind closed doors… always behind closed doors. Tensions increased, as the arguments became more frequent, until one Saturday morning, it came to a head. Storming out of Gran's room, determined and red faced, Dad called the three of us together and announced, 'Pack your bags, we're leaving.'

Maureen was directed to present herself at Margaret's house while Dad, Brother Ed and I, with our clothes stuffed into suitcases, began the long and heavy three mile walk to our Aunt Betty's home. It was a surreal experience. Dad was fraught and worked up, with deep furrowed lines on his forehead. Brother Ed and I went along obediently without understanding any of it. I remember Brother Ed asking, 'Dad, can we get a taxi or a bus or something?' to which our flustered father replied, 'No, we can't, I've got no money, just keep walking.'

Some people might find it strange that we left without tears or objections. In truth, it didn't seem so serious at the time. Besides, Dad was always our Dad. He had been our salvation and had saved us from Olga. We would have followed him anywhere, even to the ends of the Earth.

In fact, we followed him to another overcrowded flat. Our Aunt Betty was Dad's sister. She and our Uncle Tommy had three daughters and a new-born baby son. This new situation meant that all together, three adults, five children, a new-born baby and a large dog shared one toilet, a small kitchenette, a living room and three bedrooms!

It was a particularly hot summer that year and sharing a bed with my brother was one of the most miserable experiences I can recall.

4

In due course Dad and Margaret got married. The excited couple went off to Edinburgh and, after a quiet private ceremony, the new Mr and Mrs Gorman emerged. I wasn't at the wedding, none of us was. It was just Dad, his new bride and two witnesses who acted as best man and bridesmaid, all rolled into one. After the event, the four of them went for a meal, then Dad and his new wife had a night in a posh Edinburgh hotel before they returned to Priesthill on the following day.

Upon their return, we moved into number 73 Priesthill Road, a ground floor maisonette, just down the road from Gran and Uncle Ed. We had not seen them since our dramatic departure so on the occasion of our first visit, Dad insisted that we put on our Sunday best before we walked, rather formally up the hill to No 29. Gran was expecting us but was in bed, ordered there for her own good by Dr Cowen. At first there was an awkward atmosphere between Dad and the Old Girl but after a few moments, things soon brightened up. Gran shed a couple of tears and hugged and kissed us. I couldn't understand why they had fallen out but at least we were together again.

★

As we settled into our new home, Dad set to work again. In the kitchenette, which was never designed to have a dining area, our ever resourceful father built a narrow table with two seating benches. We would huddle around it as if it were a proper dining room. In the living room, he re-built the fireplace. This time, he built a bookcase into it and finished it off with miniature blue rectangular tiles. Unlike Gran's fireplace, this one had no backlight illuminations, but even so, it was a grand piece of work.

Margaret turned out to be a strong-willed and domineering woman, a real handful. She said her piece as and when she saw fit to say it. She thought that our Gran had been too soft. It was her opinion that we children had been mollycoddled and that her new husband needed to let go of his Mother's apron strings.

The loving home we had had with Gran, where we were loved for the sake of love, wanted and cherished more than things or money, where we rejoiced in simply having each other and in being a family, was gone.

But Margaret was not without her vices and weaknesses. Among my regular chores of cleaning and going to shops for groceries, I would be sent to buy Askit powders, a white powdered painkiller that came as a packet of three, which she would crave for. She was also a heavy smoker, addicted to both painkillers and nicotine, a condition that she would never rid herself of.

Her favourite saying was, 'A pound in your pocket is the best friend you will ever have'. Consequently, Brother Eddie and I were encouraged to take up part-time jobs.

'Earn your own pocket money,' she said.

I was only 10 when I started work for a local dry cleaning company. Bundled in a van with other roughneck kids, we were driven around the 'schemes' then sent out to run and knock.

'Any dry cleaning?'

The most common answer was a straight forward, 'No thanks.'

Other times it might be.

'I told you lot last week that I didn't want any dry cleaning. Why don't you listen? I'm trying to watch telly... you're spoiling my programme. If you come again, I'm gonna put the dog on you!'

Every now and again it was a 'Yes' and, with that, a heavy garment would be shrouded upon me and off I would run, to catch up with the van before it moved too far up the street. Each garment which we brought in, marked up a small commission...pocket money...hard earned.

Trouble was never far away. It was a rough business in a rough area and before too long Eddie, being Eddie, got into a fight with one of the other lads. My brother got the blame and was sacked. The offended lad whispered threateningly to me. 'As soon as he's gone I'm going to get to know you better.'

I never went back either.

We were still expected to work, so we moved on to delivering evening newspapers. This worked well enough for perhaps two years but the threat of trouble and violence was ever present. I got bitten in the face by a dog and we both got into so many fights that we eventually opted to take up morning paper rounds. Here, the world was quiet with no thuggish teenagers trying to take your money, nor dogs guarding their turf.

Our house became the central distribution point where the papers were dropped off. We would get up at 4.30 in the morning to meet the van, sort out the bundles for other kids, lay those around our porch, then set off on our runs. I had about 40 papers, Ed had about the same. Upon my return, I would normally be able to get back to bed for an hour or so before rising again for school. All this met with Margaret's approval...

As soon as our earning increased, the screw was tightened and we were made to buy our own clothes.

But Margaret was no less sparing of her own children and, within a year, her remaining two daughters chose to move out. Then, just before her 16th birthday, Maureen left school and started work as a machinist in a clothing factory. By now, she was showing an increasing contempt for Margaret; vicious arguments would break out frequently, whilst Dad looked on helplessly, torn between his wife and children.

One evening, Eddie, Maureen, Dad and I were sitting around our skinny dining table. Another foul argument between Margaret and Maureen had only just settled down and our evening meal was about to be served; Margaret hovered between the cooker and sink, banging and crashing her plates and pots and scooping dollops of mashed potatoes from pot to plate to be followed with other unappetising gloop. Her wrath was simmering briskly, barely contained, when a knock was heard at the front door. She barked, 'Go and answer it!'

Wearily, Dad did as he was told. We remained still without uttering a word. We heard him open the door and give a gasp as a familiar voice demanded, 'Where is she?'

Footsteps came towards us up the hall. Dad's voice could be heard saying quietly, pleadingly, 'Please don't interfere'.

Margaret stopped what she was doing and turned. Maureen, tearful and miserable continued to stare at the table, but Ed and I were heads up and fully aware. As we stared at the door, Gran and Uncle Eddie came into view with our fraught and worried Dad trailing behind them.

There was a stunned silence.

Gran's face was white, her breath short. It was rare nowadays to see her out of the house and rarer still to see her walk more than a few yards. She came forward to my sister and said,

'Maureen get up hen…You are coming to live with us.'

Maureen stood. Her eyes were still staring at the table. She recognised the voice but I doubt that she had any idea of what was going on. She had a look of profound sadness, a pretty girl who was lost and miserable. Gran moved forward, wrapped a reassuring arm around her granddaughter, and without inviting any discussion, the three of them, Gran, Maureen and Uncle Eddie turned and left.

Now, some might say that the greatest moment in sporting history was in 1976, when Archie Gemmill scored a World Cup qualifying goal for Scotland against Holland, or in 1966 when Glasgow Celtic was the first British club to win the European Cup. But for me and Ed, the performance of our Grandma on that day topped the lot. After so much kow towing and submission to this domineering miserly bitch, of watching our Dad pussyfoot around her, here, at last, was a Gorman who would fight. Now it seemed that anything was possible. Margaret had been beaten by the Old Girl. Now, maybe, Dad would see the light and we could all escape from this hellish existence.

As we settled around our table, Margaret festered ominously. Dad looked pale and ashen. Eddie and I ate quickly and silently but we had seen with our own eyes what had happened, and we were both brimming with pride.

★

So Maureen was home and dry and living happily at number 29 again whilst Eddie and I continued to live at number 73 with Dad and Margaret. To my disappointment, Dad never took up the lead that Gran had offered and, in the years that followed, we struggled on.

We called Margaret 'Ma' and went through the motions of being Dad's Pollyanna family. The resentments were covered and compromises were made and so, in a fashion, things moved along - but it was a miserable place and particularly hard on my brother Ed. He was young and strong, honest and painfully proud. He would never back down from a fight but he could not defend himself from the sneering derision that Margaret would frequently aim at him.

Even when the whole family came together for Christmases and birthdays and such like, there was always an underlying strain.

I began to resent my father for allowing this situation to continue and I hated my stepmother. I became withdrawn; my school grades were terrible and I convinced myself that I would have no future at all after I left school. I became a teenager and began to notice the pretty girls who were growing into beautiful young women all around me. But I felt increasingly awkward and hopelessly disconnected from the courtships that were beginning to form for other young people of my age.

I began to see Priesthill as it really was - a bleak and soulless place, a land of slab sided tenement buildings covered with mindless graffiti, communal backyards with concrete bunkers that housed dustbins set in a scrape of turf and mud. It was pointless to keep a garden in these areas as they were quickly trampled over. Empty flats were prone to arson and the Council quickly boarded these up with plywood. Dogs roamed the streets with neither a leash nor a proud owner in sight. Dog fouling was everywhere.

Everyone was friendly enough although there was a distinct sectarian divide. In Priesthill you were either a Catholic or Protestant, and bigoted passions could be inflamed and insults exchanged, when 'Faith' was brought to the fore. That being said, there was remarkable restraint, especially when compared to Northern Ireland.

A general code of conduct prevailed where you were expected to give and receive respect. 'Be courteous, but don't talk about religion because you may insult someone by mistake'. However, that rule mainly applied to the adult world. At school it was very different. When our local schools kicked out, violence and gang warfare kicked in. Opposing schools were forced to adopt different exit times to reduce the likelihood of a clash. Fighting and violence were commonplace and here the rules were quite simple; 'Don't look for trouble and don't start it. But if someone starts on you, then give a good account of yourself... remember, if you hurt someone who picks on you, he will think twice before bothering you again.'

I often thought, 'Why do we live in this place, why do we live like this? Surely Dad could move us on from here? He has a good job, he could build a house if he put his mind to it.'

It was during this time, when I was about 13, that I went to the library and, quite by chance, picked up the book 'My Lively Lady' written by Sir Alec Rose. It was unlike any book that I had ever read before. It told the story of how Sir Alec, a seemingly ordinary chap, a greengrocer, had sailed his own little boat, alone, around the world. This simple adventurous tale had a profound effect on me. From then on, in the early mornings, during the winter months with gales blowing through the deserted streets, delivering newspapers for pennies whilst the whole of the community slept, I saw myself as a lone traveller. My paper run was my imaginary voyage, and on this voyage, I was alone with my thoughts and dreams and those dreams were always of *escape*.

I would try to imagine Sir Alec sailing on through dark and blustery conditions like this. His boat, his comfortable home, would carry him through to warm and wonderful places. He didn't need to pay rent or hold down a mediocre job. He met wonderful people. He ate good food, and he had a wonderful wife. Sir Alec's life was full of courage and adventure. His life was sublime.

I dreamt of saving enough money to buy a boat and sail away from the drudgery of my existence. Once I had learnt how to sail, I would teach other people then, with the income,

I could buy a house away from Priesthill, a place by the sea where Gran and Uncle Eddie could live. And if Dad should ever leave Margaret, he could join us too.

I told John Gillen all about the book and my romantic notion of becoming a yachtsman. John Gillen was my best friend. We had met on our very first day at school. He was from a large family, mum, Dad, and seven children who lived in a 3 bedroom flat in the adjacent tenement building. Although his house was crowded and had the usual measure of family strain, it was a happy home.

In all things I trusted and confided in John and he in me. We were like two peas in a pod, always up to explore the world around us or get into mischief. We found things to do in the barren streets of Priesthill and when we finally managed to get bicycles, we explored the city, then beyond the city to Loch Lomond, Greenock and Gourock, camping and youth hostelling. When John's sister married a soldier, we cycled to Mid-Caulder near Edinburgh to visit her.

John was more level-headed than I, more inclined to see the realistic limitations behind my daydreams. He was not the type to go off sailing around the World but after he had read the book, I was surprised when he agreed that it was, for me, 'A great idea!'

I got more sailing books from the library, Eric Tabarly, Francis Chichester and Clare Francis. I read and developed an insatiable interest and, as I did, my knowledge grew.

As the next couple of years passed by, I shared my plans and ideas with Gran. She had a liking for Honeydew melon and, as a treat, I often took along a half melon which we would share. With Uncle Ed and Maureen out of the way, I would talk of my plans, sitting on a chair beside her bed, both of us with soft, sweet, cool melon dripping through our fingers.

'Now don't tell anyone about our plans Gran, not until we're ready…'

It was like a conspiracy and she, like the lady she was, played along with every notion I ever had. I had solutions for everything including her health problems.

I instructed her. 'Now Gran we need to get you better. You need to stop smoking and if you could do a little bit of exercise every day, you can have a good life till you're about 90.'

Gran would eye me suspiciously and say, 'I don't want to stop smoking. It's the only pleasure I have left'.

Worrying that I might hide her cigarettes, she made me promise that I never would. We then made a compromise agreement that she would try and cut down at least one or two ciggies a day. Whenever I checked her progress, I always found that there had been no progress.

Gran would never stop smoking.

During our conversations, I frequently asked Gran about her life. She was the youngest of six children and the only girl. She was the last surviving member of her family. She told me about her older brothers, all of whom had fought in the First World War. I had met some of them and was always interested to hear their stories. She talked about her first baby, James, who died in his cot age 6 months, and of how she had worked in the ammunition factories at Clydebank during the Second World War.

One day I asked her, 'How did you get over all these losses - your parents, brothers and baby James?'

She thought about it for a few moments, then simply said, 'Life goes on, son, life goes on.' Then she added. 'You must turn to life again Denis...'

I remember thinking that it seemed rather a strange thing to say. The word 'must' was out of context, and the way she looked at me was pained. I knew that Gran was ill, but I always believed that she would get better and convinced myself that she would be with us for a long time. She was only 65 years old.

★

It was in January, in the midst of a cold, wet Scottish winter that Gran passed away in her sleep just days away from her 66th birthday. I was bewildered and, in my grief, I turned to Gran's dearest friend, Beatrice, and said, 'She was so young and had so much to live for.'

Beatrice put her hand on my shoulder and kindly but honestly replied, 'No son, that's not the way of it. Your Gran was worn out and tired of life…'

At first, to my young, hopeful, and immature mind, that had seemed like a betrayal - for Beatrice to say such a thing. But I soon realised that I had indeed been fooling myself. It had been obvious to everyone, or at least to all of the adults and indeed, Gran herself, that she had been coming to the end of her days. She would never see my dreams come to fruition, never see my house by the sea, yet all the while … I had never understood, never wanted to comprehend that what Beatrice had said was true. And the truth hurt.

Now it was my turn to suffer loss and Gran's words made sense.

'You must turn to life again Denis …'

5

'Life goes on,' she had said, and so it did. At first I didn't want it to. I wanted to die. At the age of 15, I suddenly felt weary of the world but I was too young to give up and the pull of life was too strong. I went through episodes of guilt, I told myself that deep down I was relieved that Gran was gone because it was easier for me to get on with my life without worrying about her. I felt guilty that I had not visited her more often. During confession Father Walsh contradicted my thought, saying that it was the Devil in me, trying to make me feel terrible.

'We must never forget that Satan is like a hungry lion roaming around you and waiting to devour you at the first sign of weakness.'

His words were kind.

★

Within the next 18 months Maureen got married and left Uncle Ed's house to be with her new husband. Brother Ed wasted no time in suggesting that he should take her place at No 29 and, within a week, he was gone. I envied Brother Ed; so, Uncle Eddie, realising my want and the relative unfairness of it, would pick me up quite regularly and take me out for a treat. This was usually a Chinese meal or a visit to the cinema. I dreamed that someday I would live with Uncle Eddie after brother Ed had moved out.

An unexpected consequence of this latest movement was that life at Dad's house became much more tolerable. Indeed, there were periods of extended pleasantness; Margaret didn't seem to mind or resent me in the way that she did with Ed and Maureen and I, in return, tried to be helpful and accommodating. Margaret and John began to look like a reasonably happy couple.

I continued to dream of sailing and decided that, when I'd left school, I would join the Navy. There I could learn a trade, learn about the sea and earn some money to buy a boat.

My first inclination was to join the Merchant Navy, however, the industry was changing shape and the whole of the British Merchant Marine was suffering such decline that no opportunities at all seemed possible. That left the Royal Navy as my only remaining choice.

As soon as I turned 16, I applied to join as a ship's cook. I decided on catering, in part because of its creative manual nature and the satisfaction of producing something that others could enjoy but, more so, because it seemed like an easier thing to get into, especially with my poor education.

The entry exam included a number of tests: Basic English and Maths, mechanical recognition, a medical exam, and then an interview. After the first test had finished, I was drawn aside and taken into a small interview room where the Warrant Officer told me,

'Your education is just not acceptable...You can't even spell the word 'Chef'...you have spelled it as 'Chief'!'

I was turned down. I had failed the entry exams. It was a crushing blow.

It was my first ever experience of the brusque directness of military men - blunt and straight to the point, without soft soap. I was invited to leave the building and, as I did, I could see the other candidates going through for the next process of their application. My feelings of inadequacy made my heart ache. As I walked the seven miles from the City Centre, I even entertained the fanciful thought of throwing myself off King George V Bridge.

Then, as I walked on, a new determination began to grow inside me. Sir Alec Rose wouldn't have given up at the first hurdle, so why should I? Surely, I could determine my own future, but how? What could I do? What was clear was that, if I was going to join the Royal Navy, I was going to have to improve my education. I knew that my friend, John Gillen, as well as studying 'A' levels at high school, was attending night classes to beef up some of his other grades. I needed to find out more.

As I walked through the door of No73, Dad looked up at me. 'How did it go?' he asked. His question was anxious, his face worried.

I answered quite frankly, 'It was bloody terrible, I failed the exams.'

Dad's face fell into one of dismay and he was about to say something when I interrupted him, 'But don't worry Dad, I have a plan. Everything is going to work out just fine but I need to go out now. I need to see John Gillen right away…'

John and his family had moved out of Priesthill to another housing scheme in Penilee some 3 miles away. I told him of my disastrous entrance test and that I wanted to take a year out to study and then re-apply. Together we talked it through and decided that, as well as night classes for English and Maths, I should apply for Catering College to further improve my chances of success with the Royal Navy.

John, to support his studies, worked part-time at a nearby warehouse and he was confident that I could get work there on Sundays. He agreed to arrange an interview for me. He also explained how I could apply for a bursary which, together with the warehouse money, would enable me to pay for my housekeeping at home. I knew Margaret would insist on that. I cycled home that evening with real hope in my heart.

★

At the Glasgow College of Food Technology, I struggled through the entry tests and when the time came for my interview, I found myself in front of Mr Thompson, Mr Cushley and Miss Julienne, trying hard to suppress my nerves. When the question came, 'Why do you want to come to catering college?', my answer was both passionate and honest. 'I need this course more than any of you can imagine. I want to join the Royal Navy and having this qualification will help me. If they turn me down, then my future could be in the hotel industry but without this course, I have no future…'

There was an oversubscription for the College and, inevitably, there were many hopeful candidates who would be disappointed. However, I was not to be one of them. I was offered a place and a small bursary to help with the cost of my books and workwear. I later found out that my entry exams results were 'questionable', technically a 'Fail' but depending upon interpretation, a 'Pass'.

It turned out that Mr Cushley had been a cook in the Merchant Navy for most of his life and was twice torpedoed in the North Atlantic during the War. He liked my enthusiasm. Miss Julienne thought that I had good manners, and privately remarked that she thought that I was a very sincere and pleasant young man. The final decision lay with Mr Thompson as he was to be my form teacher. He said, 'Yes' and explained to his colleagues that it was because I'd had my hair cut before the interview.

With all the forthcoming activity of night school, college and Sunday work, I worked out that transport was going to be a considerable expense. I calculated that running a small motor bike cost less than public transport and was much more convenient. I approached Uncle Ed and he happily agreed to lend me the deposit and act as guarantor for a loan to buy one second-hand.

During this time, I began to notice a subtle change in my relationship with my Father, a trend where he would worry and I would re-assure.

'Do you think you will get this Sunday job? Do you think you can hold it down?' to which I replied, 'Yes I think so Dad. Don't worry I can do it'

'Will you get the bursary?'

'Probably, but if I don't, I'll find work on Saturdays or in the evenings...'

'You will need to be careful on that motorbike. They are bloody dangerous, you know...'

'I'll be fine Dad, I'll be careful. Stop worrying!'

My year at college was a priceless experience. I was very young and immature, more so than I should have been at that age, but doubtless a result of my upbringing and experiences. This special year, some might say a gap year, did much to prepare me for the adult world and, having finally been given some tangible opportunities, I grabbed them all. I enjoyed working in the warehouse and I loved riding my motorbike, but most of all, I enjoyed college. At every level, my life was turning from black-and-white to Technicolor.

One year later, I returned to the Royal Navy recruiting station at Queen Street and passed the exams with flying colours. On the test paper that previously had denied me entry, I scored 98%. I was accepted!

Unfortunately though, there was no immediate vacancy and it would be a further 9 months before I could enlist, but, in the event, this too turned out to be a very good thing.

Towards the end of my college course, Uncle Eddie began to complain of a discomfort in his chest; a bronchial infection was diagnosed and his condition worsened. Antibiotics were ineffective and, within a short time, he died peacefully in hospital. He was just 42 years old.

His loss had a profound effect on all of us, none more

so than Dad whose grief was palpable. He held it together, but occasionally his voice would crack with emotion when he phoned a friend or relative to give them the news. It was only then that I understood the reason why we had remained in Priesthill all this time. All along, it was Dad's loyalty and care to his mother and brother that had compelled him to stay. He had always known that one day this would happen and also, that his children would eventually leave and pursue their own lives.

He had held onto Margaret because he didn't want to be alone.

★

I now needed to support myself until the Navy could take me. A couple of weeks after Uncle Eddie's funeral, I was on my way to Pitlochry. I had acquired a residential job as a junior cook at the Pitlochry Hydro hotel. I packed a bag with all my worldly belongings and tied it to the back seat of my motorbike. Dad came onto the pavement at the front of No 73 to shake my hand and wave me off. I was leaving Priesthill for good, just as Ed and Maureen had done before me. Now, only Dad remained. I hated the thought of leaving him with Margaret but the last two years had demonstrated that with us out of the way, his life with her could balance out and they might be happy. I cracked the bike into life and slowly started to roll down Priesthill Road and into my independent adult life. I knew that Dad was standing there watching me go. I didn't look back. I didn't want him to see me hesitate.

I didn't want my Dad to worry about me.

6

I was now 18 and behaved like it. My new job in Pitlochry introduced me to other young feckless teenagers. I made the wrong sort of friends and I started drinking and smoking and got into fights.

Fortunately, the summer season soon came to an end and my sister Maureen took me in to her home in Glenrothes. I found a job working as a welder on the production line in a factory that made supermarket trolleys. It was constant brainless work, doing the things that machines couldn't do. The job entailed lifting a pre-formatted pressed wire mesh onto a welding block, which was two copper bars that separated vertically open and shut. As these bars came together, the mighty voltage powered through and welded the mesh together.

The procedure required manoeuvring the mesh through the block whilst pumping a foot control to operate the welding bars. In protest, the sparks would fly as though angry at the now and forever altered state of the steel. The smell of fused metal, the banging weld presses, wire cropping machines were all the everyday reality of 'Buko Manufacturing'. The radio, blaring out in the overhead tannoy, allowed me to hum along to a familiar tune, as my anesthetised brain commanded my body and limbs to repeat the same procedure, over and over again.

'The more times you do this, the more bonuses you

31

will earn,' said Jal, the supervisor, as he signed me off as 'competent', after my training which took about 10 minutes per machine.

It was not creative - like cooking food, nor beautiful like the deep blue sea, nor a wonderful sensation, like the wind on your sails. It wasn't any of the things that I had dreamed of, but it was a means to an end. I enjoyed earning money and the challenge of beating, or trying to beat, the 'standard bonus system'. Weld enough, bend enough and crop enough of these wire meshes, and bonuses and super bonuses could be earned. And so I whittled away the monotonous hours by trying to do just that.

Maureen was by now a mother of two. Her husband was a truck driver and was often away throughout the week. On these weekday evenings, we would sit up and talk of Dad and Gran and Uncle Ed. It was during one of these discussions that I told Maureen of my guilt, that Gran and I had never talked of our love for each other. I felt vulnerable being so open about this most personal and painful thought, but my sister understood and said, 'Gran loved you very much Denis... and she knew that you loved her... You must never doubt it...'

It is strange, but until that point, I never really knew. I was young and confused and immature, but hearing Maureen say this had a profound effect on me, and, from that point on, I never doubted it again.

I couldn't stay at Maureen's house forever and paying for my own place would have been too costly. Another residential job for a cook came up, this time in a hotel in the lovely sleepy little village of Calendar, in Central Scotland. I had four months to go before my enlistment date and so I left the presses, croppers and welding beams of Glenrothes and returned to the creative passions of being a chef.

I would soon be in the Royal Navy and my adult career would begin in earnest.

TWO

The South Atlantic

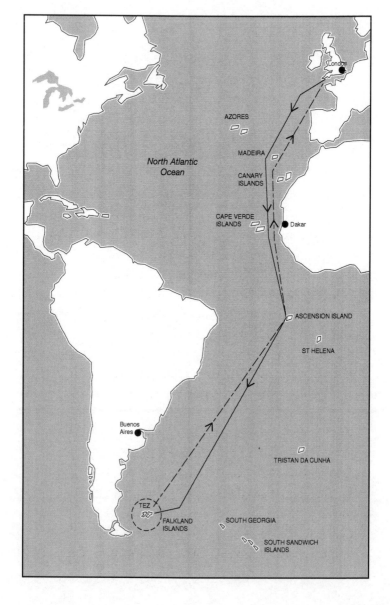

North Atlantic
Ocean

AZORES

MADEIRA

CANARY
ISLANDS

CAPE VERDE
ISLANDS

London

Dakar

ASCENSION ISLAND

ST HELENA

Buenos
Aires

TRISTAN DA CUNHA

TEZ

FALKLAND
ISLANDS

SOUTH GEORGIA

SOUTH SANDWICH
ISLANDS

1

In the fell clutch of circumstance, I have not winced nor cried aloud,
Under the bludgeonings of fate, my head is bloody but unbowed.

William. E. Henley

The new recruits from the west coast of Scotland were assembling at Glasgow Central station. We were booked on board the overnight train to London Euston. Our instructions were to make our way across London by Underground to Victoria then connect to Plymouth. At Plymouth, we would be met and taken by bus to our training base at HMS Raleigh in Torpoint. This would be our new home for the next three months.

Dad was at the station to wave me off. It was good to see him again. He was beaming with pride and said, 'Look at you, you were once so small and now my 'wee Barra' is off to join the Navy..!'

I was enjoying the attention and replied, 'I'll try and make you proud Dad, and I'll try not to mess it up.'

We were happy to be in each other's company again. I could tell that Dad and Margaret were getting on well. They had taken on a mortgage and had moved to a spacious, comfortable flat in Paisley, a much better area than Priesthill.

'Home owners in a nice area.' I thought. I was happy for him.

A commotion was going on at the platform. The recruits were getting rowdy, there would be a party mood on the train and the booze was already starting to flow. One lad had his shirt off and was being carried at shoulder height by his pals up and down the platform.

Mothers and girlfriends were fretting and crying and the noise was echoing around the cathedral-like glass roof and amplifying around the station. There were a couple of proud fathers and grandfathers, wearing their medals and old military berets. Dad knew what I would be going through in the weeks and months ahead. He had done 10 years service as a technician in the Royal Air Force following his National Service. He often said that it was the first time in his life that he had ever had a bed to himself, as he had before then always shared one with our Uncle Ed.

It was 6 days before my 19th birthday and in anticipation of this, Dad handed me a small plainly wrapped package, 'This is for your birthday, you can open it now, you might need it by tomorrow morning,' he said mischievously.

I did as he said and found an electric shaver. Surprised, I looked up and said 'Thank you. It must have cost you a packet.' It was a generous and thoughtful gift, so typical of Dad.

He smiled and said, 'Never you mind about that just make sure you have a clean shave every day or they will have your guts for garters.'

The train was pulling out at 10 pm and as the last few seconds ticked by, Dad gave me some more of his sound advice,

'Remember to choose your friends carefully', and… 'Don't forget that drink is a good servant but a poor master.'

We boarded the train. With the doors closed and windows dropped open, we waved and shouted as our loved ones cheered us away. Dad trotted along the platform briskly until our speed gathered pace. He stopped and gave me a last wave goodbye. I shouted out to him, 'I'm glad you got your new house Da, you deserve it.'

And then we were gone.

On board the train, there followed a frenetic bustle of activity. There were about 30 of us and everybody wanted to get acquainted. We bombarded each other with questions. 'What trade will you be taking? Why are you joining? Where are you from?' There was lots of male posturing and bragging about women. It was exciting, it was really exciting. Before too long, bottles of booze began to appear and got passed around and when these ran out, more was purchased from the refreshments car.

The noise grew louder and louder. The guard came along and told us to quieten down, which we did for five minutes, then it kicked off again. Several times this went on. Then one of the lads said to the guard, 'Go and shag off, go find yourself a phone box, you dirty old pervert.'

Ten minutes later the guard returned with a stern warning, 'There is a naval regulator and a senior officer on board who is threatening to have the train stopped at Carlisle and have you lot thrown off.'

This time we did as we were told and finally in the early hours of the morning, we settled down to a fitful rest.

★

The Royal Navy is full of traditions and eccentricities. Every establishment is called HMS (Her Majesty's Ship), this applies to shore bases and seagoing ships alike. Every day at 08.00hrs, a bugle sounds and the White Ensign is raised. At sunset, the bugle sounds again and the Ensign is lowered. At these precise times everyone 'onboard' is expected to stop what they are doing and stand silently and respectfully to attention. In this way the Royal Navy remembers and respects its generations of dead. Woe betide anyone who fails to pay attention. The very least you would get would be a very loud and public dressing down.

Unlike civilian employers, the Navy could punish you for any number of things. If placed on a charge, the punishment could range from loss of pay or shore leave, to a period of continuous punishment. These punishments are numbered, so for instance you could have a week of number 9's which is loss of shore leave and mustering for additional work, or five days of number 11's which is a forfeiture of pay. Also, if a sailor failed to show the correct discipline or attitude, or acquired an accumulation of minor offences, he could be imprisoned and discharged from the service. It might surprise you to know that even today the Royal Navy has the right to hang its offenders.

The Navy also has its own language; an 'Oppo' is your friend, a 'Bint', a girlfriend, to 'Trap' is to pull a girl, 'Grip' means sex and 'Squeezing' means to have the clap, a 'Run Ashore' is an evening out, 'Wets' are beers and 'Shitters' means to get very drunk, 'Gash' is rubbish and a 'Sea Daddy' is an older sailor who gives you advice.

The Navy could be tough, but it was fun too and I thrived and developed well. Life was exciting and the world seemed to be full of possibilities. I had signed up as a ship's cook and after basic training, I went on to the Royal Naval School of Cookery at HMS *Pembroke* in Chatham. From there, I was sent to HMS *Nelson* in Portsmouth for work experience before my first seagoing assignment.

2

At HMS *Nelson* we junior cooks had an easy time of it working in the spacious galley that serviced the base. I don't ever remember the kitchen getting too hot or the work being too heavy. We had civilian kitchen porters who washed the pots and pans and did most of the basic preparations such as peeling the spuds or carrying the stores into our various store rooms.

Our work pattern was relaxed. One in three days we would work late to put out the supper whilst the other two days would see us finished by 16.00hrs. Portsmouth was within easy walking distance and, on most evenings, we savoured the dubious delights of downtown Pompey. We drank in the bars, bopped in the nightclubs of nearby Southsea and had cheap takeaway food on the way back to the Base.

At the end of these sessions, we would run the gauntlet of getting past the duty officer on the gate. The act of being sober for that crucial 15 seconds became something of an art form.

Ordinarily, this shore-time period should have taken 18 months but, due to my college and previous catering work, I advanced rapidly and after 9 months I was considered fit for sea duty. All the old salts had advised me that smaller ships, such as frigates or even destroyers were more homely and more relaxed than big ships so, this somewhat homesick Scots lad requested a small ship, with a home port in Scotland.

To my disappointment, I ended up with an aircraft carrier, from Portsmouth, in the south of England.

Now, the old salts said, 'Never mind, you never get top preference on your first draft. You'll have better luck next time'….

HMS *Invincible* was a clean modern ship. Termed a 'step through cruiser', she was small by aircraft carrier standards. She carried a squadron of Sea King helicopters and another squadron of Harrier Jump jets. Due to her short length, she had a ramp at the end of the flight deck in order to provide 'lift' as the Harriers took off. Upon return, these would land vertically onto the deck. In this way, this very novel ship and her aircraft could provide the Navy with an effective aircraft carrier.

Invincible was scheduled to take part in war games in the Atlantic and Mediterranean and would be visiting Toulon, Amsterdam, Bergen then Norfolk Virginia. This particular tour would take nine months. It was an unenviable posting as it would involve a lot of sea time and little shore time.

The ship had a standing crew of several hundred, but this could swell to an operational crew of 1200 once the aircraft, and all the attendants from shore stations arrived. The galley was hot and very busy. It was aggressive and food was produced on an industrial level. It was like a factory.

Naval discipline was maintained by strictly enforced line management principles and the lower down the pecking order you were, the poorer your pay and conditions.

The accommodation for junior rates was Spartan and cramped. I had the middle section on a three tier bunk bed which was separated from the next triple set by a thin board partition. Fifteen of us slept like this in a shared compartment. Each man had a locker about the size of a small fridge. A curtain separated the sleeping area from our communal room which had a television fixed to the bulkhead in one corner.

There were no carpets and soft furnishings were minimal. Our mess deck was no bigger than two household living rooms put together.

The junior rates were separated from the senior rates. Both had separate dining and living quarters. Senior rates, such as petty officers, would share 4 to a cabin. Warrant officers and chief petty officers would share 2 to a cabin whereas Commissioned officers would typically have a cabin to themselves, (except for junior officers and midshipmen who would share 2 to a cabin).

The work was hard, constant and, it seemed to me, thankless. I began to realise that the Royal Navy was not the panacea I dreamed it would be. But I determined that the only remedy was to rise to the challenge. I also decided that if my next posting was not favourable, then I might put in my notice and return to civilian life.

After a short time of being miserable, I began to 'kick in' to my new life and as my confidence developed, I became aggressive and competitive. I became a hawk. A typical example of this was an incident that happened one day whilst I was on sink duty. I was handed a burnt 6 gallon pot with the remnants of a Madras curry stuck to the bottom. I picked it up and marched straight into the middle of the galley. Holding it aloft, I shouted, 'What the flying fuck is this? ... Who has burnt this pot?'

Everyone stopped and looked at me and Petty Officer Ray Bligh replied, 'It was me.'

I stepped forward and dangling the pot from one hand and pointing with my other straight into the black burnt cavern, I went on,

'You sir, have wasted five rations of food on the bottom of this pot and I intend to write to the Admiralty to have them take it from your wages ... Now stop pissing about.'

I turned and marched back to the sink and, as I did, I

shouted, 'You lot better sort your shit out. I won't stand for it...'

Everyone laughed. If they laughed, you would be fine. If they didn't, you would probably end up on a charge. On this occasion Ray Bligh gave me a new nickname, he called me 'Black Jock'.

I soon gained a reputation for being a strong worker and I made friends, but I wondered if this was really going to be the life for me.

3

It was during my first few months on board *Invincible* that the opportunity arose to become a ship's diver. This is not a full-time position because it is only on odd, but vital occasions that ships need to deploy divers. Cooks, seamen and stokers are needed permanently but when a helicopter falls into the sea, or an old drift net wraps itself around stern gear, those same personnel can be relieved of their normal duties to fulfil a diving role.

I volunteered for the service and *Invincible* sent 32 of us to HMS *Drake* in Plymouth to be tested for our suitability to go onto a four week intensive training course. I remembered the Calypso programmes I'd seen on telly years before. I imagined caring, compassionate instructors and, warm well-lit indoor swimming pools.

Oh no. This was the Royal Navy!

The instructor showed us the diving equipment and briefed us on our intended activity. We were to be dressed in dry suits and would run 'en-masse' through the camp and down to the creek. There, we would climb a 40 foot high platform, leap into the water below, swim across the creek, crawl up the bank of mud on the far side, run back round to the start and then, repeat the whole exercise…and that, was only the warm up!

The candidates were then to run over to the floating pontoon to be fitted with weights, lead boots, full face mask and a twin tank breathing set. A signal rope would be tied to our Sam Brown harnesses and we would be expected to jump, without hesitation, into the creek.

With all that weight, the only place to go from there was to the bottom.

The instructor emphasised the importance of clearing the pressure in the ears and explained our rope signals. One pull of the rope would be an instruction to go right, two pulls to the left, three pulls to go back, and four pulls to come forward.

A continuous tug from the candidate would abort the exercise and he would immediately be pulled out. He would of course be… 'Off the course.'

The final exercise was to operate the breathing equipment exactly as instructed. We would be carrying a set of two cylinders that were inverted. When the first tank became exhausted we were to reach behind and open the valve of the second cylinder. The instructor ended his briefing by telling us, 'Any hesitation to carry out an order, to follow a rope signal, or if you are too slow to complete a mud run, then you will fail the assessment… You must complete all of the tasks correctly in order to get a pass.'

He went on. 'This is one of the hardest courses in all the services. There is no shame in giving up. In this assessment and in the course to follow, we can only give you a taste of what you will be expected to do. The real job will throw up problems that we cannot train you for so if you have any doubts then walk away now…'

All the hopefuls held their ground. The Chief Petty Officer (CPO) Diving Instructor and his team of Clearance Divers wasted no more time. There was no small talk. No words of encouragement. Orders were direct and unfriendly. We dressed into dry suits and, on the command, set off at a brisk run down to the creek.

My greatest strength, as I saw it, was that I was a good

strong swimmer. Self-taught, I could knock out 50 lengths of a swimming pool with relative ease but, once I was wearing lead boots and all the other equipment, that would count for very little. This was an assessment of the mind more than anything. I swallowed hard and thought, 'Fucking hell'.

I quickly discovered the difficulty of running in an ill-fitting dry suit. The legs were too long and very baggy. The only way to avoid falling over myself was to grab a fist-full of bunched up material at the top of each leg and run, as it were, with my breeches hoisted up. Heat built up very quickly. My heart began to pound and perspiration started to flow.

I arrived breathless at the tower. One by one and in brisk fashion, we climbed. As I was going up, I noticed another man was passing me on his way down. He had bottled it, he was 'off the course.' As I got to the top, the man in front of me hesitated…'Don't think just go,' I told myself, and, with that, I pushed past him, ran to the end of the platform and leapt straight out. The horizon rose up as I fell straight down and plunged deep into the water. I kicked for the surface and began swimming. It was hard to swim in this awkward dry suit. The instructors were mercilessly shouting.

'Move your arses! If you don't get your speed up, you will be off the course!'

I kept going. The bank on the other side was stinking and slimy and the mud was so soft that its suction grabbed my legs and sucked me down. The secret was to move quickly over it. I passed a man who had sunk down to his waist.

'Help me, for God's sake, help me!' he shouted.

The attendants threw him a line and pulled him out, 'Are you still going?' they asked.

'You can fuck off' he said.

'Off the course.'

I ran round again. Some lads had stopped. They were coughing their guts up.

'Off the course.'

Some were too slow.

'Off the course.'

I completed the second circuit and ran to the pontoon where there was a row of attendants dressing the candidates and sending them over the side. As soon as I arrived lead boots were put on my feet and a diving set was slung on my back. Then weights were strapped around my waist, a clip was put on my nose, and a mask on my face. Hurriedly, they tied a rope to my Sam Brown and as they did, they repeated the instructions for the rope signals. Breathlessly I nodded to acknowledge my understanding. I was manoeuvred to the water's edge. I realised that every survival instinct in my body was screaming.

'Fuck this!'

But a voice inside me was saying, 'Just stick it out. You won't drown, it will be over soon enough'.

The chief instructor looked straight into my face and shouted one very clear question.

'Gorman are you happy to continue?'

I was breathing furiously, my heart pounding. My head and chest were swimming in a sea of fear and adrenaline.

I shouted back. 'Yes, I am ready',

The chief turned to my attendant and said. 'Okay send him on his way.'

With that, I stepped awkwardly off the platform and smashed into the murky water. I was held at the surface until a visual inspection of my tanks was made then the attendants slipped my control line away and I sank until I hit the muddy bottom, 15 feet below. On my way down, I cleared my ears as they had told me to do.

It was murky and green with visibility of only 3 or 4 feet and as I stomped on the mud the swirling silt arose around and engulfed me. The sound of my breathing was amplified in the water. I was expelling air at a furious rate. I closed my eyes and chastised myself. 'Goddamit, get your breathing under control!'

I felt a signal on my rope. I opened my eyes and sent back one pull to say 'I am ready', then I felt three pulls. I acknowledged with one pull and obeyed the command, stumbling awkwardly backwards. Other signals were sent. I responded.

Time passed. Cold trickles of water worked their way into my mask, the salt water stinging my eyes. It seeped in around the neck and cuffs of my suit. Although I was quite terrified and this was the most horrible hostile environment that I could imagine, I felt a sense of perverse pleasure at the thought of denying the bastards the satisfaction of beating me. A chance to prove that I was more than a cook.

My air started to drag. I reached back and opened the valve to my second cylinder. I heard a long slow deliberate hiss as high-pressure air travelled from one tank to the other. When the hissing stopped, I reached around and shut off the valve. Then I sent up five long deliberate pulls to tell them that I was completed. I was hauled out and my set was inspected. If my valve had been left open then I would have failed.

Of the 32 men who attended that day, 11 passed. Of those 11, only 2, myself and a lad called Neil Males, went on to complete the four week course.

★

At the end of March 1982, *Invincible* had completed her Atlantic tour and the ship was peacefully alongside in Portsmouth. By now, I had completed 13 months of my 18 month posting and, like many of the crew at that time, I was given general leave. I went home, put my bags down at Dad and Margaret's place, a brief 'Hello' and then headed up to Stirling University to visit and stay with John Gillen, who was now a full-time residential student there.

My birthday was coming up and I would be turning 21 on 1 April. A party was scheduled on the campus with John and his friends and then I was due to return to Dad's house where the family would be gathering for a celebration. Along with most of the population at large, I had no idea that far away in the remote Falkland Islands, events were rapidly coming to crisis point.

I had spent three days in Stirling and had not seen any television, read a paper or listened to any radio during this time. So, it was only when John and I returned to his parents' house (which is en-route to Dad's), that the news finally caught up with me. John's sister-in-law, Helen, held up a newspaper that had all sorts of crazy excitable news. What had begun as an international incident concerning a party of Argentinian scrap metal workers, who on 19 March had landed on the remote snow-covered island of South Georgia, had escalated into a full Argentinian invasion of Port Stanley in the Falkland Islands. Helen told me, 'Your Dad has been calling for you, the police have been at his house, and you have been recalled. They are ordering the Army and Navy to return from leave!'

It was true, and the papers, radio and television confirmed that this was the biggest mobilisation of Britain's armed forces since the Second World War.

The Falklands War was about to begin.

I phoned Dad right away and he confirmed everything that Helen had said. He sounded worried, then said hopefully, 'It will probably blow over and everything will settle down in a couple of days... The Police have come to the house a couple of times. I've told them it's your birthday and that the family are gathering here for you tonight, so I'm hoping they will allow you to stay until tomorrow morning.'

Dad was wrong on both counts. When I arrived at the

house two police officers showed up just 40 minutes later and the Sergeant said, 'You must go now.'

His manner was insistent but then he added apologetically, 'I'm sorry to break up your party but everyone is required to go back urgently. It's a general recall. The country might be going to war.'

I assured them, 'There's a train leaving Glasgow in an hour's time. I'll be on it.'

The policeman smiled pleasantly and said, 'That's fine. We won't bother your father again,' then said, 'I hope everything works out all right for you.'

Both Dad and I understood the situation. When you 'sign up', the Navy has first claim on you before family, friends, or any personal circumstance. I had no choice - I had to go. Straightaway, I set about packing my bag and saying my goodbyes. The hardest part was saying goodbye to Dad; he looked so worried. I tried to reassure him. 'Please don't worry. I'll write as often as I can and I'll take good care of myself.'

Dad smiled sadly then we hugged and parted. I threw my bags across my back and John gave me a lift on his motorbike to Glasgow Central. We entered the station from Hope Street, a slip road entry which allows vehicles to pick up and drop off passengers inside the station complex, next to the platforms. As I climbed off the bike, I caught sight of Graeme Petrie, a fellow cook from *Invincible* making his way. I shouted for him to wait. After a wave of acknowledgement, he waited by the platform entrance for me to catch up. Our train was at the platform, about to leave. I turned back to John. We looked at each other for a few moments not knowing what to say.

John had been my best friend since we had met on our very first day at school, when we were just five years old. Here we were, adults now.

'Goodbye John,' I said.

He tried to say something fit for the occasion and was

struggling when, I put my hand on his shoulder and said, 'Don't worry about any of that. It really doesn't suit you.'

We both laughed a little. Then I said, 'If anything happens to me, just look in on my Dad and do what you can for him.'

John breathed in deeply and nodded his head. 'Yes I'll do that for you Den...'

And, with that, I turned and ran after Graeme.

★

The train was bustling with servicemen. You could spot them easily, short hair, the way they walked, the things they said and the old fashioned, boxy, light green suitcases which are so characteristic of military issue. We were all subject to the recall and it seemed that every serviceman was on the move. The mood was business-like and purposeful, very different from the naive and excitable throng that had left Glasgow Central with me just two years earlier.

Like me, Graeme was late to hear about the recall. He had been staying with a girl, (a bint), that he had 'trapped' in Dundee and was only told to return a few hours before.

Graeme had joined *Invincible* a couple of months after me and we both knew what life would be like if we were forced to endure an extended period of sea time. The rule was simple... 'Sea time was hard time,' and the more time you spent at sea, the more likely you were to 'crack up'. Our Sea Daddies would often refer to this and talked of ratings and senior rates who had 'Thrown a wobbly,' after four or five weeks at sea, only to be 'Locked up and discharged from service,' as soon as they touched port. It is an environment where rumours, gossip and petty criticism demoralise you, where you are forced to socialise, accept ridicule but stand up to it when it goes too far. You need to read the mood and work around it. It is a place where bad news from home can throw your world into turmoil: the death of a parent, a girlfriend who dumps you, or someone close becomes ill.

It is a place where psychologically you need to be strong.

Graeme and I were the same age. Young and headstrong, we both harboured resentment against the Navy, its authoritarianism and its privilege system. Its pettiness.

When I first joined *Invincible*, I was picked on quite regularly by a leading cook who had been a petty officer but had lost his rate because of a drink-related offence. He was a burnt-out sailor with too many sea miles under his belt. I hated him and was glad to see him go when his drafting orders came up.

Graeme too had suffered some of the same general ridicule and, like me, he had a love/ hate relationship with the Navy because of it. Graeme was tall and handsome and perhaps a little arrogant. He always took pride in his appearance and was good at 'Trapping the Bints'. This invited a fair clutch of small-minded jealousies, which Graeme ignored. When we were in Norway, an incident occurred when he was ashore in a nightclub. Another sailor, whom he had never met before, for no reason, punched him in the mouth. It was a vicious unprovoked assault which caused him to have 4 stiches on the inside of his lower lip. The following day, in the main galley, his unsympathetic colleagues made sure that he was put to work on the brat pans; an act of sheer devilment because the heat from these industrial-sized skillets rose up to aggravate his wound.

In fact, the attack in the night club had been witnessed by two off duty Naval Regulators, and the Navy itself would never tolerate such behaviour. The culprit was immediately arrested and when he was brought before the Captain's table, naval justice was swift and uncompromising. The offending sailor was sent to Colchester military prison and, once he had served his sentence, he was discharged from the service.

As Graeme and I shared our journey, I pondered on these contradictions. In one sense, the Navy was a rotten and difficult path to tread but, it was an honourable institution. Some were privileged and some were from the gutter and yet, in spite of these vagaries, both Graeme and I were proud to be 'Royal Navy'.

4

We travelled all night, eventually arriving in Portsmouth around lunchtime on Saturday. The town was bustling and the taxi ranks empty. It took another hour to get down to the dockside where we saw truckloads of supplies being passed, hand-to-hand via multiple gangways up and into the ship. Above us, helicopters and Harrier aircraft were arriving from 801 (Harrier), and 802 Sea King (helicopter) squadrons.

Aircraft, men, fuel, weapons, ammunition, medical supplies, shoring equipment and spare machinery, all were arriving and being taken on board. Within minutes of my arrival, I was sent to assist in one of the main food storage areas. For hours on end, I took up a position of handling and passing on stores. Apart from a few short breaks, this went on until late into the night. The following day after a six-hour rest, we turned-to again and kept working until 6pm. Finally, all non-essential personnel were granted leave for the evening.

I went ashore to phone home. The whole of Portsmouth seemed to be alive with people. Some would ask, 'Are you a sailor? What ship are you on?' and then go on to tell me of a relative on *Invincible* or some other ship. There was an air of anxiety all around. On the harbour pier beside the train station, there was a public phone box and I queued for about an hour to use it. When I got through to Dad, I told him. 'We are leaving in the morning about 10:15 but I'm not supposed to tell you because it's a secret.'

He replied, 'Well if that's the case then it's the worst kept secret in the world.'

We both laughed nervously for a few moments then he became serious. 'I'm worried for you son, just stay strong. Do what you have to do, then come home to us.'

His voice was straining with emotion. I simply said. 'Yes Dad, I will, and you must take care of yourself too'.

I tried to lighten the mood by telling him about the five babies who were baptised on *Invincible*'s quarterdeck that day in amongst all the chaos. I promised to write, and then we said goodbye.

Invincible steamed out just as I had said, on the following morning. It was Monday, 5 April 1982 and as we went, the whole country seemed to be wishing us well. The newspapers and television were full of news about our departure. The water's edge of Portsmouth and Gosport was thronged with people who cheered and waved us away. It was heart-warming, but everyone below decks had by now some idea of the enormity of the task that lay ahead of us. We were a seaborne task force, being sent 9000 miles (a logistical nightmare) to liberate a small barren island group, covering an area the size of Wales. We would be pitched against a modern army that was well equipped, well dug in, and supported by its own substantial Navy which included submarines and an aircraft carrier. More than this, they had a substantial and well-trained air force that greatly outnumbered our small number of somewhat outdated Harrier jump jets.

We were all aware that ships are vulnerable to air attack and that *Invincible* and *Hermes*, both carriers, would be prime targets. To make matters worse we would be sailing into the very heart of a South Atlantic winter.

★

On our first night out, Captain Black talked to us from the

TV studio. From the mess decks we all watched and listened intently to our TV sets. He spoke plainly and truthfully. This was not a sound bite talk but real heart-to-heart, life-and-death stuff. He emphasised the need for professionalism to be at the forefront of every expected activity that we would undertake.

Then he told us,

'Between now and reaching Ascension Island, we will use our time constructively to train and retrain. When we get there, we will resupply and conduct as much essential maintenance as we can. We will also receive and send off mail. Get your letters written because beyond Ascension, our next mail drop will be difficult to predict...'

He finished by advising us,

'The ship needs every one of us to be at the top of our game and, I promise you, that if we do all that is asked of us, we will come through'.

It was a good briefing, one which kept us focused and ended with a touch of human consideration. One had a feeling that the 'old man' was a capable fellow.

Captain Black had only taken over the ship towards the end of our previous tour so, to most of us, he was an unknown quantity. In fact, he would prove himself to have such affable leadership qualities, that under his guidance, our ship would establish a new world record for continuous carrier operations at sea. Throughout the whole venture, incredibly, our Sea Daddies would be proven wrong, none of us would 'crack up'.

Such was the measure of the man, and his crew.

★

The submarine threat was taken seriously from the moment we left port and our course through the water sinuated in an attempt to confuse anyone who might be observing us. With blackout curtains hung on the entry and exit points to all the weather decks, *Invincible* and all her escort 'darkened ship' at night. Civilian clothes and non-essential uniforms were packed into cases and removed to the baggage store areas. Carpets were rolled up and placed in the paint store and televisions were covered and tied down with canvas.

Many ships, including *Hermes*, even threw their mattresses overboard because a burning foam mattress gives off a massive amount of toxic smoke and was seen as a considerable liability.

Captain Black, however, thought differently. *Invincible* carried up to 800 tons of ammunition and thousands of tons of fuel and aviation spirit. In modern warfare, particularly with the advent of missile technology, he reasoned that 'One Touch' could be fatal. If the magazines were ignited, the chain reaction would, quite literally, atomise the ship. Our Captain reasoned that his pilots, watch keepers, radar operators, his whole crew, would operate better if they had as much comfort and rest as he could provide. If they were refreshed and on top of their game, that, 'One Touch', might better be averted.

Consequently, he decided that *Invincible* would run the risk of toxic smoke and keep her mattresses.

Our training and preparation intensified at every level and in every department of the ship, with frequent damage control exercises in firefighting, flood control and first aid. States of alertness were reinforced. Over and over, we would practise coming to action stations and 'closing up' the ship, which meant that every watertight hatch, door and compartment was to be shut down and sealed. The call to action stations would be piped through the tannoy, 'Action stations, action stations, action stations, assume NBCD state one condition Zulu… all hands to action stations,'

This would be repeated twice more.

The 'NBCD' stood for Nuclear, Biological and Chemical Defence. To protect against an airburst of poison gas, three airtight citadels would be formed within the ship with each citadel having its own central command post which controlled the firefighting and flood containment teams within its area.

Once action stations was declared, a further Code of Condition was established. State Yellow meant, no immediate danger was detected and we were allowed to relax. During these periods, we would read, play Chess or cards or write letters. We were fed during the yellow periods when 'Action Messing' commenced; this involved a systematic relieving of each department and its firefighting teams who then made their way to the galley. Dinner consisted of one bread roll and butter, a ladle of 'pot mess', which is a thick beef stew with vegetables and potatoes, and a mug of fruit juice (either lime or orange squash). Pudding was a piece of cake or fruit. All food was served on a pressed metal tray that was picked up on entry to the dining area and handed to the mess man on the way out. Each man carried his own plastic mug and kept it on him at all times. Once a meal was issued, you were expected to sit and eat promptly, then leave the dining room within five minutes. In this way, the whole ship's company of sailors, airmen and marines, all 1200 of them, could be fed and returned to action stations within 1 ½ hrs.

The next level of alertness at action stations was, state 'Red'. At this command, all relaxation would stop. Books and board games would be stored and anti-flash gloves and hoods put on. A Red alert meant that action with the enemy was underway in our immediate area and the pipe would typically come through,

'Red alert, red alert, red alert, hostile aircraft inbound all hands close up...'

Again, this would be repeated twice.

The final command in this sequence of alertness was, 'Hit the deck-Hit the deck.' At this point every man on board would know that our outer defences had been penetrated and that imminent destruction was upon us. A standing man is much more vulnerable to the power, heat and shrapnel from a bomb blast than a man who makes himself small and lies face down. It would then be a question of survival. If we were hit, it would be up to the survivors to tackle the fires and floods, tend to the dead and wounded, and work to save the ship, to keep her afloat, to keep her moving and to keep her in the war.

Our lives were now intrinsically linked to these practices and concepts and we ate, slept and breathed them until they became second nature to us all.

It is tempting and, perhaps, even comforting to think that a ship could remain closed up at action stations indefinitely, to be ready for anything, but this is simply not possible. Our ship needed to be maintained, resupplied and refuelled. So, under cover of darkness, or in bad weather, when an attack seemed inconceivable, the announcement was made, 'Stand down from action stations. Assume NBCD state 2 condition Yankee.'

Now, the citadels were opened up and we returned to our normal duties.

Typically, we came to state 1 before sunrise and stepped down to state 2 after nightfall. But, at state 2, the ship is at its most vulnerable and a successful, surprise attack could be catastrophic.

If such an attack came, we would get an 'Action Alarm.'

This begins with an electrifying, 'Duh, Duh, Duh', coming from the tannoy, followed by, 'Action Alarm, Action Alarm, Action Alarm', all hands to action stations at the rush at the rush...!'

The bellowing, 'Duh, Duh, Duh' now hammers on.

This sound is harrowing. Every one of its mighty decibels going through you, smashing away every other thought, every other priority that you may have, thrusting you, from sound and deep sleep, into sheer, frantic, urgency and confusion, scrambling out of bunks, into passageways, up ladders, through hatches, running down passageways with watertight doors slamming mercilessly, steel on steel and voices... every one of them shouting, 'Be quick...Hurry...At the rush...AT THE RUSH!', the urgency of men on the verge of violence, their faces drawn white and grim with consternation, the feeling of adrenaline and terror coursing through your veins, of bile and acid swirling in your stomach, threatening to burn a hole right through you. Harrowing indeed.

'Duh, Duh, Duh'.

It is the most urgent of commands and it will not stop until the ship is closed down, with every man accounted for, at his designated place.

The sound of an 'Action Alarm' means,

'We have been caught out.'

If you were to experience this, as we did, you would never forget it. But, most of all, you would never forget the very real state of mind that tells you, that this very moment might be your last...

5

Invincible is a complicated ship. Some might say, she resembles a village. With her own tiny chapel, library, photographic studio, television studio, NAAFI, (Naval, Army and Air Force Institute) shop, a laundry (run by Chinese from Hong Kong) and a hairdresser.

There were three galleys: firstly, the wardroom galley provided for the officers. Then the main galley served three counters, one for junior rates, one for petty officers and a shared counter for chief petty officers and warrant officers. Finally, a tiny squadron galley, situated close to the flight deck, had a full-time dedicated cook, providing meals for pilots around their flying duties.

The wardroom and its galley, the main galley and dining areas, the NAAFI shop and barbershop were all on No5 deck. No 5 deck ran from the quarterdeck forward on both port and starboard sides to a connecting passage across the width at the forward-most part of the ship. In this way, No5 deck created a continuous loop around the ship.

Because of its uninterrupted nature, 5 deck was used as a main thoroughfare.

To the uninitiated, the insides of this great ship resembled a maze, with passageways, ladders, hatches, compartments and steel watertight doors leading off all over the place. Without a navigable system, you could easily get lost and disoriented. This was avoided by a simple system of letters and numbers that were made of luminous material and stuck in every compartment and along every passageway throughout the ship.

Each deck was numbered in relation to the flight deck. No 1 being the flight deck and No 7 being the lowest deck, directly above the keel.

Each compartment from the for'ard to aft parts of the ship was identified by alphabetical letters where 'A' was at the front of the ship and 'Z' at the back.

Other letters were added to give more precise information, 'P' for 'port', 'M' for 'midships, 'S' for 'starboard', 'F' for 'for'ard' and 'A' for 'aft'. My mess deck was in 6TPF which meant, No6 deck (below the waterline), 'T' tango (well aft, above the prop shaft), 'P' port, 'F' forward compartment.

Our tiny chapel was in '7TSF', which put it directly across the passageway from my mess and directly down one level. It may sound complicated, but knowing your ship and understanding these signs was vital, not only for speedy, efficient operations but also, if the ship had lost power and was sinking, your survival, your ability to get out would depend on it. The darkened innards of a ship have, in countless cases, taken many sailors to their grave.

We tested ourselves repeatedly on our knowledge of the ship.

★

I was the only ship's diver among the whole of the catering department and, as such, when we were called to action stations, I was released to attend a fire and repair party post at deck 5DM section, (that being at the furthermost part of 5 deck in the midships section). My role there, was to support and monitor a team of two firemen. I would dress them in thick woollen fearnought suits with each man carrying a single bottle of compressed air. It was my task to maintain and recharge their bottles and, should they be sent into a real fire, to monitor their operational breathing time.

In a smoke-filled compartment, it is almost impossible for firefighters to be aware of their time or to monitor their watches and gauges. Furthermore, it was estimated that a firefighter under such duress, would use up their air in just eight minutes. In this situation, I would be their timekeeper and inform our senior rate of when their time was up. This would ensure that fresh firefighters could be sent in, and my lads could come out before their air was exhausted.

After action stations, when the ship relaxed and went to state 2 (usually at night), I returned to the galley. Here, I was given the job of managing the beef screens and stores. The stores were situated directly under the galley on No 6 deck. Each night, I was given a list of supplies from the duty P.O. Cook and with the help of one man, we went down, found the stock and returned with it. The meat would be put to the beef screen. This was a small, cubicle-shaped room with stainless steel coverings on the walls and ceiling. It contained workbenches and a refrigeration cabinet. Here, the meat would be thawed out before it was cut into chunks and handed to the galley for their pot mess.

The Warrant Officer (WO) and Chief Petty Officer (CPO) cooks' office, the catering accounts office, the beef screen, potato store and main fridges were all situated along a narrow passageway that led to the aft end of the main galley. As well as cutting the meat and delivering the stores, I was also instructed to monitor and record the fridge and freezer temperatures every eight hours and these records were checked every day by the chief cook or chief caterer.

But at any time, a call could go out to assemble all divers. When this happened, I immediately handed over my duties to a replacement BA controller or caterer and headed for the diving assembly area. Diving always took priority over all other activities. We could be called out for any number of reasons, ranging from the search and rescue of a downed pilot or helicopter crew, to cleaning the Sonar dome on the underside of the ship.

In all, there were about 20 to 30 divers on board *Invincible*. Our Diving Officer was a somewhat eccentric, but delightfully serious, Lieutenant Commander Henry Lansdowne. He was tall and thin and wore a full beard, which made him look older that he probably was. That aside, he was certainly older than all of his diving team who were made up entirely from leading hands (killicks), junior rates and one petty officer (PO). Among the officers, he was frequently ribbed and teased. Our ship's monthly newspaper 'The *Invincible* Times' targeted him with funny articles and cartoons. Our nightly TV presenter, our educational officer, lampooned him mercilessly to the hilarious delight of us all. But, for all that, Henry Lansdowne had the unique ability to handle this mild ridicule and yet remain an impressive fellow. Behind the banter, he was highly thought of and widely respected.

Among us divers we privately referred to him as, 'Dear Henry'.

★

On 15th April we crossed the Equator and, on the following day, we arrived at Ascension Island where we dropped anchor. We were now midway between Britain and the Falkland Islands. It was here that the divers were assembled for final training and a thorough maintenance of all our equipment. I went overboard and took poker gauge readings of the propeller shafts. These indicate how much wear was going on where the shaft passed through the cutlass bearings. Then I went forward and cleaned the sonar dome. This is done, quite literally, by scrubbing it with a green scouring pad, the type that you might use at home on your dishes.

Other lads set about putting blanking plates onto underwater inlets, allowing the valves to be stripped out from inside the ship, cleaned, serviced and then replaced.

We concluded with an underwater sweep of the ship's hull. This involves divers being positioned from the keel to the surface, each spaced at 5 foot intervals. Each man was connected to a 'necklace' line, so called because the line resembled a necklace as it hung from the surface to the keel with divers clipped onto it like jewels on a chain. The line could be used to send instructions and messages by a series of pulls and tugs. In this way, divers could swim along in a uniform fashion and communicate up and down the line. This exercise is done to inspect the hull for damage or, if in harbour, to locate and deal with limpet mines.

Many of the crew were off watch, relaxing, sunbathing or playing deck hockey on the flight deck.

The divers were sweeping to the after end of the ship on the starboard side with Dear Henry in his rubber dinghy trying with difficulty to coordinate his lads around the prop shafts and steering gear. Our senior rate, a very solid PO Seaman, Steve Wills and I were on the quarterdeck. I had been diving already and was still wearing my wetsuit. I was leaning over the side shouting to Dave Houghton, a fellow diver, when I felt an irksome fellow nudge up alongside and ask, 'What's going on around here? It all looks rather interesting.'

I could see that Dave Houghton was holding a diver's line too tight and without turning my head, I said, 'Look mate I'm kind of busy right now, so why don't you bugger off.'

Then I shouted to Dave, 'Come on man give the boy some slack!'

The voice beside me said, 'Oh well, that's fine. Very good,' Then he left.

I thought, 'Who is this guy?' As I turned around, I caught a side view of him as he walked through the bulkhead door and onto No5 deck. I looked at PO Wills who was staring at me stone-faced and I asked.

'Is that who I think it is?'

Steve Wills replied, 'Yes it is, and next time you talk to him, remember to call him 'Sir'.'

It was Prince Andrew!

Whilst at Ascension, a backlog of mail was delivered and I received well over a dozen letters. I also got a box from Dad packed full of delicatessen foods: jars of meat and fish paste, tubes of mustard, tubes of spreading cheese some with shrimps, others with chives, small jars of different pickles, chutney, potted shrimps, long life cheese and a variety of savoury biscuits.

I also got a couple of sailing magazines and in the weeks to come, I spent hours reading every detail of every page. Over and over again, I pondered, examining the glossy coloured pictures and For Sale adverts. It was sheer escapism, dreaming that one day I would own a boat and sail off into the sunset.

Such a life would be blissful and free.

★

On Sunday 18th of April, *Invincible* and her escort group weighed anchor and pulled away from Ascension Island. So far, diplomatic talks had failed and, with the Army and Navy at such a heightened state of readiness, to falter, delay or turn around would have been extremely damaging to morale. Such an action seemed inconceivable to us. This meant that the only option for peace lay with the Argentinians. It would be up to them to withdraw from the Falklands immediately. They showed no such intention and so we came to the conclusion that we were going to war.

The following day, a helicopter managed to reach us from Ascension and, with it, was several bags of mail. This would be our last for some time. Dad had written to me again. He knew the significance of passing Ascension Island and anticipated the future lack of contact. He knew that the game was up and that only a forced outcome would prevail. In his letter he wrote,

'Son, if I could change places with you right now, I would do so in an instant'.

The following day, we did our last whole-ship damage control exercise and attended our last first-aid courses. We wrote our wills and were each given a Geneva Convention Identity Card. The chief petty officers (CPO's) were issued with mono jets of morphine. There were no more drills, no more exercises. There was nothing more to learn other than what we would learn 'on the job'.

There was, however, one last ship cleaning exercise for captain's rounds. The Captain wanted to visit every department and talk to his men. So we cleaned and polished mess decks and workstations, then tidied ourselves up and awaited his arrival.

I was at the beef screen, standing at ease by the open door. My work station was immaculate and I wore a fresh set of working uniform (number 8's). We could hear the Captain being 'Piped' and announced around the neighbouring departments and, bit by bit, he drew nearer to the main galley. When he arrived, our CPO Cook, Roger Davies, called out, 'Main galley you will come to attention. The Captain is on deck', and, with that, we snapped upright to attention. Capt. Black stepped into our passageway and returned the salute from our chief. He instructed him, 'Please tell your men to relax',

Roger called out, 'Main galley you may stand at ease, stand easy!'

The captain was wearing his full dress uniform and so, too, was his entourage of senior officers. This was an impressive sight. He seemed much keener to talk to junior rates, than his senior rates. When he reached the entrance of my meat preparation area, he asked me, 'What goes on here?'

My stomach was jumping with butterflies as I explained the purposes and processes of the beef screen. He took an interest in the meat tenderising machine which was bolted to the bulkhead and I proceeded to explain how it worked. As we talked, I relaxed a little and found myself looking onto a kind face. He was much older than any of us junior rates, of course, and probably even older than many of the senior rates. But what struck me most was that when he looked at you, he held your gaze in a way that a man does when he respects you.

Roger Davies, my ever doubtful Chief, made faces at me and drew his pinched finger across his mouth as if to tell me,

'Don't talk too much, don't say anything stupid, we need to move on...'

His animated expression said, 'Don't encourage him, just shut up...'

I began to enjoy Roger's discomfort, but then the Captain caught me off guard and asked, 'Do you feel confident about us going into the exclusion zone?'

I was taken aback and replied, 'Er yes ... but'

Roger's face was about to explode. He drew his finger across his throat as I went on. 'Sorry Sir, it's nothing. It really doesn't matter'.

The Captain held his gaze on me. It was neither judgmental nor harsh, annoyed or impatient. If anything at all, I would say it was kind and understanding. He insisted, 'No, please go on, please finish what you were about to say.'

I continued, 'I was wondering if our Harriers will be able to hold off the Argentinian air force.'

The captain looked completely unfazed by the question

and answered. 'Yes, I think they will. I think they will do a very good job.'

I smiled and replied, 'Thank you sir'.

I was relieved at his answer, but, more so, I was pleased that I had been able to ask the question without embarrassing myself. I was so nervous. Captain Black thanked me for my hard work and then the party moved on. As they went past, Roger shook his head at me and whispered, 'You bugger.'

I replied excitedly, 'I really didn't mean to.'

Over the many years that have passed since I stood by that door and talked to our Captain, I have often considered the effect he had on me and the many others who also spoke to him. I am sure that we were all inspired by meeting him in this way. It was, in short, a brilliant act of leadership except, I would argue, that it wasn't an act at all. Capt. JJ Black had a genuine respect for his men and trusted them, and they, in turn, did likewise.

Later that day, we were allowed one last casual walk on the flight deck. I took Dad's letter with me and read it again. I knew that, in the coming days and weeks he would have many sleepless nights and I remember thinking, 'This will be difficult for us both…'

From now on, there would be no more relaxation, nor fitness classes, nor time off.

In the evening Capt. Black conducted a 50-minute briefing which we watched on our television. He talked extensively about the carrier group, our formation, and general tactics. He talked about the forthcoming attack on South Georgia, about our Royal Fleet Auxiliaries (RFA's) replenishment ships, the new Sidewinder aircraft-to-aircraft missiles that would be used for the first time by our pilots. He talked about the new and untested Skua missiles for air-to-ground attack by helicopters. He warned of the potential dangers but added, 'We can come through this'.

Then, on a more personal note, he said. 'We are in for a long and difficult haul. You must take care of yourselves, eat well and regularly. Take rest, whenever the opportunity arises, and keep your spirits up.'

He finished by saying, 'Some crewmembers have asked me if I think we can pull this off. Well I say this to you now. I think we will piss it!'

This lightened the mood. It was always good to see an officer's mask slip and to hear them to say something 'ungentlemanly'. On that night, Capt. JJ Black had played it perfectly. His talk was very concise and we were surprised at the amount of detail that he had gone into. It was as if he was confiding in us and we felt important because of it. I can speak from the heart when I say, that in the midst of so much peril and uncertainty, and such a long way from home, Captain John Jeremy Black impressed us all, to a man. If we were to go to war, be it in the South Atlantic or anywhere else, then we would rather go with him than any other captain in the whole of the Royal Navy.

6

Looking back now, my overriding memory of the Falklands war was of the constant cold and its attendant bad weather. As we ploughed on, ever further south, the autumnal gales took hold and the cold began to permeate through the steel bulkheads and decks of the ship. The sky and sea were constantly black and grey. Rain and snow storms would blow up and when these settled, thick cold fog enveloped us. *Invincible* found herself pushing against these elements as though she were a toy in an ice-cold bathtub being splashed by an angry child.

It was always cold in the South Atlantic

I was a junior rate cook and ship's diver. At State 2, I would be tending to the ship's temperature-controlled stores. At Action Stations, I would be manning a fire and repair party post. Not one of us below decks, would have any say in the running of the ship or her actions throughout the campaign. All of that would be down to the commanding officers.

We could easily have become isolated with no knowledge of anything going on around us or in the broader outside world. To alleviate this, the captain decided that the live BBC World Service news was to be piped through the tannoy system every six hours and a general update of operations around *Invincible* and the task force, would be relayed by the Duty Bridge Officer every four hours. This openness and sharing of information helped to keep our spirits up.

Our action dress was our No.8 working rig, which

consisted of steel toe-capped boots, woollen socks, cotton trousers and denim shirt. Around his waist, each and every man carried a gas mask, lifejacket and a bright orange 'Once Only' survival suit. As its name implies, this would be put on only once - when it was time to abandon the ship. This suit was designed to stave off the deadly embrace of hypothermia and make its wearer more visible for rescue. We also carried an anti-flash hood and gloves that, in theory, give a measure of protection against the scorching heat from an explosion or in compartment type firefighting.

Although we were forbidden to carry any personal items in our gas mask bag, everyone did. The rules were relaxed as long as these items did not impede the removal of the mask. In my gas bag, alongside my plastic mug, I carried a chess set. The little plastic pieces were wrapped in a clear poly-bag, and the board, folded flat, was slid unobtrusively alongside the gas mask. Sometimes I carried a book, or a pack of cards, or paper and pen.

The constant coldness brought about another concession. We were allowed to wear woolly pullovers and carry a blanket to action stations. But, as soon as we went from yellow to red alert, these were immediately removed and stored. Prior to the Falklands, all of these things, personal kit stored in your gas mask bag, woolly pullovers, blankets, playing chess at yellow alert, would have had you swiftly placed on a disciplinary charge but now things were changed - from now on pragmatism would reign.

In due course, when we suffered our first casualties from burning ships, it was discovered that the No8 rig we wore did not offer any protection from fire and so, we were all issued with fire-retardant overalls. Also, there were disturbing reports about our 'once only' suits. The testimony of those who stepped into them was that the leg lines were tangled and knotted. These lines needed to be wrapped and crossed up each leg in order to lock out the air. Precious time was lost in untangling these knotted lines. Some of those who jumped into the water without tying up the legs found themselves floating upside down, near drowned and struggling to right themselves.

We were instructed to check and, where necessary, to alter our suits.

★

Towards the end of April, HMS's *Brilliant* and *Plymouth* were ordered to retake South Georgia. They started with a bombardment then landed a detachment of Royal Marines and Special Forces. A battle quickly got underway.

The Argentine submarine, *Santa Fe*, was operating in that area and, spotting the seemingly unarmed red-and-white survey ship, HMS *Endurance*, she surfaced and demanded a surrender. *Endurance* had other ideas. Turning her bows towards her opponent, *Endurance* drew out and rapidly armed her Lynx helicopter from her now obscured flight deck. The aircraft quickly took off and, rising vertically from the deck, she unleashed her Skua missiles straight into the conning tower of the submarine.

The damage was critical.

In desperate need of repair, *Santa Fe* retired to South Georgia, only to find that the Argentine garrison was under attack and the harbour blockaded by Royal Navy warships. By the end of the day, all would be surrendered; the garrison and submarine were out of the war, and South Georgia was in British hands again.

The South Georgia action was a morale boost for us but we all knew that the Falklands was where the true battle lay, and this would be a much tougher nut to crack.

★

Before dawn on Saturday 1 May, we entered the Total Exclusion Zone (TEZ), an event that our officers rather splendidly called our 'Interdiction of the Falklands garrison'. Our war now began in earnest.

It was on this day that we closed up for action stations for the first time for real. Reports came in that hostile aircraft were entering our area. We went to 'Red alert' and all our anti-attack measures were employed. *Invincible*'s bows were turned towards her opponents to offer as small a target as possible. We also hoped that her V-shaped bows might deflect a bomb or missile. Chaff was fired from her side. This resembled shredded tinfoil which, as it fell from the sky, would confuse a radar homing device and attract its missile away from the ship. In a further effort to draw away approaching missiles, Sea King helicopters hovered around just feet above the sea.

When an incoming Exocet missile was detected we 'Hit the deck'.

A submarine was heard encroaching upon us. A torpedo was fired. We hit the deck again.

Each time, *Invincible* was thrown into wild evasive manoeuvers and each time, our nerves were frayed.

British Vulcan bombers flew overhead to attack Port Stanley airfield. Harriers from *Hermes* supported the Vulcans with strafing and cluster bombs, while *Invincible*'s Harriers chased off waves of enemy aircraft that were probing our position.

We were like two boxers determined to prove our dominance on the first round.

Eventually, at about 8 pm, an hour or so after sunset, we stepped down from action stations. The mood on board was tense. It had been a long, hectic day. The captain made an announcement over the tannoy and gave us a calm summary of the day's events; our Harrier pilots had confirmed that they had shot down two aircraft with another aircraft, possibly two, seen limping for home. It was thought that these might have to ditch into the sea due to a likely shortage of fuel. The missile that was fired was thought to be an Exocet. It had gone wide, possibly due to a malfunction, and was tracked until it crashed into the sea about 3 miles in front of us. The 'submarine', he explained, 'was probably a marine mammal'.

(It was not until the end of the war that we discovered that the captured *Santa Fe* was the only operational submarine that the Argentinians had had. But before then, on at least two or three occasions, we had found ourselves hitting the deck whilst our depth charges and bombs rained down upon the poor, innocent ocean giants that had, for generations, lived peacefully in the South Atlantic.)

In private quarters, Capt. Black warned his officers against overreaction and, in time, our call to action stations from yellow to red alert went on in a much more considered and orderly way. Overreaction causes stress and accidents where little accidents can lead to big accidents and chain reactions. At the end of that first day, I thought, 'If all this can happen on our first day in the TEZ, then what the hell can happen over the next, God knows how long?'

The following day, well before dawn we were back at our action stations.

During the night, our Harriers had detected the approach of the Argentinian aircraft carrier '*Veinticinco De Mayo*' accompanied by its group of destroyers and frigates. It was a formidable force and, throughout the day, we moved around the ocean, probing and evading, in a deadly game of hide and seek. There were in fact two Argentinian naval groups. The aforementioned carrier group to the North-west, being monitored by our Harriers, and a separate group, to the South-west, monitored by our submarine HMS *Conqueror*. Both groups were moving eastwards whilst maintaining a position just outside the TEZ. We were directly east of the Falkland Islands just inside the TEZ.

As the day progressed, Admiral Woodward, who was in overall command, sent increasingly desperate signals to command headquarters in Northwood, London, asking for permission to attack. He was convinced that a pincer movement by the Argentinians was underway and that his task force was in peril.

Military thinking is relatively straightforward but diplomatic thinking is very convoluted. The attacking of ships outside of the TEZ would create a major international problem for the Government and the Foreign Office. Eventually, they reached a decision and much to the relief of Admiral Woodward, his request was granted. In the closing hours of 2nd May, the submarine *Conqueror* fired two torpedoes into the heavy cruiser, *General Belgrano*. Within minutes the most powerful ship in the Argentine Navy was sent to the bottom and, with her, died over 300 of her crew. There was much controversy to follow and, for years to come, debate would rage about the legality of this action and the culpability of those involved. Whatever the wrongs and rights, the effects were just what Admiral Woodward had desired. The Argentine Navy returned to port and never offered any further threat to the Task Force again.

7

The war had now escalated to a new level and, within two days, the Argentinians struck back. In a lightning quick, low-altitude raid, a pair of Super Etendard aircraft broke through our defensive ring and fired off their deadly Exocet missiles.

The first one found its target and fatally struck HMS *Sheffield* on her starboard midships section. The explosion created bilious acrid smoke and fires and a 15-foot hole just above the waterline. The second missile passed HMS *Yarmouth* and HMS *Alacrity* before falling short of us - another close call for *Invincible*.

The missile had struck *Sheffield* at the point which, in relation to *Invincible* would be on the same level as No 5 deck. The very deck where all our fire and repair party posts were stationed. The next day, these important groups were moved three decks higher and 5 deck quickly became known as, 'The death belt.' My group was now positioned directly under the flight deck, between the forward end of the flight deck ramp, and the Sea Dart missile launcher, which was to the side of the ramp. From here, we could hear every movement coming to and from the ship.

The cooks remained on 5 deck at the main galley and wardroom. They would have to take their chances. From now on, whenever we went down for action messing, there was an even greater urgency to our mealtimes as we were anxious to get back to the comparative safety of our action stations.

But it wasn't all action.

As the days came and went, there were many long hours spent waiting. I played a lot of Chess and, just like Uncle Eddie before me, I became very hard to beat. I read and wrote letters. I helped others to write their letters, or just played cards.

But there was action, elsewhere.

Invincible carried a contingent of Special Forces soldiers and they were flown ashore at nightfall and retrieved before dawn. Upon their return, they came down to the main galley for a hot meal and we could hear them talking about their night's work. They had attacked the airfield at Pebble Island, knocked out communications posts, reconnoitred areas of interest and undermined the local garrison's morale by causing havoc and destruction in whatever way they could.

Then one night, they attacked an Argentine trawler called the *Narwal*, which we correctly guessed was a spy ship. The action began with the vessel being strafed by our Harriers before she was boarded by our SBS. Some of her crew were killed and one man was badly wounded. In all, 25 prisoners where brought back to *Invincible* including an intelligence officer. The civilian crew had, for the most part, been conscripted into service.

The SBS guys that returned with them were all, to a man, well oiled! It turned out that, when they had blown open the ship's strong box, they found several bottles of booze and a load of Argentinian money. The story went that they threw away the money and started on the liquor instead.

Our surgeons operated on the injured sailor but were unable to save his life. His body was taken and laid in state on our quarterdeck all night, with two guards standing over him. It was a somewhat forlorn sight - dignified and peaceful. Just before dawn, our padre and a few attendant officers conducted a short respectful service before passing his body from the hands of men, to the depths of the ocean. The sea, where this poor man had fished for most of his life, would now be his resting place.

The remaining captives, who were mostly fishermen, were held under guard in the little chapel beneath our mess deck. In the mornings, before action stations, they were brought up to use our toilets and I remember very clearly, their rich guttural Spanish voices. They looked old enough to be our Dads and each one looked terrified. They were so frightened of causing offence that they would step aside from the urinal when we queued behind them, and we encouraged them by saying and gesturing, 'Please you go first'.

Many of us wondered how they must have felt, being captured by their enemy and then, held in the bowels of a ship that was a primary target for their own air force. We felt sorry for them.

(Eventually after the war, these prisoners were transferred to a Royal Fleet Auxiliary (RFA) and returned, via Ascension Island, to a heroes' welcome in Argentina, but not before a send-off from their temporary messmates! Prior to their departure, we cooks gifted them with HMS *Invincible* souvenirs, T-shirts, zippo cigarette lighters, baseball caps and ladies underwear. They each had gifts to bear for when they got home. I like to imagine that, to this day, their grandchildren in Argentina are still listening to improbable stories of legendary proportions from these old men.)

★

It was not long before the first call came for divers to be mustered. I was sent out with Phil Kane, a big burly Able Bodied Seaman (AB). Our mission was to recover a Sea King helicopter that had crashed and was now floating upside down on the sea.

Dear Henry briefed us, 'There is a 7ft swell running but

the wind is settling down so it should be 'do' able. We want to lift the aircraft out and recover as many re-usable parts as we can...'

We were tasked with putting and inflating a flotation device into the main compartment to keep the aircraft afloat, and then, attaching a lifting strap around the main rotor so that the aircraft could be hoisted by crane onto the deck of the ship. Phil and I had done this kind of work before and knew what to do. We needed to get there fast and work quickly. Whilst we were being flown, at full speed, to the scene, we agreed that I would go into the compartment and inflate the bag and Phil would attend to the rotor strap.

When we arrived, we could see a deployed life raft with a flashing strobe light on top that had been blown a considerable distance downwind. There was a ship approaching and a smaller deck boat was being lowered to recover the helicopter crew from the raft. We were told that they had all got out, and so, there were no bodies to recover.

It was a typical South Atlantic winter's day, grey and cold. The swell was just as Dear Henry had told us, with occasional white horses breaking. Phil jumped in first then I lined up to make my jump. I was just about to go when the winch man grabbed me and shouted,

'Wait!'

Phil was giving a signal of crossed arms, a sign of distress, the same sign which says 'abort'. He was in trouble. The winch man lowered the recovery sling but Phil was clearly becoming increasingly weaker and slow to respond. It seemed to take an age for him to grab the sling, get the belt over his head, under his arms, and lock it off. When he was eventually hoisted back into the helicopter he was shivering violently. His face and hands had turned blue as though he were a corpse with rigor mortis. He was frozen to the core.

Obviously the water was much too cold for us to operate

in, wearing just flimsy wetsuits. We had worn these because they allowed us to move more freely but we should have worn dry suits and thermal fleeces with thick neoprene hoods and gloves. Upon our return, Phil was taken to sickbay and treated for hypothermia. Dear Henry, waiting anxiously by the flight deck said. 'I'm terribly sorry, Cook Gorman. I didn't realise the water was so cold'.

There was no need to apologise, but later a signal went around the fleet instructing all diving officers to ensure that dry suits were to be worn on all future operations.

The stricken helicopter was never recovered. She sank within minutes of us leaving the scene.

8

On 21 May, the most desperate phase of the war commenced with troop landings at San Carlos Water. The Argentine air force pilots further increased their efforts and demonstrated an absolute determination to stop us. HMS *Argonaut* and *Antrim* were attacked and unexploded bombs were lodged deep inside them. HMS *Brilliant* and *Broadsword* were strafed and damaged by bomb splinters. HMS *Ardent* was bombed and sunk with 20 dead and 30 seriously wounded.

Other ships narrowly escaped as bombs fell all around them. HMS *Argonaut*, with the two unexploded bombs lodged next to her magazine and pumping to keep herself afloat, refused to retire. She maintained her position as, too, did *Antrim*, whilst this life-and-death struggle went on.

At least 15 enemy aircraft were destroyed.

Invincible was stationed to the east, away from the gun line but close enough for her aircraft to be vectored in by our picket ships to support and defend the landing area. In the space of four days, *Invincible*'s 801 Squadron Harrier group launched over 100 missions. 820 Squadron Sea Kings were also constantly pressed both day and night. The flight operations went on and on for both carriers. The war was now in the balance and the battle for San Carlos would be one of its defining moments. In the days that followed, HMS *Antelope* was bombed and sunk whilst two landing ships managed to defuse two unexploded bombs that were lodged inside them.

Four days after the landings, on 25 May, the Argentine day of national independence, the Argentines made a concentrated attack on our carrier group. The two carriers, *Invincible* and *Hermes*, were surrounded by rings of defending picket ships which carried their own surface-to-air missiles and chaff protection. They gave us an advance warning of enemy aircraft and could also, when necessary, take over control of our aircraft and vector them towards the hostile aircraft.

Nothing is infallible but the system seemed to be working well and we had deterred many probes and beaten off a number of intrusions in this way. Throughout the day, HMS *Coventry* and *Broadsword* were operating a missile trap just North of Pebble Island. *Coventry* had already beaten off an attack that day and had destroyed at least two hostile aircraft, but her luck was about to run out. At around 6pm both ships came under attack. *Broadsword* had a bomb through her side which then deflected out through her flight deck and destroyed her Lynx helicopter. Incredibly, there was no explosion or fire. *Coventry* received two hits which ignited. Fires broke out and she began to flood. She had to be abandoned and before the day was through, she rolled over and sank.

About an hour or so later, the core of the group came under attack. Our defences were penetrated. This time it was for real. This time they were very close. Below decks the tannoy clicked on and the deck officer shouted, 'Red alert, Red alert, Red alert, Hit the deck Hit the…'

The sentence was left incomplete. The tannoy clicked off. He didn't have time to say anymore. In seconds, we had gone from Yellow, straight through Red and onto 'Hit the Deck'. This was serious! For a fraction of a second, we looked at each other in astonishment. Then the chief shouted. 'Everyone get to it at the rush!'

Our section burst into a frenzy of activity; blankets, books, letters, and chess boards, in the air, being thrown into lockers.

Everyone was shouting and banging into each other. The chief was shouting, 'On the deck get on the deck!'

We scrambled to the floor and fought for a bit of space, somewhere to hide, somewhere to make yourself small, somewhere to limit the damage. *Invincible*'s engines went up to maximum power and the whole ship shuddered, as if in defiance of such harsh treatment of her machinery. We could feel her turn hard to starboard. She was trying to put her bow into the enemy. The chief continued shouting, 'Cover yourself, get your anti-flash up, cover your eyes, cover your eyes.' A voice cried out. 'Jesus fucking Christ!'

And as it did, a series of low thudding explosions rolled out, 'Putt, putt, putt, putt, putt.' It was the sound of chaff being fired all along the starboard side of *Invincible*.

My breath began to deepen and an anxious tightness stretched across my chest. In the corner, I heard a man, his voice rising in panic, 'I'm leaving. I can't stay here. I'm going into the passageway. I'm going to lie down out there.'

The chief roared out, 'Stay where you are man, on the deck and get your head down!'

I looked up. The chief had pulled his anti-flash hood down so as to make eye contact with the terrified rating. His face was red and flushed with anger. His veins were bulging from his neck and temples. His fists were made hard and tight and in his right hand he pointed a truncheon.

The rating's friend, his 'oppo,' had grabbed him from behind and pulled him so that they both lay on the deck. The 'oppo' had his arm across his friend's neck in a near stranglehold and pleaded with the chief, 'It's okay, chief, I've got him, he won't go anywhere I promise.'

Then he turned to his friend and said. 'Now hold tight you stupid bastard. I've got you, just hold tight!'

The terrified, bewildered rating waved his hands about and conceded. 'It's okay I'm not going anywhere. I'm fine, I'm fine.'

He was anything but fine and the chief warned, 'One more pipe out of you and I will fucking drop you. Do you understand?'

The rating nodded his agreement, miserably.

As this was going, on I felt someone grabbing onto and holding my left hand. It was Stevie Hiles, a fellow cook, younger than me by three years to whom I had become something of a Sea Daddy. He wanted to become a diver and would ask me endless questions about the aptitude test and training course. At the tender age of 18, Stevie was already married and had a baby boy. The chief looked at me and pointed an accusing finger and shouted, 'Get your head down.'

I nodded in agreement and, as I did, I turned and looked straight into Stevie's face. Through the slits in his anti-flash hood, I could see his pale white drawn complexion and the narrow vision of his blue eyes, piercing right into me. I gave his hand a squeeze and, with my right hand, I opened my palm and motioned to him as if to say, 'It's okay, you can hold on if you want.'

The ship continued to shudder and we heard our Harriers taking off; 'Vroom,' the first one, then moments later, 'Vroom', another was gone, helicopters were winding up and taking off and then, right out of the blue, came a shuddering explosion. 'Bang'! The compartment reverberated. This noise was unfamiliar to us. Someone shouted, 'Are we hit? Have we been hit?'

Then a split second later came another earthmoving shuddering bang. The chief replied above the din, 'We are not hit. It's the Sea Dart. We are firing back.'

Moments later, another salvo let loose and another shuddering bang ran through our cold steel compartment. Every one of us knew that *Invincible* was fighting for her life. She was in mortal danger. As this went on, I heard another voice shout out. This voice had fear but also defiance, 'Now fuck off you bastards',

The chief spoke again, a little bit more gentle, but still assertive, 'Now everyone calm down… keep it quiet lads.'

The compartment became quiet. Most of the guys had both hands cupped around their face to cover their eyes. All were lying face down. I didn't have the heart to draw my hand away from Stevie, so I lay there and pressed my face directly into the deck. Its coolness was like a compress on my forehead. I remember calming myself by thinking, 'Whatever comes through that bulkhead and up through this deck will be fine. We will deal with it, we will be fine…We will deal with it, we will be fine…'

Like a mantra, I thought this over and over again.

The moments passed by and moments became minutes, and as those minutes began to add up, the breathing began to lighten. I don't know how long we lay like that. It may have been five or ten minutes, more or less, but it ended with a click of the tannoy and the announcement, 'Relax from red alert. All hands assume yellow alert'. Our danger had passed.

Strange as it may seem, as we sat up and pulled off our anti-flash hoods, we began laughing. I noticed that Stevie was looking intently at me. He looked anxious. I guessed that he was worried that I might embarrass him by telling the others that he had grabbed my hand, so I patted his shoulder and said. 'It's okay mate. Don't worry about it', to which he relaxed and laughed too.

Cigarettes were passed out and I took one even though I'd stop smoking a year earlier. Just at this moment, the health risk seemed irrelevant. I lit up and drew the hot musty smoke deep into my lungs. It was a choking and pleasing sensation. The nicotine passed from my lungs and into my bloodstream and went swimming around my head. I enjoyed the light dizziness and slightly nauseous sensation that it caused. I closed my eyes and savoured the moment. The frightened rating was talking, protesting his innocence. 'I wasn't abandoning my post. I just wanted to crash down on the passageway. There was no room in here.'

Nobody disagreed or argued with him. If he said it was a misunderstanding, then so be it.

The tannoy clicked on and the duty officer started to speak. We settled down to listen. Exocet missiles had been fired and we had fired 3 Sea Dart missiles in response. They were unsure if any had found their target. However, an Exocet had struck the *Atlantic Conveyor*, a large merchant marine ship that was stationed 2 miles behind us, directly between ourselves and *Hermes*.

An hour or so later, darkness descended and we stepped down from action stations, but, before I went to my work post, I went first to the quarterdeck. I needed some fresh air and a few moments of relative solitude. There were other men there too, others who had the same idea, but nobody stayed for long - it was too cold.

On the horizon, I could see the remains of the *Atlantic Conveyor*. She was still burning fiercely, like a false orb of sun going down to the horizon.

The missile had struck her port quarter; fires had soon taken hold and had run rampantly through the ship, setting off fuel and ammunition.

One of the survivors from the *Atlantic Conveyor* told us what he saw. Two missiles were heading for *Invincible* when one passed through the chaff fired by HMS Ambuscade and redirected itself onto the *Atlantic Conveyor*. The second continued unabated and was brought down by our third Sea Dart. The first two Sea Darts went into the clouds where he saw the clouds explode.

As *Atlantic Conveyor* was being abandoned, a commotion broke out. HMS *Brilliant* had sent her ship's boat across to help rescue survivors and, in doing so, it had become hopelessly entangled with a life raft, until both of them were rescued by *Invincible*. Ironically, the rescued crew of the *Brilliant* complained at having lost their ship's boat and were unaware of the imminent danger that they had been pulled from.

Twelve men from the *Atlantic Conveyor* were killed, including her commanding officer, Capt. Ian North, a 33 year veteran of the Merchant Navy. Having successfully seen his men off the ship, he had been making his way down the scrambling nets, when he missed his footing and fell into the freezing water. It was thought that the shock of cold water probably induced a heart attack and he was swept away. His body was never recovered.

Capt. Ian North would later be posthumously awarded the Distinguished Service Cross (DSC). He had never married and left no living relatives, but he was not alone that day. On the land, at sea and in the air, there had been tragedies but also many extraordinary acts of bravery; helicopters flying into blinding clouds of acrid smoke, close to the steel hulls of burning ships, using their downdraft to blow life rafts out of the way to safety, men selflessly dragging comrades out of smoke-filled burning compartments, trying to contain fires, trying to defuse bombs, medics trying to save lives, padres trying to save souls.

On that day alone, HMSs *Broadside, Sir Lancelot, Alacrity* and *Yarmouth*, had come close to disaster or, indeed, were still desperately trying to contain it.

And what of the assault on us that day? It wasn't the first time that we had been attacked, nor the first time that we had 'hit the deck'. But this time, it had been different. *This* time the enemy had come perilously close. From here on in, feelings would linger that, like *Atlantic Conveyor* and *Coventry,* our luck was bound to turn, bound to run out, sooner or later.

As I stood there, looking out upon the *Atlantic Conveyor*, burning and dying, I remembered the phrase, '*When God eats he clears the table...*' and I thought. 'Indeed he does, and never more so, than when men go to war.' I promised myself then, that if I should survive this mess in one piece, I would never again in my life, take a day of it for granted.

And I can say to you, in all truth that I never have.

9

The following day, as usual, before sunrise, we went to action stations. I sat with my woolly pullover on and a blanket wrapped around me. Stevie Hiles was sitting opposite. We were playing Chess.

Whenever I played Stevie, it was always something of a forgone conclusion that I would win and so I tended to relax my concentration. The game started and, as it did, Stevie asked,

'Den, do you think we will get a big welcome when we get home?'

I looked at him, whilst casting an opening pawn forward, then thought tenderly about it for a few moments. It all seemed so distant that I had never really thought about it.

'Yes, Stevie, of course we will,' I finally said.

We made another move or two and then he asked, 'And do you think people will make us feel special?' His voice was now trailing away to something that resembled melancholy. 'Or do you think they will treat us rotten for going to war… after all… a lot of people have protested about it?'

I sensed that Stevie needed a bit of Sea Daddy morale boosting. So I casually made another move and said, 'Stevie, when we get home from this lot, you will have the world at your feet, and everything in it.' Then I smiled kindly at him. 'Oh good,' he said. He quickly moved a piece and said, 'Checkmate!'

I looked at the board, alarmed at what he'd said, then incredulous at what I saw. Indeed, it was checkmate. Nay, fools-mate! As the Americans say, I had been dry-gulched. I looked at Stevie and he was staring at me, his bright blue eyes dancing with excitement and mischief, waiting for a response.

I was almost lost for words, then I said the first thing that came into my mind, 'You little twat!'

★

The war still had a long way to go. Four days later, on 30th May at about 2:30 pm, *Invincible* was attacked again. The Argentinians were convinced that their bombs and missiles had found their mark. Their jubilant pilots claimed a direct hit with an Exocet missile and at least two 250 kg bombs, which they said had struck directly onto our flight deck. The attack had taken place with a well-combined coordination which involved two Exocet-equipped Super Etendard aircraft and four bomb-carrying A4C's. The A4C's came in first, to distract us, whilst the Super Etendard approached low and under our radar. They reported that they saw a pall of black smoke billowing into the sky.

The Argentinian population exulted at the news and massive celebrations broke out on the streets of Buenos Aires. The 'La Gaceta Argentina' printed a special edition and, with it, a photograph of our ship, fatally wounded and burning, with men running frantically across her flight deck.

The 'Times' in London had got hold of the story and printed the report and the photograph. The Ministry of Defence and government ministers were inundated with enquiries and demands for information. The news stations and media went into overdrive, trying to find out the truth. John Nott, our defence minister, was asked to confirm what had happened to *Invincible*.

Soberly and quite correctly, he said, 'If we comment on whether or not our ships have been attacked, or where they might or might not be, then our enemy can use this information against us. I cannot tell you what you want to know until it is safe to do so. Only then, will I make an announcement'.

I would later find out that on that same day, my father had gone into a Safeway supermarket and found a display of Argentinian tinned corned beef for sale. He caused a commotion and the store manager was brought out. Dad remonstrated with him angrily and, in front of an assembled crowd, he argued, 'What is wrong with you... don't you realise our sons are dying down there? ... My boy is on board HMS *Invincible* right now and I don't know if he's alive or dead. So you will take this Argentine rubbish off your shelf or you can call the Police and have me arrested!'

The store manager apologised and immediately directed his staff to clear the shelf and withdraw the product. Some of the observers looked at Dad as if he was mad, but others touched him and said, 'We understand, you are quite right'.

Dad wrote a letter to me that morning. Then, in the late afternoon, he wrote a second letter. By late evening, he had written a third. When I received these letters three weeks later, it was clear that by the time he wrote the third letter, he had completely forgotten that he had written the previous two. Such was the anxiety that he felt.

On board *Invincible*, all we knew was that we had repulsed an attack, then carried on as usual. It was happening almost every other day.

The next morning, before going to action stations, the World Service news was piped around and by then the Ministry of Defence (MOD) had made the announcement that *Invincible* was untouched and still operational....

Much as we already 'knew' that, it was only then that we had any idea of what our loved ones at home had been going through.

10

Success in war is often attributed to luck but it is also down to whoever makes the fewest mistakes. The outcome is also governed by rates of attrition and an army's ability to maintain its momentum. The British task force scored highly in these factors.

The weather, which was so cold and awful, had its benefits. When it was too inclement to fly, it allowed ships like *Invincible* and *Hermes* to rest their pilots and to conduct essential maintenance. Sometimes, the fog and low clouds were so thick that we would not go to action stations at all. This would allow us, the crew, to work, socialise and sleep. These periods were a welcome reprieve.

The bad weather favoured our soldiers too. Not only were they familiar with these conditions, having been trained in the desolate open spaces around Dartmoor and Knoydart in Scotland, but also, they were being sheltered and well fed on board ships, until the landings. Meanwhile, the Argentinians had been dug into wet and cold field camps all over the islands for weeks before our arrival.

Another by-product of the cold weather was that it saved lives on both sides as wounded soldiers lay on the battlefield, awaiting medical attention. The coldness kept the blood drawn into the core of their bodies and, in turn, this kept them alive. In a warmer climate, they would have, quite simply, bled to death.

In spite of the considerable attrition exacted against the Argentinian air force, they still posed a deadly threat and on 8 June, they attacked again. It began when HMS *Plymouth* had been diverted from the protective curtain around San Carlos water to carry out a naval gunnery support mission against an Argentine observation post. As she entered the widest part of the Sound, she found herself under attack from a group of Mirage aircraft and called for air support. By the time the air cover arrived, *Plymouth* had suffered extensive damage from cannon fire and an unexploded bomb was lodged in her mortar mounting. Nevertheless, she had shot down one aircraft and damaged two others, who were now running for home. The Harriers made a short pursuit.

It was at this precise time that the Argentines pressed home another air attack on the now defenceless RFA *Sir Tristram* and RFA *Sir Galahad*, which had Welsh Guardsmen on board, waiting to disembark at Bluff Cove. The bombs struck home and detonated. Over 50 men were killed, others were grievously wounded and burned. Both ships were abandoned. It was a sickening tragedy and the heaviest single loss of life by British forces throughout the whole campaign.

★

Six days later on Tuesday 15 June, the war ended with the surrender of the Argentine garrison at their last redoubt at Port Stanley.

There was however, still one tragedy in store for *Invincible*; on the very day of surrender, we were ploughing through a heavy sea when the ship exercised a turn which threw her sharply onto her port side at an angle of about 30°. A team of airmen were manoeuvring equipment on the flight deck when this sudden lurch caused a tractor to break its shackles and career across the deck crushing a naval airman against the island bulkhead. The unfortunate Brian 'Budgie' Marsden was knocked unconscious and rushed to sickbay where the surgeons operated on him. His internal injuries were severe and a call went out for the crew to donate blood. In all, 13 pints were transferred into him but to no avail. Brian Marsden died six hours later. He never regained consciousness.

When the news had come that the Union Jack was flying above Port Stanley, I must confess that, at first, I felt unaffected by it. I was not alone in this. The cruel loss of Brian Marsden and our time in active service had hardened us to any concept of 'happy endings'. For many of us, it would take two or three days for the message to sink in….but when it finally did, the joy of it was wonderful.

We all had our private thoughts. Many of us, especially the older guys, our Sea Daddies, had, at an earlier time, served in the ships that had been sunk or damaged. They knew many of the men who were dead and wounded. We, on *Invincible*, had treated wounded and buried three of our own ship's company, Lieutenant W.A Curtis, Lt Commander J.E Eyton-Jones and Naval Airman Brian Marsden.

My thoughts turned to a young cook, Andy Swallow, who was about 18 years old. We came through training at HMS Pembroke at about the same time. We had worked together at the shore base, HMS Nelson, whilst waiting for our first seagoing draft. Our drafting orders had come through at the same time. Andy had gone to the *Sheffield* and I to *Invincible*. We had all thought that he was lucky because *Sheffield* was due to travel 'East of Suez', and onto an extended tour of Asia, New Zealand and Australia - a fabulous trip on a homely type of ship. *Sheffield* was on route back to Britain when the Falklands war broke out. She was redirected to the South Atlantic and became the first naval ship casualty of the conflict. Andy was among the very first British sailors to die. It could easily have been me.

11

Invincible had been at sea for over 70 days but our mission was far from over. We had won the war but now we needed to enforce the peace. The captain told us.

'We will be going north to an area about 1500 miles south of Ascension Island. There we will do essential maintenance and have a short period of rest and enjoy some sunshine. Then we will return to the Falklands and patrol there until a new runway is built or we are relieved by our sister ship HMS *Illustrious*'.

We all knew that this would be a very long haul because there was no equipment on the Falkland Islands with which to build a runway and all the infra structures to go with it. Also, *Illustrious* was far from ready. She was still being built and was not yet commissioned. She didn't even have a crew.

Solemnly we continued to watch and listen. The captain went on. 'Many of our ships are in dire need of a refit and must be returned to port as soon as possible, none more so than *Hermes*. As you know, she is a very old and worn out carrier and was due to be scrapped this year...' He went on, 'The engineers on board have told us that if she ever stops her engines, it is unlikely they will ever start again.'

We knew that this was absolutely right. If the Argentines had started their war just two months later, *Hermes* would have, by then, been decommissioned, and the outcome of the war could have been very different. (After returning to Britain to a heroes' welcome, HMS *Hermes* never put to sea again).

So we went north and, as we did, a more normal shipboard life returned. We watched movies and ate normal food again. The weather began to brighten. We relaxed from weeks of active service. We had a street party on the flight deck and began fitness training again.

After we had reached our designated area, a place where the weather was settled and we would be undisturbed, we divers were called to muster in the flight operations room. Clearly, something new was brewing. We sat around restlessly waiting to be briefed.

Dear Henry arrived and began to explain our assignment. An air drop was on its way from Ascension Island. A number of Hercules aircraft were due to arrive carrying containers full of machinery parts, stores, equipment and mail. The aircraft were to fly past at low-level and would be dropping their containers by parachute into the sea. We were tasked with swimming to them and attaching lifting lines so that helicopters could lift and fly them back to the ship. This was to be an open-ocean, surface-swimming operation. There were three teams; each team was made up of two divers, with a helicopter to drop, retrieve, and transport them to the next container and other helicopters would rotate to and from the ship to carry the packages on board. At the end of the briefing, Dear Henry asked, 'Are there any questions?'

There were questions. Lots of them, of which I asked two or three. But none of us thought to ask about the threat of sharks. It never occurred to us that we were in an area inhabited by the Mako shark, a formidable predator. However, Dear Henry was fully aware and, in anticipation, had us shadowed with an additional helicopter with a Royal Marine gun crew on board. Dear Henry didn't want to worry us, so left it unmentioned at the briefing.

I was paired with Gary Campion, a very level-headed Able

Seaman (AB). We had worked together before and were happy to be put on the same team. I gave him the thumbs up and he smiled and nodded his approval in return. Without any further ado, we got ourselves ready and headed up to the flight deck. We spent the whole afternoon jumping out of helicopters, swimming, climbing, then being hoisted into the air and flown around to the next package. It was wonderful to be off the ship and swimming in translucent warm blue water. With a clear sky overhead and the radiant warm sun beating down, the pair of us laughed and joked, and repeatedly dived off the containers into the sea. There was a 6-foot swell running and this made the swimming more challenging (which we enjoyed). Sometimes, we lost sight of the containers and treaded water whilst waiting for the shape of the swell to alter and the packets to come into view again before swimming onto them.

Gary said, 'I wish I had a waterproof camera,' and motioned towards the ship. I understood what he meant, for our ship looked magnificent against the deep blue of the ocean and the sky blue backdrop.

All of our recent diving assignments had been cold and bleak and morbidly grim. This was different. This was the type of ocean experience I had longed for - the open air, living in the light, enjoying the elements around me, the warmth, the wind, the movement of the sea. Freedom.

In those few short hours, I escaped the grey steel walls of *Invincible*, her fluorescent lights, Spartan interior, endless work rotas and crowded mess decks. I embraced this freedom and soaked it up. My imagination was full of what life could be like beyond *Invincible*, when I'd have my own small boat, sailing on the trade winds to paradise.

★

Our short stay in the tropics was over all too soon and we began to make our way south again. Fresh ships were on their way to join us, HMS *Southampton*, *Birmingham*, *Danae* and *Apollo*. All were coming to relieve the worn-out and war-weary ships that needed to return to the UK. As we pressed on, the battle-damaged ships of the South Atlantic passed us, one by one, on their way home. A short announcement over the tannoy saw us rushing to the flight deck, quarterdeck and weather decks to wave and cheer for them as they passed. They did likewise. It was always bittersweet.

HMS *Glamorgan* passed by with a huge burned-out cavity on her port side just behind her aft chimney stack. She was the only ship to survive a direct hit from an Exocet. HMS *Glasgow* came by with a hole on each side where a bomb had crashed in on one side and out of the other without exploding. (During its lethal passage it struck and instantly killed one of her men. At the time, she was so badly damaged that shipwrights and engineers from *Invincible* were put on board to help shore her up and get her engines going again). As they passed, I felt proud to be part of the same Navy as them.

In due course, Admiral Woodward himself departed and, when he did, he sent the following signal,

'As I haul my South Atlantic flag down, I reflect sadly on the brave lives lost and the good ships gone in the short time of our trial. I thank wholeheartedly each and every one of you for your gallant support, tough determination and fierce perseverance under bloodied conditions. Let us be grateful that Argentina doesn't breed Bulldogs and, as we return severally to enjoy the blessings of the land, resolve that those left behind for ever shall not be forgotten.'

12

At this time, Capt. JJ Black again showed his mastery of leadership and his understanding of his men. He announced to his officers, 'We are going to relax the watch-keeping system'. They advised him, 'But sir, this has never been done before,' to which he replied, 'An aircraft carrier has never been sent on a continuous operation for so long before.'

The watch system was then changed so that most of the ship's company was only required to work on alternate days. It was a brave move because the fear, among many, was that idle hands would grow restless and trouble would brew, but Capt. Black trusted his men, and we, in turn, did not let him down.

Life instantly became more bearable. Fitness training resumed every day in the hangar. Movies were shown on our CCTV every night. The galley was given an improved budget and food was made more varied and interesting wherever possible. Educational classes were set up. The library was resupplied with books. A beard-growing contest was announced. We all delighted at showing up for work without shaving! There was a cookery contest, a Chess tournament, and a fancy dress party. There was also a Sod's opera, a performance of songs and comedy sketches, created and performed by the ship's company on a makeshift stage in the hangar. For weeks, the ship was buzzing with men making costumes and rehearsing their parts! A 100-mile marathon was announced in which 100 of the crew, in turn, ran a measured mile each, around the flight deck. Entertainers were brought down from England to perform to the whole ship's company.

Although every effort was made to make life more bearable the days still crept by slowly and inexorably. The weather would regularly play its part to taunt us, with gales blowing and seas rising so much that access to weather decks was prohibited. At these times, solid green water broke over the forecastle, down the flight deck, through the weather decks and across the quarterdeck.

Days turned into weeks - I dreamed of sailing a boat to warm sunny places, a boat of my own, a world of my own where I did not need to share my living space, where I could eat what I wanted, whenever I wanted, where life would be easy and the discipline non-existent. I dreamed of finding a girl who would share this life with me, perhaps an American or an innocent beauty from the South Pacific or even, a 'girl from next door', with red hair and freckles. I dreamed of a simple, un-complicated inexpensive life where I could escape the drudgery of mass-produced food and hot demanding kitchens.

Dad continued to write frequently and his letters were full of love and encouragement. Since we had lost Uncle Eddie, we had become closer and I knew that my joining the Navy was a constant source of pride to him. I am sure he knew that, in my crowded world, I was lonely. I would never admit it, but Dad knew and he encouraged me to stay strong. He wrote, 'You will be home soon, and have a girl on your arm.' He sent me pens, snacks, magazines, and delicatessen foods, like the earlier parcel he'd sent. I shared everything with my mess mates and they, in turn, shared their parcels. In this way we snatched moments of pleasure and luxury from our austere life.

Weeks turned into months. HMS *Illustrious* was built in record time and, as soon as she was fitted out, fully-manned and operational, she steamed directly to our lonely outpost and relieved us of our duty.

There was a mid-ocean handover of the two sister ships. We stood on the flight deck, shouting and cheering and throwing potatoes across the gap, as the ships steamed alongside each other at full speed. Overhead, helicopters turned wheels and somersaults and Harriers enacted strafing runs.

In three weeks we would be back in the UK....We were going home!

We headed north into the Tropic of Capricorn and across the Equator, revelling in glorious sunshine. Its warmth spread throughout the ship. It felt like a lifetime had passed since we had travelled this way on our way south. On we went, until at last, at 8 am on 16 September, we quietly dropped anchor at Mounts Bay in thick fog. The first Sea Lord, Admiral Sir Henry Leach, came on board along with members of the Press.

I packed my bags. I had completed my 18-month tour of duty and had already been informed that, after my leave was complete, I would be stationed at the Faslane submarine base in Scotland, for an 18-month spell of shore duty. Many others would be leaving too and fond farewells were said. We drank beer that we had hoarded and because we were unaccustomed to it, we became merry quite quickly. We sang songs, told jokes, exchanged gifts, addresses and phone numbers and promised to stay in touch.

The following morning we were called to duty at 5.50 am. Our anchor was up and we were heading into Portsmouth. The Lord Mayor of Portsmouth, the Mayor of Durham and more press members joined the ship. At 11 am, the Royal Barge came alongside and the Queen and Prince Philip joined us. They were first taken to a private cabin to meet their son, Prince Andrew, before coming to the hangar where the entire ship's company was assembled in full No1 ceremonial uniform. The Queen looked radiantly happy. Prince Philip came over to us and said, 'You are in for a wonderful welcome. The whole country is thrilled to have you back.'

As soon as the Royal tour was complete, we were ordered to the flight deck and brought to attention facing outwards on both port and starboard sides of the ship. This is known as 'Procedure Alpha' and this is practised by Royal Navy ships upon entry and exit from port.

I stood on the starboard side on the midsection, facing Portsmouth.

It was warm and the morning mist was burning off rapidly, as the ship moved gracefully across those last few miles into Portsmouth Harbour. We were preceded by two large tugs, firing water cannon into the air. Helicopters and light aircraft flew overhead with 'Welcome Home' banners trailing behind. As far as the eye could see, there was an armada of small boats of every description, shadowing us and escorting us in.

On the previous evening, Capt. Black had addressed us on CCTV. He said many things then closed with, 'I have one last thing to ask of you. When we are at Procedure Alpha, please hold fast. Do not wave to anyone, or break rank, until you are ordered to stand down. I want to show you off to the World and to your families. I want them to be as proud of you as I am...'

To a man, we obeyed his command. As we came nearer, to our astonishment, we could see the beaches thronged with people who had come out to greet us. Over two million people converged, thronging, anxious to see us, to cheer for us. To watch, to collect photographs, or maybe, simply to absorb the atmosphere, to hold onto it for a while and then to pass it on in conversation to others who were not there. Whatever the reason, we, who stood there shoulder to shoulder along the upper decks of *Invincible*, saw it and were amazed at what we saw.

We had seen the news reports of other ships returning to

port to a heroes' welcome, but that all seemed such a long time ago. We were the very last active service ship to return. We had been at sea for 166 days; five and a half months, a world record for continuous carrier operations at sea - but who would care about that? World news moves on and major events are quickly forgotten. We thought that we would have been forgotten too and, perhaps, welcomed with a muted ovation compared with those early ships that had returned.

As we neared the shore, we could hear the cheers. Onwards we came, through the narrow port entrance. On the crowded round fort-like tower immediately at the entrance, I saw a group of women holding a huge banner with the words, 'Welcome Home Valiant Men of *Invincible*.'

I felt proud and sad and joyful all at the same time. My breathing hardened and my chest felt as if it would explode. I swallowed hard. We all felt the same, but we held fast as our captain had requested. *Invincible* drew alongside the harbour wall. The tugs began to push us in and, as they did, the Royal Marine Band, which was on the shore, began to play. The seamen quickly began working on the ropes that would bind our ship alongside and bring an end to our long journey.

Still we held fast at Procedure Alpha.

Over 10,000 of our immediate family and friends were waiting on the jetty before us. They roared with joy on and on, then gradually became muted and confused as we stood there above them, not moving, not responding. After a couple of minutes, an interminable two or three minutes the tannoy clicked on and a booming voice called out, 'Men of *Invincible*, stand at ease. Stand down from Procedure Alpha.'

We erupted! We shouted with unrestrained joy and threw our hats into the crowd. The crowd, in turn, roared in response and months of anxiety, heartache, separation and difficulty were swept away and replaced with sheer unadulterated joy. Wives, girlfriends and mothers wept. The thought occurred to me that, for the first time in her incredible career, our Queen was not the centre of attention - we were.

I looked into the crowd and searched for Dad. It was almost impossible to find him in the throng. Then after 10 or 15 minutes, I saw him. He was standing with Margaret and Brother Ed. I saw him but he hadn't yet seen me. So I held my gaze on him, watching him cast his eyes backwards and forwards across the deck line until his vision was right on me.

Then I waved briskly. His head stopped. He saw me. We were looking right at each other. I lowered my hand and smiled. I felt my stomach churn and my cheeks flushed with heat. My eyes were swelling with moisture and there was a trembling in my throat. It was a familiar feeling from a long time ago, a lifetime ago. I wanted to shout but I couldn't. I wanted to run and jump but I remained rooted to the spot. I wanted to hug someone and shout for joy but instead, I just stood, smiling at my Dad. I shrugged my shoulders awkwardly and mouthed the words, 'Hello Dad.'

Then the strangest thing happened - he turned around and looked the other way. He had clearly seen me and yet now… he was looking away. I felt embarrassed; perhaps I had made a fool of myself? I continued to look, noticing now, that his hair was turning grey. He seemed smaller and older. He was still facing away from me but also away from Margaret and Eddie, with his head tilted down. Then I saw his left hand rising as if to remove the glasses from his face. Then he raised his right hand as if to wipe something from his eyes and I realised, that for the first time in my life, the only time, I was watching my father cry.

THREE

Tides of Fortune

1

'With all its sham, drudgery and broken dreams, it is still a beautiful world. Be careful. Strive, to be happy.'

Max Ehrmann

Coming home from the Falklands was surprisingly difficult. It was a slow process returning to normal living, with its normal priorities and a normal sense of purpose. I was glad to be off the ship but I missed my friends; relieved to be away from the war, and yet, strangely at odds with peacetime attitudes; they all seemed so selfish, trivial and unimportant. I was often bored and restless and found it difficult to be in company.

More than anything, I hated being asked about the South Atlantic, especially when given centre stage in some discussion. How could I explain these things and why should I? In these situations, I would politely mumble an awkward answer, then quickly move to another subject.

I had dreams; dreams that brought back the smell of spent aviation fuel and the urgent thump of helicopter engines. I could feel the heat building in my diving suit, my heart pounding and the bitter cold stinging my face as I ran across a phantom flight deck to go - where? To God knows what? Other times, in the middle of sound sleep, I could hear an Action Alarm going off, but this time, with a different outcome; explosion, fire, flood, choking in darkness, in acrid smoke, men grappling me, holding me back, holding me down, 'Get off!' I shout, but they don't listen, 'Get off!' This time I demand it and now I am punching, I am striking injured men, men who are begging for help, punching to get away from them - to save myself.

I wake up, arrested by a sharp intake of breath, bolt upright in a nest of twisted bedding, overtaken by guilt. These 'coffin dreams', with their life-like, whirling, mental sensations, were terrible. In time, it passed. Most things do, given time. And in time, good things began to break through.

I was given a shore assignment at the Clyde submarine base at Faslane. I was now, a competent worker; trusted to work unsupervised in any station around this huge galley, where we prepared and cooked for between 400 and 2,000 personnel at each sitting. No longer a rookie cookie boy, I was promoted to scale 'A' rating. I was still young but the old salts, the sea Daddies, those who had sat out the war onshore, recognised, that while they had only trained, I had done the heavy sea time - I had done everything for real. This brought me a quiet, sincere respect.

With so much sea time behind me, I had saved enough money for a deposit on a property. I bought a flat that had a sea view, in the beautiful coastal town of Helensburgh, just 3 miles from Faslane. I took on a flatmate, threw parties, went on foreign holidays, passed my driving test and bought an old banger. I received a Falklands decoration and gave a photograph of the award to Dad.

Life became wonderful again. The awful dreams faded and I stopped smoking.

★

After 18 months, I was drafted back to sea, this time, to RFA *Reliant*, a containership that had been converted to carry a squadron of Sea King helicopters. She was run by a civilian crew with a RN team assigned to maintain and operate the helicopters. She was a happy ship, full of relaxed, cheerful characters and I enjoyed being part of their company. The final 6 months of my tour were spent in the Falklands and it proved to be very different from my time spent there on the *Invincible*.

This time, we went into the South Atlantic summer and the weather was warm and often glorious. Moreover, we had time to enjoy it.

We set up a gymnasium in the hold where I enjoyed fitness training almost every day and, with our civilian captain's approval, provided that we didn't abuse the privilege, we RN personnel were allowed to build our own bar! - *Reliant* even had a tiny swimming pool.

There were parties; professional singers, dancers and comedians were flown down from the UK to entertain us. *Reliant* would anchor in the shelter of a local sound and other ships would raft alongside so that their crews could transfer to our hanger for the shows. We celebrated Christmas and New Year in this way.

We were allowed periods of shore leave for adventure training and recreation. I visited the grave of Sir Ernest Henry Shackleton in the abandoned whaling station of Grytviken on South Georgia. On another occasion, I was part of an 8 man group that went, with one junior officer in charge, to spend three days and nights living with a local family on Lively Island. Only four people lived there but, at their own expense, they had erected a memorial to the British soldiers who had died, just yards away, on this, their island home.

Our hosts were sheep farmers and, not only did they put us up in an adjacent, small, bare house but they also gave us a freshly slaughtered lamb. As we unwound from the weeks of sea duty, we went unshaven, our clothing became untidy and our attitude undisciplined. I went for long walks among colonies of penguins. I sat on the beach and watched great and small sea creatures swimming by, just yards from the shore: whales, seals and dolphins. In the evenings, we drank and sang songs, told jokes, told stories.... we were relaxed and happy.

There were no search and rescue operations nor downed aircraft to recover, no transferring of damage repair parties to stricken ships, no casualties. My diving was confined solely to training exercises in the shallow sheltered waters of Port Stanley Harbour.

Throughout my six months there, whenever I went ashore and met and talked with the islanders, I felt their warm appreciation and affection. I experienced, at first hand, just how much they valued their citizenship. It was an exciting and rewarding, experience.

★

When my time with *Reliant* came to an end, I was promoted to leading hand and instructed to attend the submarine training school. I was delighted; this was considered, by many, to be the elite of the Navy. The school was in fact, a dedicated shore base, HMS *Dolphin* at Gosport, where each candidate was subjected to an initial 6 weeks of residential, full time study. The first thing I learned was, that among the crews, submariners never refer to their vessel as a 'submarine' - it is always called a 'boat'.

We were taught the inner workings of every system on board: how water is produced, how waste is stored and ejected, how oxygen is produced and carbon dioxide is removed, how the nuclear reactor works, how a boat dives, how it surfaces, how it communicates, how it attacks and evades detection... everything. We were tested on our knowledge of every valve on board; its purpose, its importance and how to operate it. But it wasn't just about knowledge; there were frequent operational tests and exercises. It was mind boggling.

Our course concluded with a series of underwater escape exercises from a purpose built water tower, known throughout the service as 'The Tank'. We had to carry out three escapes from depths of 30ft, 60ft and 100ft - without breathing apparatus - each one, a one-way trip, with one lungful of air! However, to help speed our ascent, our lifejackets incorporated a clear plastic hood which, when pulled over our heads, would encapsulate an air bubble.

The first two escapes were made from chambers set into the side of the Tank and were reasonably straightforward. But, for all my previous diver training and my familiarity with compression chambers, when it came to the final one, the 100ft one, I was as anxious, and as apprehensive, as everyone else.

The candidate is locked into an escape pod; a steel vertical chamber, with an entry hatch at the bottom and an exit hatch at the top. The chamber is flooded rapidly from the bottom up and, as it floods and the pressure increases, it is essential that you clear your ears quickly, or they will burst. Once the pressure equalises, the exit hatch opens and up you go. The natural instinct is to hold your breath, but this would be lethal; as you rise through the depths, the continuous reduction in pressure causes the air within your lungs to expand so if you hold your breath, the expansion will rip your lungs to bits. It was drummed into us, over and over again, 'You must breathe out on your way to the surface.' …. 'You must breathe out on your way to the surface'… and every year, someone forgets, someone panics, someone dies. If you are to become a submariner in the Royal Navy, this, is your rite of passage.

My first impression of the escape tube, was that it resembled an iron lung that encapsulates the whole body from head to toe. I squeezed myself into it. The entry hatch was closed beneath my feet and, accompanied by a cacophony of noise; thundering and hissing in rapport, the chamber began to flood. This was arguably the most intensely focussed moment of my whole life which, once started, could not be stopped. There was no going back! I could feel the rapidly increasing pressure squeezing my body and pressing on my eardrums. I pinched my nose and snorted out hard. The water kept on rising. When it got up to my chest, the air pocket, now thick with pressure, was like breathing in cream. On it powered, more water, more pressure, until suddenly, the exit hatch opened and - whoosh! With my lifejacket and bubble of compressed air in my plastic hood, I was on my way. I tilted my head back and began to breathe out; steadily, slowly, feeling the freedom of my escape, up and up, faster and faster, my lungs expanding with air as if from nowhere, my ears crackling as the drums expanded, breathe out – breathe out!

I exploded through the surface, out into the air, up as far as my knees, before crashing back down. As I lay there, on the surface, I was filled with relief and splendid joy.

I completed all the tests and passed the course but, there was still more to come. I now had to serve a probationary period on one of the boats, during which time, I was treated very much as a trainee, until, the big day finally arrived.

I was invited to report to the Skipper's cabin; me, in my best No 1 uniform and he, with his full gold braid. After a short speech of congratulations, he handed me a glass of rum, in the bottom of which, I could see my gold badge, my 'submarine dolphins'. In a tradition that goes back as far as the submarine service itself, I drank the rum in one go, while catching the 'dolphins' in my teeth. Now, at last, I was a submariner - a man of the boats.

★

Life in boats was exciting but, within two years, it all came to an end.

It had been innocuous at first. It began to appear on *Invincible* and accelerated during the Falklands War. It was dermatitis; a common industrial problem, sometimes referred to as the 'housewife's disease' which is largely attributed to detergents stripping out the natural oils of the skin but, it is also known to be aggravated by stress.

The normal remedy is to apply a mild steroid cream such as Hydrocortisone or Betnovate and, within a few days, the skin recovers. However, in my case, from time to time, it would return and, each time it did, stronger steroids were needed to control it. This deepening cycle of destruction culminated in a massive outbreak when I was at sea, on the submarine Valiant.

I lost most of the skin from both hands and arms up to the elbows. It was painful and ugly and, none of the normal treatments was effective.

Upon our return to Faslane, I was relieved of my duties and taken to sickbay. After a thorough examination, the surgeon asked, 'How old are you and how long have you been in the Navy?' I answered, 'I am 26 and I've been in for just over seven years.' He looked me in the eye and said, 'That's good. You're young enough to start again.' He paused for a moment then added, 'Your career in the Navy is over'.

★

The Navy was as good to me as any employer could be. I was assigned to light duties in the wardroom where my skin gradually strengthened and recovered. Meanwhile, the process had begun that would lead to my discharge from the service. I had hospital appointments to assess my condition, including patch tests to establish if I had any allergies. I had none. I was psychologically assessed and appeared to be fine.

Eventually, I was given an appointment to go before an Admiralty Board to discuss my future. On the eve of this, I met with Lt Commander Thomas, who was assigned to advise and represent me. He explained the options that might be open to me if I stayed in the Navy and, the package of support I would receive, if I left.

The Board consisted of an admiral and two senior officers. They were in full gold braid and I was in my No 1 ceremonial uniform with gold braid badges, my diver's helmet on my lower right sleeve, with my cooks badge on my right shoulder. My good conduct stripe and Killicks badge were on my left shoulder and, on my left breast, were my submarine dolphins and my ribbons and rosette from the Falklands. I answered all their questions as best I could and then, one of the officers said, 'The recommendation from the medical board is that you be discharged from the Navy. This board has the authority to reverse that. What would you prefer to see happen?'

I answered. 'I think it is inevitable that I should leave. I can't continue the way I am…'

They asked, 'Do you have another job in mind that might be available to you in civilian life?' to which I answered, 'Not really, but I'm already doing some part-time taxi driving around Helensburgh. I could extend these hours, which should enable me to get by until I sort out something better.'

The meeting was about to wind up when the admiral asked a question that took me by surprise. He asked. 'How do feel about leaving the Navy?' I looked at Lt Commander Thomas. He gave me a smile and a short nod, as if to say, 'Say whatever you feel.'

I tried my best to explain. 'I have mixed feelings about the Navy. Sometimes I have loved the life and other times I've hated it…but in all things, my strongest feeling is one of pride. I am proud of the Navy, I am proud to have been in it, and, although I might be leaving the Navy, I don't think the Navy will ever leave me.'

There was a silence for a few moments, then I was invited to leave the room while the officers talked in private. A few minutes later, I was ushered back in.

The admiral at the centre of the table began. 'Leading cook Gorman, we have unanimously agreed that you should be released from the service and, we feel that you will be happy with this decision. You have an excellent record of service and we would like to thank you for your hard work and commitment to the Royal Navy. We wish you every success on your return to civilian life.' It was the right decision, but it meant the end of a great adventure.

On the day that I was demobbed, I had to hand in my equipment, workwear and uniforms before signing myself back into Civvy Street. When the time came to hand over my No1 ceremonial uniform, with all my gold braid badges attached – the milestones of my seven years in the Royal Navy – I faltered. I asked the Wren behind the desk, 'Can I keep it?' She replied, 'You are not supposed to, but sometimes they will let you buy it back for £35.' 'That's okay I will happily pay,' I said quickly. She went to the end of the room to consult with her senior rate. He flicked through some papers, found what he was looking for, then said something to her. When she returned she said, 'It's okay you can keep the uniform and, don't worry about the money.'

2

As part of my re-settlement package I had trained to become an HGV driver. I now had the licence but there were no vacancies anywhere within 30 miles of my flat. It was as good as useless. I applied to join the MOD police but they turned me down. I attended a night class in Clydebank Technical College to learn about computers, which bored me to death. I got a job selling double glazing but, after six weeks, I ran out of customers.

My dermatitis was still a problem; it would flare up viciously, just from washing myself with a bar of scented soap and for the next three years, I was unable to wash or shower without first wearing rubber gloves that sealed around my arms.

Other health issues plagued me; I began to suffer from excruciating stomach pains and, after a brief stay in hospital, I was diagnosed with a duodenal ulcer and was told that I would need to take daily medication for the rest of my life.

I was having to take on more and more taxi driving and, eventually, I was forced to the conclusion that I would have to take it up full-time.

Trident was the smallest of the three taxi firms in town. The owners, Gordon and Ellen Morton, operated it from a little shack, built onto the side of their house. They had been the only ones to offer me work while I was still in the Navy and they now agreed to take me on full-time. Since buying my flat, I had acquired a working knowledge of Helensburgh and with Gordon and Ellen's patient help and guidance, I became proficient at my job.

With our proximity to Faslane, it was not unusual for me to find an old shipmate climbing into my cab. We would talk about the old times and all the goings-on as I drove them back to the Base. Our journey over, they would walk away into the life that I once had - and I would drive back to town for another hire. I missed the old life but I enjoyed the comparative easiness of my new one; the lack of discipline, the absence of heavy sea time.

I had never expected to stay in the taxi business for long but, I got on well with Gordon and Ellen and, as we got to know each other better, I became a key member of their team. It turned out to be a fun job and I started to enjoy myself, chatting up girls, finding out where the parties were, and gate crashing them at the end of the night. I bought an answerphone and became creative with the greetings that I left on it.

(Polish/Italian accent)
'This is the Holy Father Papa John Paul II. I'm taking messages for Brother Denis who is currently flagellating himself on the taxi ranks of Helensburgh. Leave your name, number and a message after the tone... Then go forth and multiply.
(Singing in a heavenly voice...) Amen.'

'Beep.'

It went down well and, after a while, a kind of fan base grew up with equally creative messages being left in response. After a month I changed it to,

(Upper-class, dithering voice.)
'This is Prince Charles. I've decided to take up residence with a scruffy little fellow called Denis. If you wish to leave a message for him, just say whatever you like, but if you're calling for me,

*remember to start with 'Your Royal Highness' and make sure
you grovel copiously before you ring off.*
I must go now. I'm taking the corgis for a walk.'

'Beep.'

I grew to love Helensburgh and its people. It's a picturesque town, big enough to have everything you might want and yet small enough to remain personable and friendly. The town had a population of about 15,000 with new blood continuously coming through, as the Navy base rotated its personnel and its contractors. Glasgow was just 22 miles away so, I could visit Dad, family and friends as often as I liked.

The opportunity came for me to buy a car with an operator's plate from an owner/driver who wanted 'out' of the taxi business. I bought it and Gordon and Ellen agreed that I could rent a radio from them and continue working at Trident. This meant that, once I had taken out the rental I would be able to keep all my fares and, after allowing for my running costs, I would be better off. I was the only owner/driver on Trident's books; all the other drivers were driving the company cars and were paid on commission.

I prospered and, over the next three years, I even took on two part-time drivers to work my car. I was able to pay off my mortgage and was starting to save for my boat.

Gordon, Ellen and I had become close friends and they knew all about my dream of owning my own boat and sailing off around the world. Ellen said, 'Why not rent out your flat, sell us your car and we'll run your plate until you return? You're much too young to be sitting on the taxi ranks of Helensburgh.'

Her offer was tantalising. It was starting to look as if my boyhood dreams could be coming true.

★

I had been directed to pick up a hire at the residence of the Commodore of the Clyde Submarine Fleet. Standing by the gate was a blonde Wren, in full Royal Navy uniform. She had a lovely face, a slim figure and blonde hair that was gathered neatly and tucked under her hat.

We chatted throughout the journey and as I dropped her off at her destination I found myself inviting her out for a meal at my favourite Italian restaurant. She accepted, and although I didn't know it at the time, my bachelor days were over.

Jessica Jane Pember was fun-loving, dizzy, light-hearted and generous and, before very long, we had fallen in love and my life was changed completely.

In May 1990, when Jess came out of the Navy, we got married.

It was a grand affair in the sleepy village of Dunchurch on the outskirts of Rugby, her family's home. I pushed the gold band onto her finger and there it sat, contentedly, beside the Sapphire and two diamonds that I had placed there two years earlier. My brother Eddie was my best man and he was really on form, so too was Lionel, my new father-in-law. Dad wore his smart old suit and Margaret wore a new hat and dress. Among the large contingent of family and friends, was my boyhood friend, John Gillen and, only revealed on the day before, Stevie Hiles, the same Stevie Hiles who had grabbed my hand eight years earlier when we were together on *Invincible*.

Within a week of returning from honeymoon, I had put my flat up for sale and arranged for Gordon and Ellen to take on my car, my operator's plate and my drivers. I said my goodbyes to Helensburgh and headed off to the Midlands, to start again, at the very beginning. I was 29.

3

We had decided to start a new life in Rugby and then see where life took us from there. Dad had also been making plans; he had retired and he and Margaret had decided that they would move to Malta. Everything was changing.

Our new home was a rundown semi. With a DIY book and what scant savings I had left, I decorated the house, fitted a new kitchen, bathroom, windows and doors, repaired the fence, built a new gate and repaired the garage roof. We couldn't afford a second car so I bought a broken-down moped and fixed it up.

My skin and hands had steadily been improving and so I decided to have a go at catering. I landed a job at a local factory as a chef/manager of the canteen. I held it down. Then one day I forgot to take my stomach pills and nothing happened. I stopped taking them. I went to night school to study management.

We began to prosper and in among all of this, Jess after 22 hours of labour, brought our daughter into the world, a raucous little mite with liquid blue eyes. Baby Amy had a habit of gathering her breath, filling her lungs to capacity, and then ripping a roaring wail, demanding attention. Jess and I had a set response. After the crescendo, we accused each other. 'That's definitely from your side of the family…' It was hard-going constantly living from one pay cheque to the next but we were happy. We were good together.

★

We had been living in Rugby for 5 years and Dad was making his annual trip to the UK. Having already been around the family in Scotland, we were his last port of call before his return to Malta. This time, Margaret was not with him and I sensed that all was not well, that he was a troubled man. He looked worn out and tired and when I asked about Margaret's absence, I was given the terse reply, 'I don't want to talk about it and if you keep asking, I will leave tomorrow,'

I persuaded him to stay, to rest up and recharge his batteries and, in return, I promised to lay off the questions. It was good to have him to ourselves and, as the days passed, he began to open up a bit. He reminisced more than usual about Gran and Uncle Eddie, his time in the Air Force, his court case with Olga. As he became more relaxed, he even talked about Margaret. 'She's not herself these days. Sometimes she looks at me as though she hates me. She hardly ever leaves the house and she is so difficult. I think it's the painkillers she takes.' Tentatively I said, 'She has always been difficult...growing up with her was often miserable, you must know that?' He replied, 'I know that, son, but they have not all been bad years... I still love her.' I was surprised because this was the first time that he had ever admitted that they had not always been 'good years'. Perhaps now he was seeing her flaws more clearly?

On our way to the airport, he told me. 'I've written my will and I intend to send it to you.' My immediate question was, 'Have you talked to Margaret about this?'   'Aye, I've talked to her,' he replied. 'She'll come around to it. She just needs time to think it through.'

Now I understood her absence. I knew Margaret too well and I remembered her attitude to money. She must have disagreed with the contents of the will and was showing her anger by refusing to come over with him. I pleaded, 'Don't discuss it with her anymore, you'll only make life miserable for both of you. Just post it to me privately. Please think about what I am saying.'

In the ten days that Dad had spent with us, the colour and fullness had returned to his face. I wanted him to stay, I wished that he would never go back. I said, 'Dad, I don't know what's going on in your head right now but, if you are in any trouble, please come and stay with us. Jess and Amy both love you and we will look after you. Margaret is a mean woman. She always has been and she's not worth it. Please think about it, okay?' and with that, I put out my hand to shake and say goodbye. He stepped through my hand, hugged me and said, 'I love you son and I'm very proud of you. Don't worry about me, I'll be fine, but if I need help, I'll let you know.'

Three weeks later, a package dropped through the door. Inside there was a large, red envelope and a brief letter. 'I have left the envelope holding my will unsealed. Read the documents and then seal it up. It will save hassle later…'

Phoning Malta was expensive but this time I didn't hesitate. When I got through, Dad tried to sound cheerful but I sensed an awkward atmosphere. After some small talk, I reminded him of our conversation at the airport. 'I've spoken to Jess and she would love to have you visit again and stay as long as you like,' the obvious inference being, 'You can stay for ever.'

My last words were, 'We all love you Dad, remember what I said.'

It was the last time we ever spoke. Three days later in the midst of yet another domestic argument with Margaret, my dear father, the best friend I'd ever had, suffered a massive heart attack and died. He was 62 and, like Gran, he was old before his time. He had kept giving until there was no more left to give.

★

Dad had spent five years living in Malta and I like to think they were among the happiest he had ever known. It seemed only right that his bones should remain there forever.

It was a large family gathering with all of Dad's and Margaret's children and some of her grandchildren coming to say their fond farewells. Dad had many friends. Every house in St Pius V Street, where he lived, had black bands tied onto the shutters. A senior clergyman was brought in to conduct the service at the Nazarene church in Sliema. He arrived in a chauffeur-driven car and people crossed themselves as he went past, or kissed his hand if he got close enough.

Dad was to be buried in the family crypt of his friends and neighbour Leli and Mary Borg and they and many others turned out to pay their respects. It was an emotional, heart-rending experience. Just after we had sealed the crypt, from out of nowhere, his Maltese friend, Raymond, jumped onto a high platform and shouted, 'Come now everyone, let's give him a round of applause. John Gorman was a good man!' As crazy as it may sound, we stood there in the sun and clapped our hands. Indeed, a lovely gesture.

Margaret revelled in her role of widow; dressed in black, wearing solid gold rings, bracelets and necklaces, chain-smoking and gobbling pills, I never saw her shed a tear or say a kind word about him. She looked older but she was still the same forceful character that she had always been. She said to Maureen, as if chastising a child, 'Yer Dad's deed and he's no comin back...'

I told them all that Dad had sent me his will and that I had put it into the hands of a solicitor in Scotland. 'When we all go back, he will open it and sort everything out. There will be no Irish parliament. We will do what the old man wanted.' They could do nothing other than agree.

★

Mr Graham Yeoman sat comfortably behind his large desk while we squeezed in around the opposite side on a variety of odd-shaped chairs and stools. He was a young-looking, somewhat small and spindly man with an innocent face and pleasant broad smile. He spoke comfortably and confidently with a broad, somewhat funny Aberdonian accent.

I first used his firm when I bought my property in Helensburgh and had had a number of dealings with him over the years. I liked the man. He had a sharp, well-educated intellect and I knew that what he lacked in physical stature, he more than made up for in mental ability and shrewdness. He had moved to a new office in Clydebank and here we gathered, the angry, the crafty, the bereaved and the greedy, waiting to hear what was in store in the red envelope. He announced, 'I have already read the will and have studied its contents and ramifications. In a few moments I will read it to you and then explain what it means and then we can gather in some signatures and this will allow us to begin the winding up process of the estate.'

Margaret was impatient and Graham, picking up on this, immediately placated her by saying. 'Let me first of all assure you, Mrs Gorman, that although some of this might sound complicated, your husband has, in fact, made a very generous provision for you.'

His spindly fingers worked through the papers then, matter-of-factly, he read out Dad's handwritten will, which ended with the words, 'These are the last wishes of a man whose main regret in life is that he never saw more of his grandchildren.' Maureen said, 'I knew it, I knew he would mention his grandchildren.'

Margaret said, 'What does that mean? When will I get the money?'

Graham ignored Maureen and, looking comfortably at Margaret, he smiled nonchalantly. Margaret held his gaze, her face like stone. He answered, 'Half the money is yours to do with as you please and it will be deposited in any account of your choice as soon as the estate is wound up. The remaining 50% will be put into a legally binding trust fund for your exclusive benefit for the remainder of your life. Denis and Edward are to be the trustees. They will have a legal responsibility to protect this fund until the end of your retirement. Then it will revert to Denis, Edward and Maureen exclusively.' Margaret's face was like thunder. She had wanted it all.

This woman knew the price of everything and the value of nothing and yet, strange as this may sound, I would have gladly given her everything and more, if only she had been kind to my father. To the end of his life, and beyond, poor old John had tried to cover for her and here she was, none the wiser, still grasping.

Eddie, Maureen and I could never forgive Margaret for her treatment of our Dad and, from now on, our family relationship became a business one. Nevertheless, her effect on our lives remained destructive as she repeatedly made unacceptable demands on the trust. We were forced into a whole gamut of argument, counter argument, legal opinion and adversarial return. Stress and strife followed and tore away at what had once been a very harmonious family.

Margaret and I were never to see or speak to each other again. However, I understand that, five years later, on her last night, she was heard to say,

'I know I didn't treat John well…but I did love him.'

4

It had been an uncomplicated birth but Jess was exhausted. As she rested, I cradled our new-born in my arms and described everything to her. 'He's a wriggly little fellow. He looks like your dad, Lionel. He's really wonderful.' Baby Matthew cried a little, a gentle cry, so different from the raucous sound his sister made. I sat on the edge of the bed, took her hand and said, 'He's perfect, Jess. Thank you.' It was a Polaroid moment.

For me, family life is full of Polaroid moments but, however rewarding it might be, it is not always easy. Jess and I were in our mid 30's when Mathie was born and, with a growing family to support, I threw myself into my work to create a better life for us.

Since arriving in Rugby, I had gone from being a cook in a factory through to sales management for a wholesale food company and I now moved on to a career in banking with Barclays. It was time-consuming, mind-bending, interesting, challenging and exciting. At last, after years of manual work on low pay, I had a prestigious job in management.

Financially, we prospered. Tatty old cars were replaced and we moved to a detached house. But, I was so wrapped up in my dreams and ambitions that it didn't occur to me that Jess might not feel the same. In fact, at heart, she didn't want to be the wife of a bank manager. She was ill at ease with the erudite, polished social scene, the high achievers and incisive thinkers. Jess was not of that world and was at a loss to support me in it.

She had neither the confidence to pull me out nor the ability to develop and stay within.

She strayed….and in what seemed like the blink of an eye, my marriage to this beautiful, generous, fun-loving girl was in crisis. By the time the problem became apparent to me, it was too late. Jess saw another life for herself and wanted out. Nothing I could do, or say, could change her mind. It became a heart-aching, angry and bitter time but, shouldering my disappointment and hurt, I tried to think of our kids and to do the right thing.

While the threads of our marriage were picked through and undone, I left our family home to live in a caravan, at a local site that provided low-cost pitches for migrant workers. In the mornings, I would emerge with my smart suit, polished shoes and briefcase and leap from one paving stone to the next to avoid the mud and puddles. My fellow campers emerged with worn, high visibility vests, concrete encrusted boots, pot bellies and a rough, cheerful manner. They were HGV drivers and quarrymen from the nearby concrete plant.

My office attire brought out the politeness in them. 'Good morning Denis, how are you today?' they would ask and I would reply, 'I am unloved and almost bankrupt but, goddammit, I am still living the dream!' They would laugh and we would give each other the thumbs up.

This was my public face. My private thoughts were more grounded. Nineteen years had passed since I came home from the Falklands war. I thought I'd come a long way from being a Navy cook and a world away from my humble beginnings at Smilum and Priesthill. I thought I'd found the perfect girl. Our children and our home had been the cornerstone of all my achievements and ambitions, my identity. Now I would find myself staring at the mirror, 40 years of age, after all that work and effort, wondering how it had ever come to this. Here I was, standing on Square One, almost broke - and worse - *alone!*

It was agreed that, if I provided a new house for Jess and the kids, I could return to the family home. With legal bills, ongoing maintenance and cars to pay for, I would be mortgaged to the hilt. In order to survive, I would need to earn substantial bonuses every month and, every month, I would have a sword in my back until all these costs were discharged.

In 2001, after six months of campsite living, I returned to the family home; to the emptiest house and emptiest feelings that I have ever known. I struggled on throughout the winter of that year. My stomach and dermatitis began to play up. Then I prolapsed a disc in my back which caused throbbing pain and semi-paralysis in my legs. My relationship with Jess became bitter and irreconcilable; achingly, I would come home to the dark, cold and empty house, remembering the poem;

evening brings the memories I can't forget,
with empty echoes as I climbed the stairs,
from empty rooms,
and empty clothes that fall and drape on empty chairs

I would warm up the house, cook a meal, then sit by the fire with poly bottles of high octane cider. I would put on some music, ramp up the volume and drink; drink to wash the pain out of my back, to relax my mind, to accentuate the music, to cheer me up and to help me sleep.

It became my nightly ritual and yet, in the middle of all this, I performed well at work. Now alone, I would work late most evenings and some Saturdays. I was given the chiding nickname 'The estates and trusts king' and the bonuses kept coming. I won major convention awards every year and I saw more of the world with Barclays Bank than I ever did with the Navy, and all of it in opulent, five-star luxury. Nevertheless, I was a hollow man, running on nervous energy, with a void of emptiness burning through me.

It was my friend, Mark, who brought me to my senses. Prior to my taking the job with Barclays he and I had worked together in management at Booker Cash and Carry. He was a big lad with a positive attitude. During his marriage breakup, I'd been his friend and had brought him home to the family for meals and companionship during his troubles. Now that I was in need of a friend, he was repaying the debt in spades. During my worst periods he would phone me every night, sometimes for an hour at a time, offering lots of constructive advice. 'You have to move on Den,' he would say.

It was his idea to put up a whole-year planning chart in the dining room and, when the kids next visited, I announced, 'We're going to make plans for every Wednesday night and every weekend that we're together and also, we're going to plan fantastic holidays!' They loved it.

I bought a guitar and a manual to occupy some of the empty times. I bought an old sailing dinghy and spent hours refurbishing it. Then, one day, I climbed into a tree to rescue a kitten. Just a ball of fur with fleas. She was perfect. To the delight of my children, I adopted her. Now, I had another heartbeat in the house and she has remained my housemate ever since. I remembered Gran and her advice, 'You must turn to life again', and Dad saying, when we were at the train station saying goodbye, 'Remember, drink is a good servant but a poor master'. I was ready to act upon his advice. Drink had served its purpose so, I replaced cider with tea.

Divorce is cruel. It robbed me of everything that I held dear and left me bereft in every way that a man can be. It almost destroyed my soul. Emotionally shattered, I knew that it would take a long time to recover but, however faltering, every long journey begins with its first steps. It was hard but, bit by bit, piece by piece, ever so slowly, I rebuilt my life.

5

Five years later, in the autumn of 2006, having recently bought an old and, somewhat rundown, 23ft sailing cruiser, I was flicking through the pages of Practical Boat Owner (PBO) magazine when a particular article caught my eye. The story covered the single-handed transatlantic Jester Challenge (JC) which, earlier that year, had set out from Plymouth, England and finished in Newport Rhode Island USA. As I read it, I was drawn further in. The glossy pictures and bright cheerful faces of the skippers conveyed adventure and optimism on a grand scale. It began:

'Sitting in the cabin of his little Westerly 22, Bill Churchouse has a grin from ear to ear. He's about to take his tiny boat single-handed across the Atlantic via the northern route, and he's relishing the challenge.

'Too many friends have died suddenly in their 50's,' he told us. 'Life is for living, and this is something I have always wanted to do.'

To realise his ambition, Bill has joined the Jester Challenge, an unofficial transatlantic race for small cruising yachts. There are no rules, no official organisers, no committees, no fees and no sponsors. In a world awash with high-powered sailing events and high profile professionals, this is something of a culture shock. Better still, it brings real adventure back into the realm of the amateur yachtsman.'

The feature moved to Pete Hill of *Badger* fame, an

experienced sailor whose partner at the time, Annie Hill, had written 'Voyaging on a small income.'

'Once again (his) boat has had a minimal fit out, with no electronics save a hand held GPS, and no radio. Peter, perhaps one of the most relaxed sailors you will ever meet says he manages to live his cruising lifestyle on an income of just £2,500 per year, another advantage of owning a small boat.'

I was hooked. My imagination took off. I thought of Jacques Cousteau and remembered the feelings of joy and adventure I had had when, as a child, I watched his programmes. I thought of Sir Alec Rose and remembered a time when I believed that all things were possible. I cast my mind back and remembered our air drop in the Atlantic, leaping from helicopters into the warm translucent blue sea, swimming and climbing onto floating boxes with aircraft buzzing around and our ship sailing serenely by. What a sight! That had been the closest I had ever come to emulating those feelings of my youth.

And now, all these things had passed. Looking at myself now, what did I see? I asked myself, 'How did I lose those dreams, those desires, and those beliefs?'

Here, in this article, I saw an opportunity to bring all my boyhood enthusiasm back to life. It clearly demonstrated that money wasn't a barrier, nor was a modest, low-cost boat, nor qualifications, nor clever electronic equipment. All that was needed was the heart to do it and the will to see it through. I thought of Gran, Uncle Eddie and Dad, and their attitude to life. Lastly I thought of my time on the quarterdeck of *Invincible* on the night I'd watched *Atlantic Conveyor* burn and, not for the first time, I found myself thinking - *Time is precious ...waste it wisely.*

I read on. The Atlantic challenge was due to be repeated in 2010 but a shorter voyage from Plymouth to the Azores was scheduled for 2008.

'The Atlantic,' I thought, 'would be a foolhardy venture,

but the mid-Atlantic islands of the Azores, with the right weather window and going south into a warmer climate, might not be so bad. I was fully aware that, when it came to sailing a small boat alone, across an ocean, my time in the Royal Navy counted for nothing. The one thing I *had* learned was that the sea was enormously powerful and completely indifferent! My boat was untested, I was inexperienced, but... I wrote to Ewen Southby Tailyour, the co-founder of the JC.

'I have a 23-foot boat but no offshore sailing experience. Would it be possible for me to join the next Jester Challenge outing to the Azores?' He replied, 'Certainly. You're exactly the right type of candidate. Welcome aboard.' I found myself smiling.

It was the beginning of a new adventure.

FOUR

The Azores

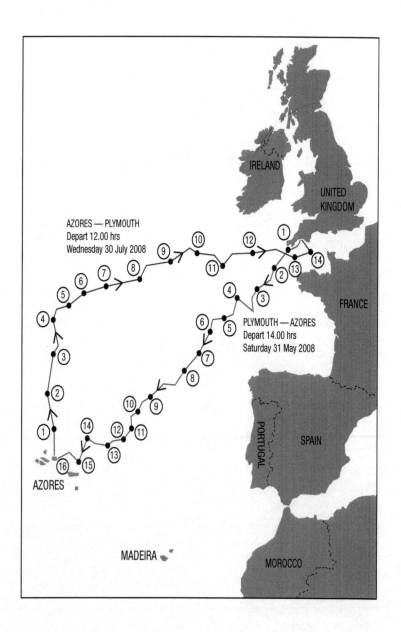

AZORES — PLYMOUTH
Depart 12.00 hrs
Wednesday 30 July 2008

PLYMOUTH — AZORES
Depart 14.00 hrs
Saturday 31 May 2008

IRELAND

UNITED
KINGDOM

FRANCE

PORTUGAL

SPAIN

AZORES

MADEIRA

MOROCCO

Prologue

The first ever single-handed transatlantic yacht race took place in 1960. The idea was the brainchild of Blondie Hasler, a retired Lt Col of the Royal Marines, famed for his exploits during the War when he led a daring raid on the German ships in the harbour at Bordeaux. Under cover of darkness, he and his men had paddled through the harbour defences in canoes and had sunk six enemy vessels. They became known as the Cockleshell Heroes.

In the 1950's, after the War, Hasler found himself becoming more and more interested in the idea of single-handed sailing. He turned his inventive mind to the task of designing an easily-handled sailing vessel which could weather all sea conditions with relative safety. He took a 25-foot 'folk-boat', enclosed the cockpit and fitted a simple Chinese junk sail which could be controlled from the hatch, while standing inside the cabin. With his friend, Jock McCloud, he designed and built a wind-powered self-steering system which could also be controlled from the same position. He named the boat 'Jester'.

He then came up with the idea of a race across the Atlantic for single-handers. This had never been done before and the whole idea was considered by most of the sailing establishment to be crazy. He found four other like-minded sailors and on 11th June 1960 the five boats crossed the start line in Plymouth bound for New York. There were no fees nor prizes and four of the boats were under 30 feet in length.

They all succeeded in making the crossing. Francis Chichester drove his boat hard and was the winner, whilst it was said that Blondie, who came second, had worn his cardigan and slippers throughout the voyage. It was reported that this larger-than-life character spent the evenings enjoying fine food and wines and entertaining himself playing his ukulele.

The event was considered to have been successful enough to be repeated and, four years later, the second race attracted 15 entrants and, four years after that, 47. However as the event grew in stature so, too, did its commercial aspect. It soon became far removed from Blondie's original intention of using the race to encourage the design and development of small, safe, seagoing sailing boats. The free-wheeling adventure that he had envisaged became swamped with entry fees, rules, handicaps, boat inspections and big money sponsorship. The boats became bigger, faster and costlier until, ironically, a minimum boat length of 30 feet was introduced which would have disqualified four out of the five founding fathers from competing in the race that *they* had started! But before then, Hasler had sold his boat to Mike Richie and moved on to other things.

In later years, he wrote of a wish that a second series transatlantic event might be made available to ordinary yachting enthusiasts so that they could race each other once more, or simply challenge themselves and their boats.

Mike Ritchie came from the same mould as Blondie and went on to make many successful transatlantic crossings in *Jester* during which he survived a number of severe storms and knock downs. Finally, on 15 July 1988, 500 miles south-east of Halifax Nova Scotia, a massive rogue wave hit her, smashing a gaping hole through the side of her cabin and ripping off her forward hatch. Mike was rescued by the 60,000 ton bulk carrier the *MV Nilam*, but Jester could not be saved.

She had been more than a boat to Mike, she was something

special, an iconic yacht, an art form, a historical vessel but more still… a friend. That might have been the end of it except that sometime later, whilst giving an after-dinner speech to a group of wealthy businessman, he attempted to describe these feelings. As he spoke of losing *Jester*, he wept. Taken aback, the audience were moved by what they saw and proposed to Mike that they could club together to build a replacement yacht. The Jester Trust was formed and funds flooded in. The new *Jester* followed the plans that Blondie had meticulously detailed.

After Mike Ritchie's retirement from sailing, he pondered the possibility of realising Blondie's dream of reintroducing a transatlantic event for ordinary yachting enthusiasts. He got together with Trevor Leek, the new owner of *Jester* and Ewen Southby Tailyour, the author of Blondie's biography. They began planning for an event to take place in 2006. When it came to the question of a name there was no disagreement.

It would be called 'The Jester Challenge…'

1

Out of the night that covers me, Black as the pit from Pole to Pole,
I thank whatever gods may be. For my unconquerable soul.

William. E. Henley

At the time when I threw my hat into the ring for the Jester challenge, scheduled for 1st June 2008, I knew nothing about the Azores. My initial research told me that they consist of nine small volcanic islands that lie in the mid-Atlantic and belong to Portugal. They are about 800 miles to the west of Lisbon and 1250 miles to the south-west of Plymouth. The weather is generally mild, but as the only flights go via Lisbon, they are not a popular holiday destination. This exclusivity somehow made the quest to reach them by small boat all the more exotic and I loved the idea of it.

My boat was called 'Tipexe', a standard production Virgo Voyager, a 23-foot sloop made of glass fibre. She was designed as a small family coastal cruiser ostensibly for weekends and short holidays. She had changed hands many times and I bought her for less than the price of a second-hand car.

I got what I paid for! She was shabby, she had extensive osmosis, a scourge of water blisters on her glass hull, her propeller shaft leaked, the wire rigging was old and rotten and her steering linkages were worn and loose. I had, however, already put on a new and expensive 'Sea Feather', self-steering wind vane that was currently untested. I had a lot of work to do before I could take her out into the Atlantic.

★

In January 2007 I attended a 'Jesters' get-together at the Master Gunner's Arms in London. It was an uncomplicated affair; you just show up, pay at the door, mingle with the crowd and then grab a seat when the food was ready to be served. The guest speaker was none other than Mike Richey himself. At 90 years old, he had retired from sailing but was still fit and active. I hung on his every word as, in his gentle, weathered voice, he spoke of sailing and his knowledge of many Atlantic crossings in *Jester*.

I also met some of the characters who were featured in the magazine article namely, Bill Churchouse and Roger Taylor. Although I was something of an irksome enthusiast, as yet unproven, they didn't seem to mind my many questions, whilst I tried to find out more about what I had let myself in for. These people had actually done what I had only dreamed of but, nevertheless, they made me welcome and I felt as though I belonged in their company.

Back in Rugby, I spent every free evening reading sailing books and making extensive lists of everything from food and clothing to buckets and flags. Throughout the winter, whenever I had a free weekend, I would drive down to Hayling Island Yacht Company and work on *Tipexe* until eventually, after a lick of rejuvenating paint, I was able to stand back and announced, 'It is done!' It was time to get her back in the water.

There was, however, one last finishing touch; that awful name *Tipexe* had to go! I wanted something special, something that had a story to it. I settled on the name '*Auld Meg*', after the horse, Meg, that had gathered up her pace to carry her reckless master, Tam, to safety in the wry, heart-warming Robbie Burns poem 'Tam O Shanter'.

The name of the famous tea clipper *Cutty Sark* also came from this poem. *Cutty Sark* was the witch who chased Tam and Meg with deadly intent until Meg jumped across a stream of silver water and carried them to safety. I imagined that *Auld Meg* might look after me in the same way with the Atlantic being our silver stream and the witches from hell being the wild wind that would chase us.

2

Practical work and mental preparation are all very well but more than anything I needed to get out on the water to test the boat and my ability. The summer of 2007 was a particularly blustery one, with many yachtsmen preferring to stay in port or take only short coastal hops. Nevertheless, with two weeks' leave booked, I planned a round trip across the Channel to France, an initial distance of 64 miles, then onto the Channel Islands and then back to Poole. My good friend, Mark, agreed to join me for the first three days to get me to France, from where, I'd go on alone.

In the last week of June, Mark and I were ready and keen to go. We had two weather reports, one good and one bad. We made the classic mistake of choosing to believe the good one. At 04.00hrs, with equal measures of enthusiasm and naivety, we set off from Poole to Cherbourg in a boisterous force 6 in rough seas, all the while believing that the wind and sea would settle down to a favourable breeze to take us across. We were in for a rude awakening...

Mark quickly became seasick then flaked out in the saloon. In the kerfuffle of getting him laid out and managing the boat, I missed the next scheduled weather forecast which, had I heard it, would certainly have persuaded me to return to Poole. Instead, we continued and, before long, the wind shifted and strengthened. By now, we had come too far south and had drifted too far to the east to have any reasonable chance of returning to a favourable home port. The only option left, was to press on.

I woke Mark after 12 hours and, like a scolding mother, I bundled him into the cockpit wearing nothing other than his underpants. I hoped that the cold air and clear horizon would nip away at his seasickness, wake him up and clear his head. I began to pass up his clothes, a sock here, a vest there, 'Where is my lifejacket?' he asked.

'I'll give it to you when you're dressed,' I replied.

'Pass my mobile phone. I need to phone Debbie,' he demanded.

I told him, 'Your mobile's no use. We went out of range 10 hours ago. Stop thinking about Debbie and get yourself dressed!'

Over a sandwich and a cup of tea I summed up the situation,

'We are off course, the weather is set to deteriorate further and we are very unlikely to make Cherbourg!'

I went on to explain that we would shortly be crossing the shipping lanes and, with us travelling at just 4 knots, we would be trying to weave our way through a busy stream of big ships doing 20 knots. The visibility was coming and going, varying from good to 300 yards and I needed Mark in the cockpit to help as lookout. We needed to be prepared for the worst; suited and booted, lifejackets on and the life raft ready to go.

We pressed on and, with every ship that came into view, of which there were many, our hearts would drop in dread. After three long hours, I was able to announce with confidence that we had made it through. But we were now well off course and had lost the favourable tide for Cherbourg. Our only remaining alternative was to head for the fishing village of St Vaast, some 20 miles to the east of our original destination.

Here, in the darkness and rain, after 20 hours of difficult sailing, I made another colossal mistake when I wrongly identified a navigation light. We grounded onto the hard granite slab banks that lead off from this picturesque French town. 'Bang!' and 'Shudder!' Our iron keel took the full force of the strike and a loud metallic ringing ran straight up the mast and down the steel shrouds. We fell on our side, scraped along, then, with the wind still pressing hard on our sails, *Meg* took off again.

'Quickly! Helm over. Take us out the way we came in,' I shouted, as I scrambled below. I made a quick check around, grabbed a lantern and, within moments, was back in the cockpit. Mark had done his best to turn the boat and take us back out from the shore but, in the confusion, he was now steering us through the middle of a nest of rocks. In the torchlight I could see them, just yards away to the left and right, each one capable of tearing a hole straight through us. I let the mainsail out sufficiently to slow the boat down and told him, 'She's dry below so just do your best to get us out of here,' and with that, I grabbed the boathook and moved on to the wet pitching foredeck in the hope that I might be able to spot, or push us off a rock.

It was an alarming experience but we were lucky in that we struck when the tide was high and the water was still. We got off but, standing there on that foredeck, I felt like a criminal who had committed a heinous crime that I would forever be ashamed of.

★

Two days later, with handshakes, hugs and a good friendship still intact, Mark got the bus from St Vaast to a ferry connection at Cherbourg. Within the hour, *Auld Meg* and I were heading there too, catching the notoriously strong tides that sweep around the Cotenin peninsular.

The wind was initially helpful but, as the day unfolded,

it strengthened and shifted and began pushing against us and the tide. This made for lively conditions. A lot of water was breaking over the deck and running into the cockpit. Now alone, the steering, navigation and management of the boat became even more challenging but this, I reasoned, was just the sort of hard-earned experience that I needed.

The wind strengthened and, in the midst of this near gale, I realised that we were running out of tide. When it changed direction, as it does every six hours, we would be swept all the way back to where we had started. We needed speed, but the wind was blocking us. I abandoned sailing and tried motoring but, on its own against the wind and waves, the motor couldn't cope. In the end, I motor-sailed (a combination of engine and mainsail), working the boat in tacks, first one way then the other, to windward. It was slow and tedious and required me to be on the helm the whole time, exposed to the wind and spray, cold and damp. The sea was rougher than I had ever experienced on a yacht but all I could do was cling on and keep going.

Sometime into this, I noticed from my cockpit position that water was surging up past the bilge boards on the cabin sole. I quickly lashed the helm and went below to pump out, all the while wondering if the grounding at St Vast had disturbed the keel. After what might have been 30 or 40 heavy strokes, the pump became light and I heard a reassuring gargling sound as air was being drawn up with the dregs. I threw off an inspection plate and looked down into the keel. Everything seemed okay but water was still appearing there at about a saucepanful every 30 seconds. Where was it coming from? I pulled the engine covers away and there, to my great relief, I found the problem. It was the neoprene seals that sit around the cockpit sole; they had deteriorated and, with so much spray coming over, the water was washing straight past them and into the bilge. *Auld Meg* was sound.

On we went with me now having to regularly go below to pump out until, two hours later, we arrived in Cherbourg.

★

The summer gales continued and I was holed up in port for another five days as one foul weather report followed another.

When the weather finally broke, there was much excitement and eager anticipation to get away. By the time the tide turned favourable, the marina had a mass exodus of boats breaking out for the Channel Islands and other French ports. *Meg* and I followed and set off for St Peter Port on the island of Guernsey. I was so excited to be sailing again that instead of following the others and motoring to keep up with the tide, I tried to sail the whole way. Wrong again!

Meg and I fell behind schedule and, by the time we had reached the narrow, rock-strewn Russell channel leading to St Peter Port, it was dark and a strong tidal stream was set against us. It took over two hours, with the engine on full power, to cover the last 2 miles. It was another hard learned lesson.

My shakedown voyage ended with a fine and fast solo passage across the Channel from Alderney to Poole. After 18 hours, I dropped *Auld Meg*'s anchor into the calm sheltered waters of Studland Bay. With that splash came a deep satisfaction that, despite my many mistakes, my boat and I had done really well. We had overcome all our difficulties and had learned invaluable lessons.

I had already started a 'to do' list for the next winter refit and, with this, I was hopeful that we would be in good shape for the Azores the following year.

The next day, I put *Meg* on her mooring in Poole and, after a fond farewell, I drove to Corsham to spend the night with Mark and his wife, Debbie. I felt fit after all the activity and fresh air of the past two weeks, I had lost weight, had a deep tan and a stubble around my chin. After a hot shower, a hearty meal and a couple of glasses of wine, Mark and I had a 'heart to heart'. I told him everything and finished with, 'I believe that *Auld Meg* and I are beginning to shine through.'

Mark was not so convinced and when he asked me, 'Den are you sure about all of this? What about all the cockups that keep happening?' I looked him in the eye and replied, 'I've never been surer. Besides, a man who has never made a mistake, has never achieved anything in his life...'

3

The start of the 2008 Jester Azores Challenge was scheduled for Saturday 31st of May. At the beginning of that month, I arranged for a long weekend off work so that I could move *Meg* from Poole to a temporary mooring in Plymouth.

The weather was calm, bright and clear with a light south-westerly wind. With my experiences of last summer still fresh in my mind, I carefully worked out the tide times and, by the end of the first day, I had motor-sailed, efficiently, from Poole to Portland where I spent the night at anchor. At first light on the following day, with another favourable tide, I took the inshore passage around the treacherous Portland Bill then pressed on across the soulless Lyme Bay. I pulled in for a further night at Salcombe. Plymouth was now within reach.

The following morning the wind had risen and suddenly my plans looked as though they would be foiled. 'It's as rough as guts out there,' said the Harbourmaster. 'Once you get past the breakwater, you are going to have a very tough time of it. It's blowing in hard, from the West.'

The Harbourmaster knew his stuff. He had lived in Salcombe all his life and knew the sea and tides around this coast very well. I took his advice and waited until the wind had died down and the tide became favourable again. As the day wore on, yachts and powerboats came in with strained-looking skippers and sick-looking crew. I was getting concerned that

I wouldn't be able to get to Plymouth in the limited time available.

By late afternoon, the Harbourmaster gave me the 'thumbs up' and a few hours later, as evening was drawing in, I closed in with Plymouth. I noticed a small yacht off my port quarter heading in the same direction and, as we drew closer to each other, I realised that it was Bill Churchouse's *Belgean*, the very same boat that was in the 2006 article that had introduced me to the Jester Challenge.

I called over. 'Bill… Bill, go on the radio… channel 15.' He looked up and waving back he shouted, 'I don't have a radio!' I was lost for words……

★

Three days before the start, I returned to Plymouth. As well as my one-month entitlement of annual leave, Barclays had agreed to my request for two further months without pay, allowing *Meg* and me an uninterrupted period of three months for the voyage. After so much planning and preparation, here I was at last, back on board. Now, I could give up the reins of everything onshore and concentrate completely on this one great endeavour.

I motored *Auld Meg* the 400 yards or so from her mooring into QAB Marina and, as I came in and the normally empty visitors' berth opened up before me, I saw lots of small boats tied up there. I joined them and, throughout the day, many more arrived until we were rafted three and four deep. The buzz of expectation and excitement was palpable and everywhere people were talking, exchanging ideas, comparing equipment and visiting each other's boats.

The yacht, *Lucy*, was tied up next to me. Her Skipper, John Margarson, invited me on board and put the kettle on - he reminded me of Captain Birds Eye from the fish fingers adverts.

Lucy was a 28ft Kelt; modern, light and fast, very different from my humble *Meg*. John told me about his earlier sailing adventures, how he had built a 42ft Wharram catamaran and sailed it around the world. When I suggested that, with all his sailing experience, he must be familiar with the use of a sextant for navigation, his response was, 'Don't waste your time with all that bloody nonsense! How many GPS's are you carrying? 'When I answered, 'One,' he said incredulously, 'One! Just one? You get your arse off to the chandlers and get yourself a spare – or two, if you can afford it. If that GPS goes down and you start piss-arsing about with a sextant, you'll be lost in the Atlantic for weeks.' That was John - assertive and kindly.

That evening I headed over to *Belgean* for a visit. I had taken to Bill. He was optimistic and cheerful and seemed perfectly happy living on his little boat. The thing that struck me most about *Belgean* was the modifications he had made to improve her strength and safety. He had built an observation dome into his main hatch so that he could keep watch from inside the boat, he had blanked out three of the windows with solid wood and covered the cockpit over to prevent the sea from flooding in. His only electrical equipment was a handheld GPS which ran on cell batteries. For lighting, he used paraffin lamps which gave his cabin a warm cosy feeling. His engine was a modest 5hp outboard.

Over a cup of tea and a tumbler of whisky I asked him to tell me what it was like at night, offshore and alone. 'It depends', he said, 'sometimes, when it's very quiet and flat calm, the stillness is complete. It's like being surrounded by cotton wool. Other times you'll be sailing along normally and then, after its gone dark, it'll start to blow up.' He looked at me and added, matter-of-factly, 'It often blows up at night...'

I tried not to show any emotion as I said, 'Mm. Interesting.'

★

My Gran and Uncle Eddie.

A youthful picture of my dad.

A typical scene from Priesthill, taken in the early 1970s.

Capt JJ Black. After the war he was knighted and went on to become Admiral of the British home fleet.

Invincible is escorted into Portsmouth with an armada of well-wishers.

Invincible's triumphant return, 17 September 1982.

Den and *Auld Meg* approach the start line of the 2008
Jester Azores Challenge.

Terciera, a typical party on the pontoon.

Bill and *Belgean* entering the Azorean harbour of Velas on the Island of Sao Jorge.

Den, Amy and Matt, painting our colours on the wall at Terciera.

2010 Skippers' dinner (L-R): Roger Fitzgerald, Stan Snape, John Margarson, Den Gorman and Bill Churchouse.

Den and *Lizzie*-G on their way across the Atlantic.

2010 Trevor Leek and *Jester* coming through the start line.

As we come off the continental shelf we are surrounded by Beluga whales.

Igor and Rory blast off a cork. They are the first to arrive in Newport.

Standing on *Cookie*, the skippers gather to say goodbye to Rory (L-R): Den Gorman, Thomas Jucker, Rory McDougal, Roger Fitzgerald and Tony Head.

Rory and *Cooking Fat* set off for England.

My dear father, John Gorman.

The next afternoon, the skippers' briefing was held on the deck of Ewen Southby Tailyour's boat, *Black Velvet*, a beautiful 35-foot Tradewind. Ewen was a white-haired retired Lieutenant Colonel of the Royal Marines who gave the impression that he liked to grab life by the horns. I was about to ask why his boat was called *Black Velvet* when his assistant, Amanda, handed the answer to me in a plastic pint tumbler. It contained half Guinness and half Champagne.

Ewan began his briefing which, accompanied by much jocular banter, boiled down to details about the start and finish lines and not much else. 'There are no inspections. Your boat, and what you carry in it, is all down to you. Just try not to use your engine... if you have one,' and with that, as the rain began to come down, we all signed soggy disclaimer forms together with details of our next-of-kin.

Later that afternoon, I paid a visit to Roger Taylor on *Mingming*. Roger had recently published his book, *Voyages of a Simple Sailor*, and I wanted him to sign my copy. It was the story of his early adventures and sailing experiences and how they led to his purchase of *Mingming*, a 21ft junk-rigged Corribee into which he had built foam-packed compartments, thereby making her virtually unsinkable. He had no engine at all and carried a minimum of electrical equipment. He then demonstrated how he could reef her junk rig down from full sail to virtually nothing and back again and all the while standing inside the hatch of his main cabin. I had no doubt that Blondie would have approved.

All this made me think about my preparations to *Auld Meg*. She was after all, no more than a standard production boat without any such modifications. Had I done enough? Was I ready?' Offshore there would be no coastguards or handy ports to run to - it would be just me.

★

On the evening of the second night before our departure, we had a group dinner at the Royal Western yacht club. We were entertained by Jake Kavanagh, a PBO journalist who had a talent for stand-up comedy and we spent the evening eating, drinking and laughing. As I turned in that night, I gave a thought to my kids. Amy couldn't make it but Mathie, with my friends, Ian and Claire, would be coming down to see me off. I wondered how he would feel witnessing over 40 small yachts heading out to sea with his Father on one of them.

4

It took an hour or so for the spectators' boat to get organised and to move into position. Our 'shore time' was up and 'the fleet' was starting to cast off their lines and move out. I whacked on *Meg*'s engine to warm her up and cast off John Margarson and *Lucy*. He shook my hand and said, 'Okay, nice to have met you Denis. I'll see you down there. We can go for a beer or two okay, yeah?' I tried to appear calm, 'Sure thing mate, I'll look forward to it,' I replied.

It was a bright sunny day with only faint breezes, too little for the engineless boats to get to the start line on time. I turned *Meg* around and picked up a line from *Mingming* to tow her and Roger out. We were on our way. At last we were on our way!

My mouth was dry and I found myself bungling everything I handled. At one point, I was steering *Meg* and *Mingming* into the path of an incoming cross-channel ferry until Roger, who was calm and a good deal more composed, directed me onto the correct heading.

As we approached the start line, I dropped Roger's line and we wished each other 'good luck'. Up went the sails. Off went the engine, away with the electric autohelm, and down went the servo blade. *Meg* was now self-steering by the wind.

The spectator boat came into view and moving forward to the shrouds I shouted. 'Mathie, Mathie...' And then I heard a little voice shout back excitedly, 'Dad, Dad!' A skinny little arm and head pushed out from the bulging crowd at the guardrails of the boat. We both waved vigorously. A lump came to my throat. I waved with moist eyes and choked emotions. None of my well-laid plans had taken account of this.

Black Velvet was anchored at one end of the start line. Ewen, Mike Richey and Amanda, were on board along with a crowd of other guests. It seemed that a party was going on with Amanda cheerfully recharging the glasses. Her voice carried across the water, 'More Champagne, more Black Velvet?' And then, 'Go on, have another!'

BANG! The 10-minute gun went off and a barrel full of talcum powder was discharged which blew back all over Ewen. 'Have another drink, Darling,' said Amanda.

Five minutes later, he raised his shotgun again and pulled the trigger. Click, nothing; it was a dud cartridge. Ewen unloaded the gun and shouted, 'Bang, that's your five-minute warning.' We all laughed. I turned *Meg* onto a heading straight for the spectator boat. I knew I couldn't win the race but it would be good to be the first to cross the start line, the first to go past the spectator boat. Perhaps I could snatch a moment of glory for Mathie.

I slackened the mainsheet to hold off the speed....Ewen lifted his gun for the third, and final, time. This time there was no misfire, both barrels went off simultaneously, 'BANG!' White powder filled the air. I pulled in the mainsheet and adjusted the wind vane. Running forward to the shrouds, I shouted, 'Come on you guys, let's hear it for *Auld Meg*!' And with that, as I crossed the start line, they cheered a series of hurrahs. I looked at Matt and shouted, 'I'll see you soon, I promise,' and, smiling bravely, he waved back.

Eventually, the spectator boat did one last sweep of the fleet, hooted her horn goodbye and headed back. We were now alone and, in a funny way, I welcomed it. All the social niceties, the worrying, planning and scurrying about were over. It was time to get on with the job. This was long-distance sailing; no deadline, no hurry, no point in worrying about the tide, a case of letting the forces of Nature do what they want and simply, going with them.

The wind fell away to almost nothing and I drifted over to the eastern breakwater. I was detached from the main fleet who were stuck around *Black Velvet*, each boat trying to make its way in the very light airs that moved around us. Here I came upon *Moonbow*.

'Hi Stan,' I shouted. Her skipper, Stan, a white haired chap, wearing glasses, came to his main hatch, 'Hello Den, how are you? That was a lovely send-off, don't you think?' 'Sure was, but I think we're going in the wrong direction.'

'Oh I'm not bothered,' he said, 'I'm going below to make a stew. There will be plenty of time for the Azores when the wind picks up.' Then he disappeared below.

Before long, a light breeze picked up and *Meg* pulled away. To my surprise, within the next couple of hours, we were in front of most of the fleet. I had closed to within 2 miles of Eddystone Lighthouse when the wind dropped completely and I had my first experience of the stillness that Bill had described. One by one, as our first evening drew in, each boat switched on its navigation lights. It looked like merry Chinese lanterns strung along the coast to the west and east of me. Curiously, I noticed that little *Mingming* had the brightest lights of all.

The breeze returned and very soon I could see that the fleet was catching up. I tried trimming the sails but, no matter what I did, *Meg* seemed to be slower than the others. One by one they went past and pulled steadily ahead. *Jester* glided by, not more than 100 feet away on my port side, then *Mingming*.

To keep pace, I decided to fly the cruising chute. This is a large, colourful balloon-like sail, similar to a spinnaker, used for running downwind. Already, I was breaking my own rules because, to put up such an awkward, difficult sail in darkness and fly it all night can be foolhardy. If the wind strengthens, the boat can become unmanageable, and you can find yourself in trouble. Even so, I decided to have a go, thinking that this would give me an advantage. I was wrong. The sail filled and collapsed and made an irritating crinkly, crackling noise. After 3 or 4 hours of fruitless perseverance, I gave up. I brought the cruising chute down and stowed it away. I concluded in my journal,

'Meg is not a fast ship, even with this gigantic sail.'

As *Auld Meg* and I bore on through the night, I thought of Mathie and Amy and, in my thoughts, I wished them a safe and sound sleep and kissed them good night. I pondered about this crazy voyage that I had locked myself into. 'I must be mad', I thought, but I was happy. I was having the time of my life.

I had decided that until I was safely out of the English Channel and into deep water, I would have to maintain a vigilant lookout for ships. Consequently, I planned to go through the night, taking only 15 minute catnap rest periods.

5

Throughout the next day, the sailing was excellent. On the first day we had clocked 75 miles. We were to follow this on the second day with 102. I noted the following in my diary:

'*Regular cat napping, not too tired. Hopefully out of the shipping lanes by sunrise tomorrow.*
Eating well, porridge, cheese and tomato sandwiches. Afternoon tea, tuna and pasta casserole. Eating plenty of ginger and garlic with my main course to keep seasickness at bay.
Boat is dry and everything is working…'

As our second night closed in, the wind dropped to a dead calm and a heavy mist descended, creating a halo around my masthead light. I was still in the shipping lanes and I began to feel nervous, my every sensation alert, absorbing the stillness, the gentle swelling motion, the shroud of isolation, the ever-present threat, its every nuance belonging to a lone mariner. I felt very much alive, but not alive enough to stay awake!

I slept through my next 15 minute alarm and, three hours later, when I awoke, I found bright sunlight flooding through *Meg*'s cosy little cabin. The wind had joined us again and the mist was gone. I checked the horizon and monitored the radio. Nothing. We were probably miles behind everyone else, but, even so, it felt fantastic.

Meg began to fly along, but the sky had the tell-tale streaks of mares' tails - a series of long wispy clouds that indicated a likely change of weather. Sure enough, at the end of the day, our third since leaving Plymouth, a strong wind of about Force 6 came up. The seas rose and white horses began to appear. Under reduced sail, *Meg* bowled along with water breaking over her bow and the wind humming through her rigging.

As we sailed on through the night, we moved from the Sole Bank, (typically 100 to 150 m deep), out into the deep Atlantic which drops off to over 4000 m. By lunchtime, we were in perfect sailing weather, bright, fresh and clear. The ocean, now deep blue, began rising into magnificent gentle swells which looked awe-inspiring but were relatively harmless. The boat rose and fell with hardly any sensation at all, like a baby being cradled by Mother Nature. I sat for hours watching. I was mesmerised. By now, our position was about 360 miles to the south-west of Plymouth.

With this sea change, I extended my sleep periods to an hour. The effect of this was almost instantaneous and I started to feel more refreshed. It felt good to be alive. I soaked up the vista as *Auld Meg* dipped and swayed along. The world around me was unhurried, uncomplicated and without demand. I was content.

★

On our fourth morning at 05.00, I woke to hear squealing and slapping sounds. I clambered on deck to find the sea around me awash with dolphins, hundreds of them, dancing around *Auld Meg* who herself was charging along with them. They cut under the bow and darted through the gap between the keel and rudder. They leapt alongside as if challenging us to a race. 'What's this?' I hear them say in their high pitched voices.

I wanted to grab one and rough him up around the cockpit, the way you would with your pet dog on the living room floor, then release him so that he might say to his friends, 'That guy is a nutter…but he's good fun.'

I laughed. After 15 minutes or so, they got bored and moved on. We were alone again.

The morning was cool, grey and overcast but, as we approached noon, the wind and sea calmed and blue skies began to break through. The Atlantic swell returned in dark blue intoxicating swells 20 to 30 foot high. It is something I could never tire of.

My desired course was to head south-west at 240° but, as we crossed Biscay, the wind began to strengthen and move onto our nose. I could either tack to the south or to the north-west. Neither option was good. To go north-west would be well off course and a course to the South would lead us towards the shipping lanes and Spanish fishing fleets around Cape Finisterre. Racked with indecision, I settled on the southern option.

The following morning, on our fifth day, about one hour before dawn, a huge ship appeared from astern. Fearing a close encounter, I erred on the side of caution, changed course to the north-west… and stayed there.

As the morning wore on, the wind strengthened, the sea began to rise and white horses began to gather. Before long, *Auld Meg*'s smooth and comfortable motion was gone and we were hammering and crashing through the waves. My movement around the boat became increasingly difficult and, at noon, I decided to 'heave to'.

'Heaving to' is a tried and tested method of riding out a storm. It involves setting the rudder and sails in opposition to each other, so that one is trying to steer the boat into the wind, and the other, to turn it away. When the two forces are in balance, the boat drifts slowly downwind at about half a knot, leaving behind a slick of smooth water and swirling eddies which have a calming and smoothing effect on the oncoming seas. I had

practised this manoeuvre in calm seas but, this time, it was for real!
When the operation was completed, I stayed on deck for well
over an hour, nervously watching, balancing the tiller and
adjusting the mainsheet. I was pleased to see that my slick
was running off nicely and having the calming effect that I
desired. By now, the wind and sea were intimidating; as far
as the eye could see, the previously rather attractive-looking
white horses, were rolling and breaking ominously. Then the
rain closed in, very heavy, and with it the visibility reduced to
perhaps a hundred metres. It looked like this was going to be
our first gale.

I felt a long way from home; I was wet, cold and hungry
but still I stayed out there watching until sharp cramps in my
stomach told me that I needed the loo. It was time to leave *Meg*
to fend for herself. Reluctantly, I went below.

Up top was noisy, scary, wet and cold. Inside *Meg*'s main
cabin, it was relatively quiet, dry, warm and snug. The boat
was heaving about but bearably so. I began to feel confident
that my little Virgo Voyager would ride this out.

For those who have never been to sea, it is difficult to
imagine how awkward it is to function on a small heaving
boat. You move about like an orangutan grasping every odd
and angular hand and foothold, leaning and wedging into
every available nook and cranny, every mistake rewarded with
a bump and a bruise.

I made a hot meal, cleaned up and then finished off with
two or three cups of tea. Every half hour or so, I would stick
my head out of the hatch to check the horizon and see how
Meg was doing. Content that my little boat was managing
admirably, I eventually wrapped a sleeping bag around me,
wedged myself into a corner of the saloon and closed my eyes.
Warm and content, with a full belly and a mind without fear, I
slept.

After 9 hours, the wind abated. The new wind that

followed gave a welcome change of direction and we got moving again. *Meg* and I had done well and I was in a self-congratulatory mode. Evening was drawing in and it was time to eat again. As I lifted a pot out of the locker, I noticed water at the bottom of the well. I went on to check the bilge and there I found a further 4 or 5 pints sloshing around. I pumped it out then watched for a few minutes to make sure that no more was coming in. I wondered where it had come from. During the gale there had been a lot of water washing over the decks but there had been no sign of it coming through the hatches. I had, however, done some work on the rigging points on the deck; could it be that this had weakened the seam between the deck and the hull? I went on deck to check the area and the seam but I could find nothing wrong. I was perplexed.

By now, night was drawing in and it was time to switch on the masthead navigation light. 'Click, click, click, click', I repeated, on and off – nothing. The masthead light was knackered! With its newly installed bright and efficient LED bulb which only drew 3 ½ W of my precious battery power, it was my main light, the highest and therefore the most visible to shipping. I switched on the less efficient deck-level lights to find that only the front one worked! My rear white light was also out of action. I put my head in my hands.

After a few moments of thought, I clambered around below, dug out my spare oil lamp and rigged it to the aft guardrail. It was a poor substitute. Quite apart from it swinging around, it illuminated the whole cockpit, making it very difficult to see anything out there in the darkness. But there was nothing more I could do until daylight so I went below thinking,

'All this after just one gale… And after all my preparation and planning.'

★

I had a restless night, and by first light on the following morning, I was ready to start work. I suspected that the problems with the navlights were due to corrosion in the wiring and wasn't the sort thing that I could fix at sea. Instead, I took my LED bicycle lamp which I had been using as a cabin light to ease the load on my boat batteries and attached it to the stern rail facing aft. It was unconventional but it worked and was a distinct improvement over the oil lamp.

Now for the water leak. During the night another 3 or 4 pints had collected in the bilge but now that the weather was much calmer I felt certain that no water had come over the suspect deck area. Then it hit me - Perhaps the water wasn't coming from the outside of the boat at all!

The main water tank was on the starboard side in the aft quarter berth locker. I crawled down the quarter berth, lifted the cushions and locker plate and found my problem. The water tank was a flexible bladder type and it was soaking wet, with water and air gargling through the seals at the top of the bag. The rough weather must have strained it and, as the boat rocked and rolled, water was seeping out to begin its journey to the bilge.

My first thought was to decant it, but I had no suitable receptacles; it had a capacity of some 30 L and was far from empty. Better to carry on using it as it was because at the rate it was leaking, I was only going to lose a gallon or two. I was carrying 20 litres of spare water in jerry cans plus a further 15 x 2 litre poly bottles. On top of this, I had 10 litres of skimmed UHT milk and, by any reasonable estimate that should be more than enough to get me to the Azores.

I reflected on my situation over a cup of coffee. We were into our sixth day, the navigation lights were improvised and the main water tank was leaking. It would take another 10 or more days to get to the Azores. What would the Prudent Mariner do? Would he play it safe, head for the nearest land and retire from the event?

On the plus side, we had weathered our first gale, the emergency navigation lights were fine, the boat was strong and I had plenty of water. What would Sir Alec Rose do? Surely, he wouldn't give up, so neither would I!

6

On the evening of that sixth day, I noticed a triangle of three white lights on the horizon behind me. It was a ship. I was feeling tired but decided to wait until she had passed us before turning in. I went below to get my hat and gloves and returned five minutes later. I could now see a triangle of white lights plus a red and a green. This was a big ship and she was coming straight for us, and fast. Within another five minutes, she would be right on top of us. I got onto the radio, channel 16.

'Security, security, security,' I called, 'Yacht *Auld Meg* to motor vessel, please respond?'

No answer. I repeated again and again. It was no use. I grabbed the lantern and illuminated my sails. I directed the beam to their bridge deck and started flashing. As I was doing this, I disengaged the steering gear and threw the helm over to turn *Meg* off to port.

The green light on the ship disappeared and the vessel passed down my starboard side just 300 yards away. She was huge. I breathed a sigh of relief, then tried again on the radio. Still no answer. I sat for a few moments to gather my thoughts, then put *Meg* back on course.

Was it a close thing or was the bridge officer simply swinging by to have a look, without wanting to talk? I think this was possible. But it was unnerving, and so I resolved to be more disciplined and maintain a better lookout.

I told myself, 'What does it matter if you get tired? You can sleep in the Azores, or when you get home, or when you are an old man in a nursing home. For now, you must be on your guard, you must be vigilant, you must be strong!' I resolved that from now on I would get up every half hour to check the horizon.

I went below, turned in, and awoke four hours later!

★

The following day, our seventh, my position was 12° 18' West, 45° 30' North and we were heading due South. The wind was light and we were rolling and slopping about in a tedious motion. I was cross with myself for heading north-west for those 8 hours before the gale and, on top of that, 'heaving to' for a further 7 hours. I had been too cautious and I now imagined the rest of the fleet, maybe 100, 200 or even 300 miles to the south, picking up the easterlies and heading west like the clappers.

I had my cruising chute up and it was doing its usual thrap, crinkle, thrap routine as it filled and collapsed in the light breeze.

'You're driving me bloody daft,' I muttered aloud as it continued, 'thrap, crinkle, thrap, crinkle...', Then, '...crinkle, crinkle, thrap!' Then more loudly, 'thrap,' then softly, '...crinkle' then louder still 'thrap.' 'You are driving me mad!' I screamed. 'Crinkle,' it replied, then, 'Thrap'.

'I'll bring the bloody thing down,' I thought but decided to have a cup of tea first.

The day was warm and sunny. I had laid my wet clothes and cushions outside and they were all dry. 'The miracle of the sunshine,' I observed pleasantly to myself as I took them below. Everything was stored again and *Meg*'s cabin was warm and cheery as sunlight streamed through the windows. I was about to light the stove when I heard a mighty blowing sound - 'Whuft!' I stopped.

I popped my head over the main hatch. I could sense something moving, something near, then over to my starboard quarter about 50 yards away, I saw the water move and the head and back of a large whale broke the surface. 'Whuft.' The vapour from his blowhole rose 6 feet. I watched transfixed. This creature was enormous, easily the size of *Meg* and probably a good deal bigger. The great whale, probably a bull, circled the boat two or three times picking up speed and getting closer each time. I found myself breathing quickly and I could feel my heart pounding. 'Where is he going with this?'

He cut quickly across the front of the boat and arched out of the water as he passed, so close that I could easily have stepped off the bow and onto his back. He went around again but, this time, further away.

At 90° to our starboard side, he stopped and lined himself up as if to attack. He started heading straight for us, blowing hard, his vapour shaft rising vertically from his bulbous head. Just before he reached us, he dipped below the water and, as the great beast passed underneath us, *Meg* lifted slightly then settled again.

'Holy fuck!' I muttered under my breath.

The whale broke the surface about 30 yards off our port side, blew hard, arched his great back and dived away in effortless motion. He was gone.

I sat down and breathed deeply. My hands were shaking. I looked at the clock. It was 09.00 hrs. I closed my eyes, 'Thrap, crinkle...' The noise went on, but this time I didn't hear it - My only thought was, 'How close was that?'

Forty minutes later, the whale came back, circled one more time, then left for good. I would see whales again, both going to and returning from the Azores, but I would never see behaviour like this from any of them. This creature really unnerved me and for the next two or three days, I was anxious. It was hard for me to relax or sleep. Whenever I heard something strange, I would jump up to look out in case he had come back.

I have no real idea what it was all about, whether he was just being curious, or amorous, or even defending his territory. Who can tell? However, one thing is certain that if he had failed to take that dip under, then *Meg* would have been sent to the bottom, I would have taken to the life raft and this story would have had a very different ending - if it was ever to be written at all.

7

The next few days were warmer and the wind light and variable. I strove to get my little boat to the South West. I spent hours adjusting sails and steering gear so that *Meg* 'held a course'. Even if it were only at 2 knots, that would be a 50-mile day! Holding a course became a constant preoccupation and was demonstrated repeatedly throughout my logbook:

Tuesday 10th June day 11.
'From 14:00 hours to 19:00 hours we have covered 12 miles. Today has been really hard going. I have changed, reefed, shaken out, boomed out and lashed back the sails constantly, The wind has been light from the East and, try as I might, I cannot get Meg to run downwind. She backs her mainsail and runs off South-east or North-west or anywhere but South-west! (Which is where we want to go!) So frustrating.'

Later on the same day I wrote:

'My hands are hardening with all the rope work, so much work for so little gain.'

Wednesday, 11 June. Day 12.
'There was only a zephyr of a breeze, I loosened the lead lines from the steering gear, with less wind this seems to need more flex

in order to adjust. We headed south at 210°, our desired course
is 250°. No matter - we moved about 2 to 3 knots very gently'.

Once *Meg* was sorted and a course was held, sleep and
food were the next priorities. I checked over my fresh fruit
and vegetables every day and any that were starting to go soft,
black or bad, were trimmed out and used straight away. In this
way, I wasted very little and had some interesting and delicious
meals.

On a typical day I had fresh orange and grapefruit segments
followed by French toast with fried tomatoes and mushrooms
for breakfast. At lunchtime I had Spanish omelette with
chutney and home-made chapatti bread. In the evening I had
steamed rice with sultanas and red capsicum with a home-
made vegetable curry made up of potatoes, carrots, onions and
lentils followed by caramelised bananas and evaporated milk.

I always made an effort with food and, when the weather
permitted, I never missed the chance to be creative.

In the evenings I enjoyed listening to music. This was an
unexpected bonus; imagine listening through headphones,
as you go through the night on a calm ocean with countless
stars above you looking close enough to touch, satellites going
by low and fast from one horizon to the other, their shining
white colour so distinct from the flashing navigation lights of
aircraft. And in our wake, as *Meg* disturbed the bioluminescent
life in the water, there were thousands upon thousands of
bright flashing diamonds….just sublime!

I was visited by dolphins, whales, turtles, Portuguese
jellyfish and numerous seabirds. I tried to appreciate my
surroundings. I enjoyed reading and finished Roger's book,
Voyages of a Simple Sailor, at the end of which I thought, 'I wish
he had written another hundred pages', because I enjoyed it so
much. Then I started 'Skeletons for Sadness.'

By now, the water in my leaking water tank had turned

foul. Even with the addition of water purification tablets, it was undrinkable. I still had all my emergency water so I decided to have a cockpit bath. Sitting naked in the cockpit with only my harness on. I washed myself from head to toe, firstly with seawater and saltwater shampoo, then rinsed it off thoroughly with the water from the foul tank. My whole body tingled with approval.

I was contented and happy, enjoying the voyage and living the dream.

★

On Thursday 12 June, our 13th day, we recorded a 24-hour distance of 98 miles. We were moving fast and holding a near-perfect course for the island of Terceira. I estimated that we would arrive in about three days.

But as evening fell, I noticed a heavy nylon fishing rope dragging behind the boat. It had caught on the bottom of the skeg, at the hinge where it met the rudder. It was an ugly thick light blue rope and was trailing about 15 feet behind.

After much difficulty, I dragged it up with the boat hook but, despite much pulling and tugging, it refused to come off. It was nearly dark and I needed to reef the sails for the night so I cut off what I could and left the rest until the morning.

During the night the wind started picking up. By 01.30hrs the sea was rising and breaking and the wind was screeching and whistling in the rigging. Lying in my bunk in the snug cosiness of the cabin, it was easy to tell myself that there was no need to go up top, that it would soon settle down and go away.

This, of course, was wishful thinking and, after half an hour of cowardice, I had to bite the bullet. Poor *Auld Meg* was being tossed and strained against her will. She was crying out for my help and it was my responsibility. This was my half of the bargain between us; I would look after her and she would look after me.

As I opened the hatch, my warm soft face was struck by a blast of cold, moisture-filled air. The strength of wind was shocking and the darkness was intimidating. I took a deep breath and broke into the cockpit. The sails needed reefing which is easy enough in calm conditions but on a night like this, the strain on the headsail control sheet was enormous. Once released, the sail thrashed and shook so violently that it threatened to burst itself or tear the rig apart. I ignored the sound and worked quickly until it was wound away.

The mainsail was next. I now had to leave the cockpit and go out on deck to the mast. I took another deep breath, whispered a Hail Mary and up I went. I was now fully exposed to the elements. I remember the darkness, noise of water, wailing wind, swish of spray, violent movement, slippery footing, tenuous handholds and ensnaring harness lines. There was no other way and it had to be done, so I got on with it.

Back in the cockpit, I sat for a while assessing the situation. Now that the mainsail was reefed right down, *Meg* seemed to be okay. I tried unrolling a little of the headsail and we started to make some worthwhile, albeit uncomfortable, progress. I shook out some more and soon we were banging and crashing along, wonderfully fast. We were on the edge of our capabilities, the edge of the decision to keep going or 'heave to'. I clung on and sat up all night monitoring the situation. When daylight broke, it looked even worse than I thought it would. *Meg* was charging along with solid water and spray coming over her bow and landing all over her deck. It was like a mad fairground ride.

By mid-morning the wind had increased further and I sat in the cockpit for over an hour, just watching and listening, ready for action. The wind and sea were stronger than we'd experienced near Biscay, on our fourth day. This time, however, from what I could see, *Meg* was coping fine. Furthermore, we were going in the right direction. Gingerly, I let out a bit more headsail and teased the main sheet and steering gear into fine adjustment, then after another 20 minutes, I decided to go below.

All day we hung on, thumping and rolling along with the sound of the wind shrieking and constant torrents of spray pouring down on us. Inside the cabin, the air was laden with moisture and everything became damp. I spent the day fully clothed and prepared to go on deck in an instant. I wedged myself in tight and draped my unzipped sleeping bag around me. I nodded off repeatedly but then a sudden jerking would shake me back into fatigue-weary consciousness. It was too rough to prepare food or to make a hot drink. Instead, I drank squash and ate a few biscuits. I tried to read, but the motion made me feel sick. Instead, I listened to music. I wrote in my journal,

'It is a horrible day! Meg is banging and crashing and rolling, watchkeeping is pointless. The barometer dropped 6 mb and then a further 3. I decided to keep pushing on as long as we can. The only one good outcome is that we are travelling fast and pretty much in the right direction. This kind of sailing stretches your nerves! If the sea rises much further or breaks more heavily then I shall need to heave to...'

8

At 04.00 hrs on the following morning, the gale began to blow itself out. It had lasted for almost 28 hours, during which time we covered 77 miles, which gave us a running total of 1130 miles since leaving Plymouth. It was now only 120 miles to Terceira.

The late morning brought sunshine and a gentle swell of about 1 metre and what little wind there was, was now coming from the wrong direction. I needed to get rid of the rope around *Meg*'s rudder. I was lucky that it hadn't yet interfered with our self-steering gear and I was anxious to get it off. Clearly, I was going to have to go over the side. This is a risky business. A sudden breeze could easily blow *Auld Meg* away and leave me stranded.

I stopped the boat, dumped the sails and lashed the helm. Then I rigged a boarding-ladder and fixed a generous scope of lifeline from my waist to a secure handhold in the cockpit. With my snorkel and mask on and carrying a sharp knife that was attached with a lanyard to my wrist I made one last check. Wind… settled, helm… lashed, sails… tied down, lifeline… secure and laid out, sharks and jellyfish …none.

I leapt over the side and, as quickly as I could, I cut the thick ugly blue rope away then, without wasting any time looking around, I scrambled back on board. It was a refreshing experience but one I was glad to put behind me.

Meg needed tidying up and I needed some hot food. I

allowed myself an hour or so to get things done before getting underway again.

I laid a course, close hauled into the wind, but it was carrying me too far north. At 17:30 hrs I changed tack but was then heading too far south. It was disappointing and frustrating.

As if in consolation, during the night I was accompanied by the brightest full moon of the whole voyage. It was a magical night. I felt as though Mother Nature was giving me a gift of unsurpassed splendour which, in the early hours, she topped off by giving me a wind from the north. I could barely contain my excitement as I turned *Meg* onto a starboard broad reach and headed due west, straight for Praia da Vitoria. As we skipped along, I shouted, 'All the way from Plymouth to Praia da Vitoria on zero gallons of fossil fuel. Try beating that, EasyJet!' When daylight came I could see clouds on the horizon, a sign of land. I felt like a child on Christmas Eve, full of eager anticipation.

I studied the harbour entry chart, double-checked the GPS, recalculated my distance, and then went up top to have another look. At 11:00 hrs I could see the distant outline of the island. There was no doubt. The island that we had worked so hard and travelled so far to get to, was now before our very eyes. I gently slapped *Meg*'s cabin top and said, 'Well done old girl.' And all the while I asked myself, as if in disbelief…'Could it be real…have we really done it?'

Ten minutes later, the wind fell away and within twenty minutes we found ourselves floating on an oily calm sea with no wind at all. I calculated our distance. Thirty miles to go.

Bugger!

I wanted to sail in. Would the wind come back? Well, of course, but when? At what strength and in what direction? To combat my frustration, I decided to give the boat a clean and tidy up.

Still there was no wind; we were in the flattest calm you could imagine. The sky was blue, the world was full of warmth, *Meg* was going absolutely nowhere and I was a strong swimmer.... 'Why not?'

I stowed the sails, lashed the helm, put on my snorkel and mask and, as naked as the day I was born, I jumped in. I dived down and swam under the boat from bow to stern along her entire length. Seen from underwater *Auld Meg* seemed to be bobbing peacefully on the roof of a world that was thousands of miles wide and thousands of metres deep - audacious, fragile, slick and somehow perfect.

Finally, I swam out to the side for about 100 feet and turning, I looked back at my yacht just floating there. It was... magical. Then the memory came flooding back to me of swimming in the South Atlantic all those years ago and looking back at *Invincible* as she slowly passed by. I had recaptured the moment.

Back on board, I treated myself to a sponge bath in the cockpit with lashings of freshwater then dressed in fresh clean clothes. It was midday, there was no wind and Praia da Vitoria still lay just a tantalising 30 miles away. I was too excited to read, I had listened to enough music, I wanted to hear the sound of people, to go for a beer.

I looked at the chart. If I put the engine on now, I would be in before nightfall. That made sense. With my compromised navlights, I really shouldn't spend another night at sea and I was going to be last in anyway. Having watched every boat pass me on that first night, having taken the wrong tack when the wind was on the nose, and having stopped the boat during our first strong wind, I was bound to be the last boat to enter port.

'Who would care that I whacked on the engine for this last millpond stretch?'

The trouble, however, was that I had an aversion to the noisy racket that the engine would make. A couple of days earlier, I had tried running it for an hour to boost up the batteries and after 40 minutes I had ended up shutting it down. I had grown to love the gentle sound of sea and sail and found the engine terribly intrusive.

After a few more minutes of hesitation, I said, 'To hell with it!' And I whacked it on!

The next hours chuntered noisily along. Green hills and brown land came into view sitting majestically on a sea of perfect blue. God's own picture of paradise in watercolour.

'Was I at last a single-handed sailor?'

Yes, I was and I had fulfilled a dream that I had held dear throughout all of my adult life. As I motored those last few miles, I felt a rich and quiet satisfaction in all that *Meg* and I had done.

9

After all my fretting about being left behind, I was astonished to find that I had completed my voyage in an impressive time. *Auld Meg* was the first boat under 25ft to arrive. My passage had taken 16 days, 4 hours and 15 minutes which placed us 20th overall out of a fleet of 42. 13 boats had retired, most of them around the time of the first gale.

After the trials and tribulations of a long, single-handed voyage, somehow it felt good entering a port called Praia da Vitoria, which translates, 'The Beach of the Victorious'

On my first night, a barbecue was held on the pontoon. I was gifted with mugs of wine, fistfuls of bread and chunks of delicious grilled chicken and beef. I was unsteady on my feet, my sealegs being to 'blame'. As our supper began to wind down, spit spots of rain started to fall and I announced, 'You are all welcome on board *Auld Meg* for a nightcap.'

A healthy crowd took me up on the offer and stayed late into the night. They drank everything I had and I drank everything they had. In the days that followed, we celebrated each new arrival with similar parties, eating, drinking and singing.

My time alone in the Atlantic, overcoming all obstacles and completing the voyage, gave me a credibility that was equally felt by the other new skippers who, like me, had come offshore for the first time. There was a buzz of happiness all around and many exciting stories were recounted.

It was like being on that train again on my way to join the Navy, with a bunch of new recruits.

★

Happy days melted into one another and, as they passed the remaining boats arrived in port. In company you could often hear someone say, 'I can't believe I'm here!'

Between all the merriment and socialising, I had serious work to do; *Meg*'s wiring needed attention, her flexible water tank was rotten and leaking, the grab rails and upper woodwork needed sanding and varnishing. I spent the mornings and afternoons working on these problems, then, whenever I had had enough, I wandered off to another boat to ask for a coffee break or I might interrupt my work if someone chose to visit me.

Trevor Leek (*Jester*) was a helpful and a frequent visitor, as was Rupert Smith, the skipper of *Niord*, a 28-foot Vancouver. On one particularly hot day, I spent hours cramped into the cockpit locker trying to repair a broken wire which led to the aft navigation light. It was hot, clammy and claustrophobically awkward. Meanwhile, Rupert was repairing another faulty connection on a wire that led under the headlining of the main cabin and on up to the masthead. Everywhere was a mess with stores and equipment, tools and headlining panels all over the place. It was depressing.

I had managed to get the aft light working again but the masthead one still refused to work. 'It must be another dry connection,' said Rupert 'Let's have another go tomorrow. I'll pop by in the morning.' I breathed a sigh of disappointment as I felt the pangs of frustration. 'Sure thing,' I said, 'but for now, I have got to get out of this bloody awful mess.'

I wandered over to *Moonbow* and called down the companionway, 'Stanley my boy how about getting your old pal an ice-cold beer? I've got to get off *Meg*. She is driving me nuts.' Stan laid out some beer, an octopus salad and bread for lunch. It was a welcome relief - so civilised. *Moonbow* was tidy, well laid out and comfortable. She had a moulded interior and her deck head was smooth to the touch, quite unlike *Meg*, with her foam-backed vinyl roof lining which constantly sagged. *Moonbow* was a proper little yacht with bigger wider bunks, rich deep upholstery, a separate forward cabin and vastly superior locker space. At the same time, in a modest sort of a way, she felt purposeful and tough.

Stan had specific locker areas for fruit and vegetables, tinned foods and a cool bilge space for drinks and dairy products. We were talking about these things when I asked, 'So what will be the next great voyage for you and *Moonbow*? Stan affectionately touched her mouldings and said, 'Well, after we return home, we shall go no further together. I'm getting to a point in life where I need to slow down. I would like to change her for a little motorsailer to go local sailing around the south of England and France, one with an enclosed wheelhouse to keep me out of the elements.'

I could see his point. Stan was 68-years-old and had been sailing for 25 years, which included a dedicated five-year cruise around the Atlantic, Caribbean and East Coast of America. In order to keep sailing into his retirement, he needed the right boat. We sat quietly for a while and then I said, 'Stan, show me around *Moonbow*, I think I would like to buy her.'

10

I spent five weeks in total in the Azores, two of them voyaging and touring other islands. The first island was Graciosa where John Margarson joined me on *Lucy*. After he set off for England, I went on to the famous yacht haven of Horta on the island of Faial. Here, I met up with Bill Churchouse on *Belgean* and Richard and Amanda on *Sprinter*.

Together, the four of us took the short ferry ride to the island of Pico, climbed the 7,000 foot conical shaped Mount Pico and walked above the clouds. Two days later, Richard and Amanda set off for England and Bill and I returned to Terciera in time to meet my kids who were flying in for a two-week holiday. We found only two Jester Challengers remaining, Alan Charlton and George Jepps. The news which they told us was sobering. Boats that had made a safe passage down were now having a tougher time going back. *Tahiti Belle* had broken up and her skipper, Nick Barham, had been rescued by a passing ship. Alexei Federouk, had pushed on for the USA, lost his mast and been spotted by an American fishing vessel which reported that he was proceeding under a jury rig. Paul Feasey's catamaran, *Stingray*, had had her windows stove in and was heading for La Caruna to make repairs and *Dolphin of Fowey*, with skipper Nick Bridges and his son Andy on board, had lost her rudder and, God knows how, had managed to put into the Scilly Islands. This list was further added to when, within a week of Alan Charlton leaving, we heard that his keels were leaking and he was heading for Lisbon to make repairs.

I thoroughly enjoyed two whole weeks staying in the luxury of a hotel with Mathie and Amy. We spent time on the beach and explored the rest of the island. During this period, George Jepps left closely followed by Bill. I was now the only Jester left and after an emotional farewell to the children at the airport, I returned to the boat alone.

Without wasting any more time, well provisioned and having made numerous improvements and repairs, we set off on what I hoped would be a less troublesome return than my friends had experienced. I planned to head due North, to a mid-Atlantic point, where I would find Westerly tailwinds that would carry me East towards England. I chose this route as an additional challenge. Feeling as I did, that after this summer, I might never have the chance to engage in such a voyage again, I wanted to be able to say that I had at least completed half an Atlantic circuit.

It was a brisk start with sustained periods of near gale-force winds. We bowled along handsomely but it wasn't easy. For the first couple of days I was distinctly fragile and I had all the symptoms of mild sunstroke. I needed to acclimatise. I was further depressed to find that the fore hatch had developed a drippy little leak and there was nothing I could do about it until we next reached land.

But things began to improve. My appetite and my strength returned, and then there came, 'an omen'. In the early hours of our third morning, in the black of night with no moon or clouds, the stars and Milky Way put on another magnificent display. This panoramic show was interspersed with bright satellites travelling from horizon to horizon and many meteorites entering our atmosphere. One in particular, it must have been a big one, left a long trail as it travelled low and fast from east to west directly above us with flames billowing off the back of it. I could almost hear it. It was a breath-taking spectacle.

The following day, our fourth, another sign arrived. I was sitting in the cockpit eating my morning porridge, when I heard a familiar 'Whoosh' of a whale blowing out his spout. Alongside, there surfaced a magnificent specimen; a square headed creature of some 30 feet in length a mere 50 or 60 feet off my port side. He was as calm as you like, and seemed to enjoy swimming along and looking us over. I was mesmerised. I was surprised that I felt no fear at all and I could not help but smile broadly at him. Indeed, it seemed as though we were both smiling at each other. After 15 or more minutes, he was gone and, as he went, I remember shouting after him, 'I hope you live long and prosper.'

But were the meteorite and the whale good or bad omens?

Two days later, as we approached our mid-Atlantic point, the sky began to darken and fill with clouds. The wind began to build and, with it, came a gentle but persistent hum in the rigging. I began reefing down the sails until they were at their smallest. By nightfall it was raining heavily and this continued all night. On and on it poured, hard and relentlessly. The bleak morning light began to break through and now I could see how the sea was developing around me. I had hoped that the weather might have improved but the morning was not revealing this at all. The wind was strong and the rain, which had been so heavy all night, was now giving itself up to dry interludes of about 20 minutes. The clouds, however, showed no signs of blue or thinning out. The sea was rushing from the south-west in waves which looked to be taller than my mast. Breaking white horses were everywhere. I sat in the cockpit trying to figure out my next move. Generally speaking, at such times as this, it is possible to develop a feel for what the weather might do next. You watch and observe and usually you'll anticipate correctly if the weather is likely to improve, get worse or stay the same. On that morning, everything I saw and felt told me that things were going to get worse, much worse.

I checked my chart and plotted our position. The open sea was all we had and this would be our strength, for if *Auld Meg* could cope, then the abundance of sea room would keep us safe. I stored all the loose items away and strapped down the bunk cushions and locker lids. I brought down the mainsail and lashed the boom to the deck. Once done, I moved forward to the mast and put on the storm trysail. Surveying the scene, I felt satisfied that I had done all I could for the boat. I made a lunch of soup and biscuits and then made some corn beef sandwiches which I put into a Tupperware tub for later. I was nervous.

Auld Meg was running fast but, as time passed, she began to feel more fragile, rocking and dipping a little harder. Then she began to bang and crash. The wind was still rising and the humming through the rig became a shriek. By early afternoon, I decided to heave to, which turned out to be a wise decision because, within the hour, we were in the teeth of a full gale, the wildest and most violent that I had ever encountered. I wrote in my diary:

'It's up to you, Meg, to look after me now…'

I sat in the cockpit for a while, to look around and evaluate the situation. I had no way of knowing at the time, but I would later discover, that we were being overtaken by the tail end of tropical storm Cristobal. I went below and tucked myself into the driest part of my bunk and left the weather to do its worst and for *Meg* to do her best. At 22:00 hours I wrote;

'I am certain we are in the middle of a severe gale or storm. We are riding along comfortably but any notion to try and sail would be ridiculous. Thank God, I have plenty of sea room. I've made a comfortable bunk and sandwiches but I can't sleep or stomach anything to eat.

I miss my kids and all my dear friends. Hopefully this will break before too long.'

There was no moon that night and the low inky black clouds

were like giant writhing snakes that blotted out every star in the sky. The night around us was completely black. There was the high screeching wind, the roar and hiss of curling breaking waves, the thumping of rogue waves against *Meg*'s hull, and the dissipating water spraying over her entire length and entire height.

There was a rapid flapping of a tiny trysail as it bravely rounded *Meg* into each wave; there would follow a hard pressing 'Thunk', as she'd fall off and be caught again by the wind. In *Meg*'s cold, damp, contorted little cabin, I could hear her creaking and groaning and feel my heart thumping as we both waited anxiously for the dawn to arrive. But we had to hang on till the following afternoon for the storm to pass finally.

★

The remainder of our voyage continued to be boisterous with many episodes of thrilling sailing. On one occasion, I spent a whole afternoon surfing through the Atlantic swell, perhaps 60 feet high, and visible as far to the left and right as I could see. At the crest of each wave the unabated wind made contact with my goose-winged sails and 'whoosh', off we would go from 6 up to 7, then 8 knots into the trough until the wind was blocked out and we would slow down again until the next wave raised us up to repeat the cycle.

On and on we went, eating well, working day and night, resting day and night, reading in the daytime, music through the night. On and on managing the sails, tending the steering gear, logging our position, cooking food, keeping clean, being happy.

At last we entered the English Channel to be told by the Radio 4 shipping bulletin;

'The unseasonal weather continues, sea state moderate to rough,

wind south-west force 5 to 7, veering south-east. With likelihood of severe force 9 later...'

I studied the charts. Falmouth was our nearest safe haven but that was too far away; the gale would be on us before we got there. I wasted no time in accepting that our only option was to meet the gale head on and to ride it out.

When it came, in these shallower waters, the seas were chaotic, but no more than we had experienced before. I found myself surveying the scene without any fear or apprehension. Blue sky was breaking through the clouds and *Meg* was riding comfortably. Occasionally, a combination of waves would collide to windward and this would roll into the cockpit, draining away almost as quickly as it had come.

I retreated to my bunk and remained catnapping for six hours. By 17:00 hours, things were moderating. Falmouth was so close, a mere 30 miles to the north. I evaluated that, if I got underway, I would be crossing the shipping lanes and entering an unfamiliar harbour in the dark. On the flipside, however, Falmouth is not a difficult harbour to enter and many yachtsmen have done this at night. Together with that knowledge and our hard earned confidence, *Meg* and I headed for land.

★

At 02.00 hrs after a voyage of 15 days and 14 hours I dropped *Meg*'s anchor into the calm sheltered waters of Falmouth's visitors' Yacht Haven anchorage. My first instinct was to clean and tidy the boat but then I thought, 'Why bother? Leave it till tomorrow, you silly sod.' I was tired. My hands were hard, my face weather-beaten, my hair a mess, my head fuzzy with fatigue and my eyes and eyelids were dry and heavy. I was stiff and sore. I poured myself a mug of wine. It was, after all, a time for celebration.

I settled into my bunk and contentedly sipped my wine. It had been a hard voyage but worth it. I thought about my kids. It would be good to see them again and, hear all their stories and recall our adventures in the Azores. I thought about going back to work, back into the mainstream of everyday life. What a contrast!

I thought about the sea, its indifference, its great power, storms, wind and waves, its panoramic views, its endless horizons, its great and small creatures. And then, I thought about its peace and tranquillity, its calm restful swell, the dry warm sun, the clear sky, its peace and tranquillity...its peace and tranquillity... its peace...

FIVE

Newport Rhode Island

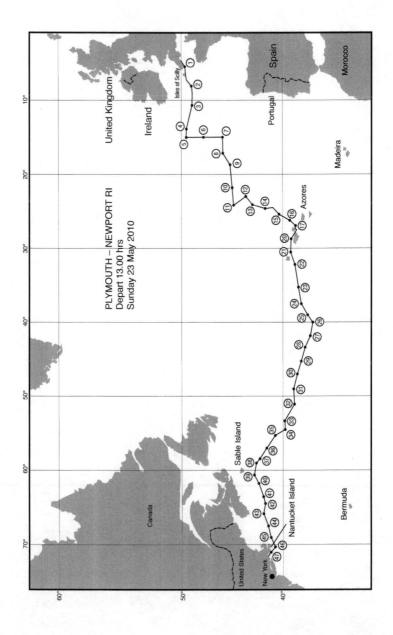

PLYMOUTH – NEWPORT RI
Depart 13.00 hrs
Sunday 23 May 2010

1

You are a child of the universe, no less than the trees and stars, you have a right to be here and whether or not it is clear to you, no doubt the universe is unfolding as it should.

Max Ehrmann

In September of 2008 I went home and prepared to return to my job at Barclays. I was not looking forward to it. Over the previous couple of years the job and the company had been changing. An influx of fresh-faced predominantly American directors had brought with it an aggressive management culture. We were expected to submit reports twice a day demonstrating our activity levels, with details of phone calls, appointment bookings and appointments completed, along with the projected gain ensuing from any business that might be written.

There were time-consuming computer compliance procedures, overbearing emails and the constant pressure to write more and more business.

The poorer performers were weeded out by being set virtually unachievable sales targets.

For many years I had enjoyed my work. I believed that good financial planning helped to bring calmness, structure and order into one's life. I had seen at first-hand how my dear Father had tried and failed to do the same and I saw the consequences of this failure.

When I first started, the job was centred upon, 'doing your best for the client' and, 'gaining business through the identification of client needs…' I had built up my knowledge and reputation, added a measure of rapport, offered a viable solution and, le voilà, the deal was done, to the benefit of the client, the company and myself. My success had not been brought about by sales targets or the ego of some slick director, or even money. It was through my empathy for my clients, supported by the belief that the work I was doing was good and beneficial.

Upon my return, I was informed that I was to be moved to cover another area some 30 miles or more away from my home. It was known as a disadvantaged area and, to go back to the very beginning of creating a new business base there, was a body blow. All my complaints were brushed aside. I was given the option…. 'Take it or leave it!'

Perhaps my character, when angry, leads me to make dramatic gestures or my new-found sailing experience had changed me. Irrespective, my resentment boiled over and I left the company.

It was at this time that the simmering news of sub-prime lending and non-solvent banks exploded onto the media and so began the world's greatest-ever banking crisis. The stock markets crashed and government fiscal policies around the world went into meltdown. The credibility of financial institutions was utterly dashed. Fortunately, my reputation had not gone unnoticed and I was soon offered a position with the Halifax. After attending their 3-month training course, I started my new job with as much commitment and enthusiasm as I could muster, but I soon discovered that the sales culture within the Halifax was just as aggressive as Barclays.

They were all making the same mistakes.

It felt like the re-tread of a bad movie. The job was miserable and I was struggling to believe in what I was doing. I snatched moments in between the pantomime of getting through the day. Standing in front of my office window, looking out, with hands in pockets and my tie loosened, I would dream of sailing. The feel of rope in my hand. The sway of a yacht on the ocean. I remembered meeting people who were wonderful to be around and of times when everything I did was an action of choice, without ulterior motive.

Running parallel to these events, I contacted Stan to see if we still had an arrangement for me to buy *Moonbow*. We had. He was keen to own a Marina 75, a pretty little motorsailer with an enclosed cabin, and I, for all my affection for *Auld Meg*, felt it was time to move on. I scrubbed and polished *Meg* until she looked her very best and put her into the hands of a yacht broker in Plymouth. In November 2008 we received an offer. I consulted with Stan and the deal was done. *Moonbow* was mine.

In January 2009 the Jester Challenge met for its annual meeting at the Punch Tavern in Fleet Street. There was a good crowd and a wonderful atmosphere. Speeches were made and anecdotes recounted then presentations followed. For those who had crossed the start line there was a green tie with the Jester Challenge logo embroidered. For those who had completed the voyage a handmade Darlington crystal commemorative paperweight was awarded. The inside was engraved with an image of yacht *Jester* and the words 'The Jester Azores Challenge 2008'. Then underneath a single word that stirred my heart, 'Finisher'!!

It was a wonderful gift and a superb evening. Speculation was rising as to who would put themselves forward for the next Atlantic outing in 2010, which coincidentally fell on the 50th anniversary of the very first single-handed transatlantic yacht race. The room was buzzing with questions and enquiries and reasons for going or not going. The first names into the ring were John Apps, Bill Churchouse, Roger Fitzgerald, John Margarson and Trevor Leek. In my heart of hearts I would have loved to join them but I ruled myself out. My commitment to my new job came first. I had a home to run and my children to think of.

No. This outing would not be for me.

I drove home to the Midlands that night with my treasured paperweight on the seat beside me and fanciful thoughts in my head; the Atlantic, the broad wild untamed Atlantic, with its shipping, icebergs, endless depressions and Gulf Stream and, the 50th anniversary of the first race to cross it single-handedly.....The very audacity of it.

★

Stan and I had become good friends. My new boat, *Moonbow*, was in winter storage at Payne's yard in Emsworth, relatively close to Stan's house in Arundel. Meanwhile he had found and bought a charming little Marina 75, '*Sabrina*', which would remain in Makum on the Eiselmeer in Holland, until he sailed her back to England in the summer. In the interim, he volunteered to help me fit out *Moonbow* with the electronic gadgets that I had bought. With his years of sailing experience and electronic circuitry at the BBC Stan was too good a gift to pass up. I accepted his offer and it was agreed that I would take leave in April and together we would get *Moonbow* ready for the season.

As the time drew nearer my consternation over my job was increasing. I confided with my close friends and it was Stan who said. 'If the job is that bad, pack it in! Life's too short to put up with that load of crap.' Then I found to my surprise that others began to agree with him. When I spoke to Amy and Matt they said. 'You will be fine Dad. You'll find another job doing something you like when you're ready. Don't worry about us.'

I agonised over the decision. If I did quit my job there would be no going back. I would be finished with banking forever. It would be a big risk. What I was sure about though, was that deep inside, I really wanted to sail my boat across the North Atlantic to the USA. Such a voyage would not save the world, or make me rich and famous. But after my previous voyage to the Azores, I felt that this forthcoming Atlantic challenge would be the fulfilment of my long held dream. To turn away would be a personal betrayal.

What to do?

April came and, with it, my much welcomed leave. Stan and I had been working on the boat for the past couple of days and had fallen into a pleasant routine of stopping for lunch at the Boaters Arms, a family run pub at the neighbouring Thornham's Boatyard. Here they provided home-made lasagne, pies, roast dinners and curry and a pleasant atmosphere, all for just £6.50 a head. We sat down to eat and I said to Stan, 'I have an idea and a proposition for you.'

Stan smiled and said, 'Okay, what is it?'

I nervously bit my lower lip and began, 'I've decided to resign from the Halifax. I want to take the summer off and do some sailing and I would like to take you to Holland on board my boat. We can sail together to Makum to pick up *Sabrina*, and from there we could sail single-handedly, but in convoy, back to Chichester Harbour.' I paused then added, 'At the end of the season I intend to find whatever temporary work I can through the job agencies around Rugby. Then next spring I'll take the boat to Plymouth for the Jester Challenge, and cross the Atlantic…'

Stan looked at me and an excited smile broke across his face, 'I think that's an excellent idea. I'd love to help you in whatever way I can.'

I took another breath and said, 'There's something else, I've decided to rename *Moonbow*. I want to call her *Lizzie-G.*'

Stan was still smiling but his excitement showed a little surprise, 'Of course, call her whatever you like. She's your boat. But tell me who is *Lizzie*-G? You've never mentioned her before. She must be someone very special.'

I smiled back, perhaps a little reflectively and said, 'Oh, if you saw her she wouldn't stand out in a crowd. Just an ordinary girl by most standards I suppose.'

I felt more confident now and relieved that I had not offended my friend. So I opened my hands and explained honestly,

'Lizzie was the dearest girl I ever knew. Lizzie Gorman was my Gran.'

2

We had a memorable sail with overnight stops at Dover, Dunkirk and Nieuport, in Belgium. We then entered the inland waterways of Holland and worked our way across the open lakes and narrow canals. We passed through Edam, the Makermeer, Amsterdam and then across that great northern enclosure, the Eiselmeer itself. We visited Hoorne and Stavoran until finally we came to Makum where Stan's boat, *Sabrina*, was moored.

During this time I gleaned a lot of information from Stan about the now renamed *Lizzie-G*. How to bleed the engine, change an impeller, top up the cooling water, change the fuel and oil filters and reef the sails. He also showed me how to use the Global Positioning System (GPS), to plot a course and to continuously monitor the boat's progress along it. The GPS is rather like a sat-nav in a car, but without any roads.

I also purchased an Automatic Identification System, (AIS), which Stan had fitted into the boat. This electronic device, quite simply, tells you when a ship comes into your area. It has a little alarm that, when set, can wake you up or draw your attention when you're otherwise preoccupied. This was a fantastic piece of kit. Not only was it useful in avoiding the risk of collision, but it also gave the name of each vessel so that they could easily be raised by radio.

(With AIS however there were two drawbacks. Firstly it needs to connect to the GPS system in order to orientate itself with the ships in your area. Without a good GPS signal hooked in, it could not work. Secondly, only ships of 300 tons and above are required by law to transmit the signals required by the unit. This means that smaller vessels such as fishing boats, powerboats and yachts could go undetected).

If I had had this equipment two years earlier, my channel crossing with Mark would have been much less difficult. We would have been completely aware of all the large vessels as we crossed the shipping lanes and, would have completely avoided the rocks, and kept out of the shallows, around St Vaast.

On the way back from Holland, Stan and I sailed into the picturesque village of Wivenhoe where Bill Kippen, Paul Feasey, George Jepps and John Margarson, fellow Jesters from 2008, came to visit. It was good to see them and catch up on all the news.

I loved my new boat and her existing and new equipment but all the time, I was acutely aware that I was jobless and living on scant savings with no immediate prospect of a decent job or good earnings. Sometimes I would fall into mild despair and always Stan would offer encouragement.

Eventually we parted company in Chichester. I cruised on to Alderney, then Falmouth, then back to Studland Bay, all the while, practising my skills with my new GPS and AIS equipment. After all there was no particular hurry to go home. At Studland Bay I fell upon Bill Churchouse who was anchored there with *Belgean*. It was great to see him again and to reminisce about our voyaging to and from the Azores.

We spent a week sailing in company as I slowly headed back to Chichester to haul out for the winter. But there remained one last major job to do to *Lizzie-G*. I decided to repaint her and transfer her topsides from their original dark blue to a light and bright sky blue, the same colour as *Lively Lady,* Sir Alec Rose's boat.

She was now as pretty as a picture and in every sense I felt she was ready to go.

3

It was September when I returned home to the Midlands. I had been gone for five months. It was time to clear the cobwebs out of the house and get a job. I needed to earn enough money to pay my way, but also, save enough to carry me through the following summer and across the Atlantic.

I had it in mind to blow the dust off my old HGV licence, to gain some experience and find regular work. I gained this licence as part of my resettlement training when I left the Royal Navy in 1987. I had been unable to get anywhere with it then, and doubted, after all these years, that I was going to find someone to entrust me with 46 tons of fully articulated truck now.

A stroke of luck came by when I bumped into an old friend, Geoff Pilling, who I had not seen for at least eight years. We went to the pub, and over a couple of pints and a large bucket of fried chicken, Geoff listened. He was just as I remembered, with a generous girth and an even bigger personality. Geoff was the sort of man who liked to help everyone. He wiped his greasy fingers across his yellow T-shirt and said, 'Problems are temporary, there's always a solution...'

And sure enough Geoff had a solution. He offered to introduce me to his friend, Jimmy Ryan, who was a self-employed haulier. As we parted he said. 'Don't worry Den, I'll get you sorted...'

A couple of days later, I got a call from Jimmy. He wanted

me to help him run his truck up and down from the Midlands to the shipping terminal at Felixstowe. Jimmy knew that I had been out of circulation for a while.

Whilst he drove, Jimmy talked me through the characteristics and particulars of the vehicle. It was agreed that when my turn came to drive, he would supervise me. It all seemed like such a good arrangement.

Halfway down the A14, it was time for Jimmy to take a break and for me to take over. But first, we pulled in for dinner. For the first time in my life I was in a truckers café, and before me was fried eggs, chips and beans, a slice of bread and butter and a mug of brown tea.

'Couldn't be better.' I thought.

As we ate Jimmy said. 'Geoff tells me that you've been driving in South Africa, America and on the Continent?'

I looked perplexed and corrected him. 'Oh no Jimmy… I went to those places when I worked with the bank and before that with the Navy… I've never driven in any of those places…'

'Oh, must be my mistake, I thought that's what Geoff said… But you did quite a bit up in Scotland didn't you?'

Again I corrected him. 'Jimmy, the only time I drove a truck in Scotland was when I passed my test, and that was 23 years ago.'

Jimmy's face dropped. He looked at me horrified and muttered, 'That lying fat bastard… I'm gonna kill him!'

Jimmy was on tenterhooks as I took the wheel of his precious truck. It was quite the most terrifying experience for both of us. But Jimmy was brilliant, good-hearted, a rough-diamond, a good teacher.

Over the next two weeks he taught me how to follow a satnav without leading the truck into a trap, adjust the suspension, complete vehicle checks, connect and disconnect a trailer, work the vehicle around busy town centres, roundabouts, dual carriageway and motorways, reverse on and off bays. He introduced me to gatehouse and security procedures for entering yard sites, how to operate the warehouse bay doors, ramps and safety lights, to operate a digital tachograph, to calculate journey times, mandatory breaks and working time directives that govern all licensed HGV drivers. Lastly and most importantly, he taught me how to talk like a trucker.

After two weeks, my high visibility vest was dirty and my boots were scuffed. I knew I was a great pretender... But my luck held.

We were now into the last quarter of the year and the demand for temporary drivers increased as Christmas approached. I found that despite my inexperience and limited credibility, I was able to persuade the local driving agencies to give me assignments. When asked 'How long have you had your license, mate?' I would nonchalantly, and quite honestly reply, 'Oh ... about 23 years.'

With a quick check of my licence they would say, 'Okay. Off you go', and hand over the keys and paperwork.

The solution I'd been looking for had been found. This type of work is transitory, with job assignments being issued on a day-by-day basis. This facility of flexible labour suits many clients but it also suits drivers who want extended periods of time off. The agencies are happy to accommodate this as they have a regular flow of workers coming and going. Throughout the winter I worked intensively and saved up for the coming summer. All the while I was safe in the knowledge that when the time was right, I could go away sailing and whenever I came back, I could begin earning again.

It was perfect.

4

It was a blustery day. Clear and bright and cool with plenty of blue in the sky interspersed with white fluffy clouds scudding from one horizon to the other. A great day for sailing. It was May 2010. I had been in the Plymouth area for the past 14 days, marking time and waiting for the start.

I had no permanent job, no wife or girlfriend and my kids were quite settled with the idea of my absence. It had been arranged that they would come down to wave me off and if all went well, I would have them flown out to America to join me for a holiday. In the meantime, there was nothing left to be done other than to enjoy my free time and get myself acclimatised with life on board again.

*

It was three days before the start and, just as we had done two years earlier, I made my way into QAB marina where the visitors' pontoon was reserved exclusively for us. The place was bustling with activity. Last-minute jobs, people climbing masts, rigs being tensioned and stores and equipment coming and going. There were yachting journalists milling about, wives and girlfriends, well-meaning and curious spectators who ambled across to see what all the fuss was about. There were many familiar faces amongst the skippers.

Others were new to me but as is the way with this

fraternity, self-made introductions, a smile and a handshake, soon produced new acquaintances. Some of our friends who had done the Azores had come down to wish us well and send us on our way. George Jepps, Paul Feasey, Nick Bridges and Paul Mead were the most familiar to me, along with Stan who was tied up alongside with *Sabrina*.

The next couple of days passed quickly. A skippers' briefing was conducted by Ewen on the pontoon adjacent to *Black Velvet*. Glasses were charged with a healthy supply of Black Velvet or, for those who preferred, a mug of Plymouth gin or a beer. The gin had been given to John Margarson who wrote to the Plymouth Gin Company and asked if they would like to sponsor us. To his and our delight, they responded by sending 15 bottles of their finest Blue Label which John in turn had victualled to Ewen.

Ewen decided that *Black Velvet*, which shared our pontoon, would be left open for any of us to come on board and socialise at an improvised bar which had tonic water, bitter lemon, lemonade and, of course, gin. He announced, 'Bring your own drinking vessels. The bar will be open 24 hours a day until the start.'

Three bottles were put aside as gifts to our hosts in America. One bottle to George Pike, another to the Commodore of the Newport Yacht Club, Norm Bailey, and a third to be put behind the bar at the Newport Yacht Club as a gift to the parishioners there. These were to be carried by three different boats who were thought most likely to get there.

During our briefing, one of the group called out, 'Ewen, what is that flag you're flying?' I looked up and recognised the light blue colours of the Falkland Islands. I had not seen it for many years.

Ewen explained, 'Today we are approaching the 28th anniversary of the liberation of the Falklands and as a patron of the Falklands and the Royal Marines Veterans Association, I like to show my respect by hoisting the colours.'

We all gave a polite round of applause. There was of course more to it, but Ewen was not the type to go into details. Since his involvement in the war he had revisited the Falklands many times, offering his help and his influence to any good cause that would assist the communities, as well as being a champion for the Royal Marines and veterans' institutions in the UK.

I remember looking at the flag and thinking of how much life I had lived since then, and of how much more there was to come.

5

The five engineless boats were the first to manoeuver off the dockside and out past the protective wall of the marina, where they raised their sails, and made their way slowly to cover the 3 miles or so to the start point.

Jester, Mingming, China Blue and *Cooking Fat* were permanently engineless but *Astro* was different. Her skipper, David Graham, had removed the engine, fuel tanks, propeller and its shaft and bearings, simply to make *Astro* lighter and more streamlined in order to give her greater speed and a faster passage.

I was surrounded by madmen - and I loved them all!

★

As I said my goodbyes to Matt and Amy, I was very aware that their emotions were being hidden behind a thin veil of confidence and brave smiles. Jess, now remarried, brushed my shoulders and said, not without affection, 'Look at the state of you. You always were a scruffy devil...' Then, more seriously, 'You take care out there Den. Don't do anything stupid. Keep your harness on. Remember you have the kiddies to come home to...'

It was kind of her to show some concern and I reassured her...' Don't worry Jess, it's only sailing. I'm going to take it easy, eat a lot, sleep a lot and read my books...I'm looking forward to the peace and quiet…' I squeezed her hand and kissed her cheek.

They then left, with all the other well-wishers, including my friends, Mark, Debbie, Ian and Claire, to board the spectator boat at the ferry point opposite our marina entrance.

Our visitors' pontoon was now strangely quiet. A pregnant pause hung above us as we waited for the spectators' boat to get underway. As I waited, I fidgeted restlessly. I started up the engine. Too soon. I knocked it off again. Then I realised that I hadn't taken the sail cover off the boom. That should have been my first job. I took it off and stowed it and I remember thinking that it would not be needed again for many weeks. I found my hand shaking and my mouth was dry. Was it nerves? Apprehension perhaps? Or excitement? Was it fear?

After 20 minutes the engines started to flash up and, in turn, I switched mine back on. John Apps and *Glayva*, who were rafted to the outside of me, decided to move off. I undid his lines, pushed out his bow and dropped his coiled-up bowline safely inside his guardrails. John gave me a smile and with his jocular Aussie accent said, 'Thanks for that Denis. Have a nice voyage. I'll look forward to meeting up and sucking down a few cold beers in Newport.'

Newport. It seemed so far away, *it was so far away*, pretty much the other side of the World.

I felt a sense of panic as I realised that I would be the next to go. I told myself. 'Just don't drop your lines over the side.' I was starting to imagine a mooring line tangled around my propeller, a stalled engine and *Lizzie* drifting helplessly around QAB marina, when …

'Are you all right?' came a familiar voice.

It was Paul Feasey, and beside him stood Paul Mead, my fellow Jesters from two years earlier.

I drew a breath and answered, 'I don't know what's come over me but my nerves are shot. Man, I can't stop shaking.'

Paul Feasey smiled, 'I know exactly how you feel. I get it every time I set out. Most of the guys are feeling the same. It must be especially bad for those that have got family to wave them off... It's a big emotional thing you know.'

I nodded my agreement and asked if they would help me to slip my lines.

Throughout the process the other Paul, Paul Mead, was quiet. His face was strained and his eyes were filled with moisture. As they were about to push me out, I shook his hand and said, 'Don't worry mate, it will be your turn someday.'

He nodded his head in agreement but couldn't speak. I knew that Paul had been unable to get time off work to do the Challenge, and I guess that the sight of his many friends setting off to fulfil a dream that he had long held dear, was hard for him. As I motored away we shouted goodbyes to one another and I began to settle down a little. As I passed through the marina entrance, I heard cheering. Looking across, I saw the spectator boat with my family and friends on-board. They were initiating a cheer that was taken up by everyone else.

I decided to make a show of it and, ducking down below I came back up with my hand operated fog horn. I pumped it up, then, steering *Lizzie* with my foot, I revved up the engine and swept past the spectator boat whilst waving and letting off blasts of the horn. I shouted,

'Three cheers for *Lizzie-G*, hip hip...'

To which they added, 'Hooray, hooray, hooray'.

This seemed to set a precedent and as each boat came out, they also did a fly-past.

I put away the shorelines and fenders, hoisted the main sail, rolled out the headsail and put on the auto helm. The day was bright and the sea oily and smooth. The breeze was gentle and interspersed with calm. Not a good day for brisk sailing but a kindly one for the spectator boats. We made our way to the start point where *Black Velvet* was anchored and waiting.

Ewen was watching the time and his trusty Purdy was again loaded with cartridges stuffed full of talcum powder. There we gathered and began vying for positions on the start line.

I was crossed bows and sterns with *Ella Trout III* and *Triple Venture*, *Fluffy* and *Marta*. These were all fast boats but, they could not race away yet. Just like me, they were waiting for the gun and their release. I wanted, if possible, to cross the start line in front of them and to hold them off for as long as I could.

The 10-minute gun went off. The wind fell away to nothing. The vying and movement stopped. I hoped the start would not be a damp squib, wallowing aimlessly on the wrong side of the start line as the spectator boat headed for home. That would be disappointing. The five-minute gun went off and still no change. We lay about with sails and sheets slapping as we wallowed gently from side to side on the swell.

The minutes slipped by and cats' paws started to sweep and move around us. It looked like a breeze was coming in from the east. I tapped *Lizzie*'s helm over and positioned us up for the start. The cats' paws were followed by a firm rippling breeze. We started moving and as the last seconds were counted down, *Lizzie* came up to something akin to her full hull speed. The gun went off and Ewen shouted, 'That's it. Off you go.'

The spectators cheered as Scott Turner, a proud Scots lad who skippered *Altamira*, an old 21-foot Westerly, was first across the line. He looked bemused as he found himself in front of the pack with yachts bearing down and rushing around him.

I shouted, 'See you in America Scott …Yahoo!'

Tony Head and Roger Fitzgerald passed me on my port side and I began to fall back as they blocked my wind. Through the muddle of yachts, I saw Stan and *Sabrina*. I waved goodbye and then *Dolphin of Fowey* closed in and her skipper Nick Bridges called out, 'Denis, this is for you, Godspeed and good luck.'

He had a glass of whisky and made a deliberate point of holding it up and drinking to my voyage. I was almost moved to the point of tears. Here was the man who, two years earlier, had nursed his stricken yacht, without a rudder, into the Scilly Isles. And he was drinking a toast to me? I waved back and shouted, 'Thank you Nick, thank you.'

We rounded Penlee Point. The spectator boat would be going no further, so I made my way over to wave a final goodbye. Duncan Lougee on *Vaquero* was running alongside under full sail. He had set his steering gear, gone to the front of his boat, leaned through the pulpit, and spread out his arms to impersonate Kate Winslet in her *Titanic* scene, 'I'm flying, Jack, I'm flying.'

It looked spectacular... And funny.

I looked up at the spectator boat. I could see that Matt and Amy were both crying and Mark was comforting them. It had all been too much. My own emotions began to buckle. I knew I must not show it but I felt terrible and a wave of guilt came over, that was so strong... I waved, and shouted, 'I'll be all right I promise, God bless you...'

Then, with my heart and head and stomach churning, my face flushed with heat, and tears welling in my eyes... I turned *Lizzie* away and we headed for the open sea.

6

Within an hour of breaking out of Plymouth Harbour the wind fell away. Fickle zephyrs and breezes followed and these called for constant adjustments to the wind vane and alteration to the sails. I noticed many of the other boats pulling ahead. Just as I had done two years before, I became convinced that everyone was making better progress than I was. Were we overweight? Poorly balanced? Should I have bought new sails? As I agonised through the long afternoon, I became more and more doom laden and fatalistic.

I made some soup but it didn't lift my spirits. Then darkness fell along with the last of the wind. *Lizzie*-G slumped into a powerless wallowing lop on an uneven sea swell. Everything banged and clattered. The mainsheet slapped and slatted across the traveller and the sails slapped and cracked as *Lizzie* threw herself from side to side. It was intolerable, an uncomfortable noisy racket, with no purpose other than to wear everything out.

At 21.30 hrs I decided 'we are going no further tonight'. So I stowed the sails and lashed the boom to the cabin top. The rolling increased but at least the noise settled down and with that, I too settled into a cycle of 15-minute cat-naps. Up and down for the whole night.

The morning brought with it bright sunshine but still no wind. I heard engine noises approaching and went out onto 'the upper array' to investigate. A Royal Navy Sea King helicopter was skimming 100 feet off the deck and flying around us. It was the same type of aircraft that I had flown in years before. I waved to the lads as they circled around, they waved back, then moved away. The phone rang. I was surprised!

I scrambled through the shelf at the back of my starboard bunk to find it. I was over 10 miles offshore and I hadn't expected that my mobile phone would have a signal.

It was Mark and it was good to hear his voice. We chatted, and after he had told me what things had been like on the spectator boat, I said, 'I'm thinking of jacking it in. It's not fair on the kids…'

As strange as it may seem, I was actually quite serious about quitting. Looking back, I can laugh at myself but at the time, after spending a difficult sleepless night, constantly worked over by my parental emotions, I was in a poor mental state. Mark proceeded to calmly and thoughtfully reassure me that I was an experienced yachtsman, prepared for anything, and my kids would be just fine. He was right, of course, and our chat was just the tonic I needed.

Soon afterwards, Stan phoned too. We had a good chat and, like Mark, he encouraged me to go on. The signal was fading so after saying our goodbyes I switched off the phone and put it safely away in a Tupperware box. These two phone calls did the trick and helped me on my way. My mood was further improved when I managed to pick up Scott Turner on *Altamira* on VHF radio. He was wallowing just 5 miles behind me at a dead stop. The sight of the other yachts overtaking him and pulling away, had convinced him that his boat would be the last one into Newport. Now it was my turn to offer up some re-assurance.

'Not at all,' I said. 'There are lots of slower boats than yours and besides, there are going to be many variables. You might find a better route or wind and your boat might perform comparably better on the ocean…'

I must have sounded so experienced...

Scott was encouraged and his mood picked up. He was a really nice guy who, like me two years earlier, was taking part on his first offshore voyage. We talked about heavy weather tactics and I advised him, 'Always reef down before nightfall and if the going gets really tough, just heave-to and go below. Stay out of the elements as much as you can...' Then I added, 'Don't worry about your boat Scott, she will take care of you. Remember, you are the weakest link ...not the boat.' Scott thanked me for the encouragement and advice and, with that, we agreed to stay in touch every 12 hours.

By the end of our first 24 hours *Lizzie-G* and I had only covered 58 miles, but more importantly, I had swept aside all my fears, doubts and guilt and was firmly resolved to see the voyage through.

7

I opened the Admiralty chart before me. After 24 hours we had covered a pitifully small distance and the empty ocean between us and America looked enormous. It was all very depressing. Then at 18:00 hrs precisely the wind suddenly sprung up out of the north-east, good and strong, *Lizzie* took off on a near-perfect course of 265° at 6 ½ kn. At last, after 30 wallowing hours, we were on our way!

In this strong wind, the sea soon became rough and as *Lizzie* twisted and rocked away, her hull flexed with the pressure and movement of the water around us. She began to give off her characteristic creaking and groaning. *Auld Meg* had been quieter simply because she had a moulded interior. *Lizzie* had carpentry and this noise came from the pressure and micro fractional movement where the timber mouldings joined. I didn't mind. The noise meant we were moving.

As the afternoon wore on, I tried to contact Scott but the distortion was so bad we had to give up. This would be our last contact. The sailing was good but not particularly comfortable. I tuned to Radio 4 for the Shipping Forecast and to listen to the news. I slept. I read my book. Little by little, the wind and sea lost its sharp edge and things started to settle down. As night fell, I made a delicious savoury pasta with smoked sausage, tomatoes and mushrooms. *Lizzie* was coping well.

On our third day we were still bowling along at 5 kn on a near-perfect course. The sun was out. The sky and sea were a magnificent spectacular blue. It was too good to miss, so I took the opportunity to strip off and with just a harness on, I topped up my tan and enjoyed the unclouded joy of it all. I slept well and spent time daydreaming with hardly a care in the world. As we passed noon, I recorded a 24-hour distance of 100 miles, then two hours later, we crossed over the continental shelf of the Great Sole Bank and into the deep ocean proper. It was the best day so far until... at 15.00 hrs two industrial-size fishing boats came into view. When I looked at my AIS, which should have raised the alarm, I could see that it was frozen.

I raised the deck officer on one of the boats and he told me that my radar return was, 'not bright' which meant that my 'Sea Me' radar transponder was also not working. This was a huge concern, as these instruments were my protection, my first line of defence when I was sleeping or in fog or going through rough weather. I had no idea as to what was wrong or how to put things right.

As the afternoon gave way to evening, the wind strengthened and by nightfall I settled for two reefs in the mainsail and one in the head. It was too rough to sleep in a bunk without the risk of being thrown out so I slept on the cabin sole. Knowing that my 'Sea Me' was probably useless and the AIS only working intermittently, my senses were tuned up. It was during the dead of night, at its darkest point, when I had unwittingly fallen into a deep slumber, that suddenly the AIS alarm went off.

A ship! But where? Was it close?

I leapt up from my makeshift bunk, scrambling frantically to get to the screen, to the hatch, to see what was going on. As I came to my feet, *Lizzie* lurched savagely and I was thrown across the cabin and smashed into the cooker area. The fire extinguisher broke off its mountings and I felt a sharp pain run up my thigh. I was in agony but that would have to wait. I looked outside. I checked the AIS screen. The ship was 8 miles away and passing to the north. The AIS had done its job.

I reset it, then put the extinguisher into a locker before it decided to fly about and do any more harm. My leg was bruised but other than this it would be okay. I could so easily have broken it, or my arm, wrist, ribs or skull? On this occasion I was lucky. I shuddered at the thought of it then did the only sensible thing left open to me.

I went back to bed.

8

It was mid-afternoon, on our sixth day out, when the first proper gale struck the fleet.

I remember this well. We were crashing along at full speed on a beam reach when *Lizzie* was picked up and thrown hard onto her starboard side. I was down below at the time. I felt the wave approach but it wasn't predictable like the others. Then I heard the roar of water breaking off. Instinctively I grabbed the handhold immediately above my head. I just knew this was going to be bad, then BANG, a shuddering concussion blow that echoed and reverberated; that shook everything inside *Lizzie* like an earthquake and pushed us right over. *Lizzie* was on her side, broached, her mast flat against the water.

I was holding onto the deck head hand holds now looking face-to-face with the ceiling that should have been above my head. I found myself standing on the starboard window which was now beneath my feet. As I looked down I saw that the window was pressed against solid green water. To my right, I could see tons of water pushing past my Perspex washboards like an uncontrollable waterfall, wild and untamed, flooding right over the cockpit. I remember muttering under my breath, 'Come on baby. Come back up.'

Then, as she started to rise, I felt another wave quickening its pace and another roar descending upon us and 'BANG' we were over again. This time, however, it went dark and as I looked above my head I could see the same solid green water pressing against the skyward window blotting out the light.

My heart quickened even further. I feared that the windows would burst against the pressure of sea. We were caught inside a curling wave, caught beam on, and were momentarily under water with tons of it washing and cascading over us. It passed. The reassuring dissipating hiss followed and *Lizzie* came up with clean decks and a cockpit full of water which quickly drained away.

It was after this that I hove-to and spent the next few hours riding it out as the weather and sea deteriorated even further.

This event told me that although *Lizzie* was good and strong, her windows could be a vulnerable weak spot. With that, I made the decision that instead of ploughing on into heavy weather to take advantage of course and speed; I would opt for a slower and safer tactic of heaving-to early. Moreover, the answer to the question 'What route should I follow?' was now clearer in my mind. Our repeated broaches had convinced me that a northern route with cold water, prolonged strong weather and bigger breaking waves could, on another day, stove in our windows.

From now on, whenever we were confronted with a headwind and I had to choose between going to the spikey North or the warmer gentler South... I would go South!

9

For the next few days we battled against headwinds of Force six and above. The sea state was rough and life on board *Lizzie-G* was very lively indeed.

My charted passage clearly shows that, for days on end, *Lizzie* and I were being forced further and further to the South of our desired course. As these hours of frustration turned into days, and these days gathered up, I started to doubt my earlier decision, convinced instead that had I turned North, I would have found a favourable wind to take me West. Time, and the constant wearing down of the sea, its motion, its discomfort, isolation and the sheer lack of worthwhile progress, all played their part. Before too long I convinced myself that every decision I had made, had been the wrong one.

In splendid frustration, on the seventh day I wrote;

'13:00 hrs position. North 48° 4' 44' West 14° 52' 25'
Today's total distance 92 nautical miles... South!!'

On and on we pounded, close hauled and hard into the wind. The most uncomfortable direction in which to push a boat. Try it for an afternoon and it is tedious. Try it for days on end with no sign of a let up, and it will test the charity of a Christian nun.

It is no wonder that windward sailing is referred to as 'beating' into the wind.

In these rough conditions, *Lizzie* rocked and pitched so

violently that my bunk lee-cloths were ineffective. During the night I was frequently thrown out of bed, or would wake up in a nest of twisted rope and cloth. The cabin sole was always a better place to be, wedged firmly between the two bunks; it was snug and secure, but it was damp.

With so much spray coming over the cockpit, sea water was seeping past the locker lids. From here it worked its way forwards until it leaked from underneath the main cabin bunks and through to the cabin sole. The very place where I was lying down.

I tried my best to stop it, soak it up and block it. I put foam mats down to keep me off the damp spots, but most of the time, these things only worked for a short period. At its worst, the water could be as much as an inch deep as it sloshed up and down the length of the cabin before finding its way past the bilge plates.

This was all so grimly depressing.

There was of course one easy fix. Instead of beating close-hauled and into the wind, I could crack off onto a beam reach. This would keep the sea spray out of the cockpit and away from the locker lids. The water ingress would stop and this would be more comfortable...but that would take us even further off course.

Doggedly, I persevered.

These conditions often worsened during the night when the wind increased, in bursts, to Force 7 and 8. The seas would rise to formidable heights and poor *Lizzie* would be pounded relentlessly, with shock waves running through her flexing hull and her rigging shaking violently. I would lie in my damp sleeping bag thinking, 'How much more of this can she take?'

I knew that I was pushing her hard, much harder than I would have under any other circumstances or for any other voyage. Each night, I would balance my near impossible objective with my determination to carry on.

10

This part of the voyage was uncomfortable, frustrating, difficult and lonely, but I had expected it to be all this and more. However uncomfortable, it was not enough to put me off. And besides, it wasn't all bad. I managed to have a cockpit bath on two occasions and this was utterly refreshing. I had more good meals than bad and I found plenty of time to read. Although, during this first 14 days I only averaged 60 miles per day, I told myself, optimistically, that I was always drawing nearer to Newport.

Nevertheless I could not ignore the list of problems that was developing and causing real consternation about the voyage. *Lizzie-G* was riddled with electrical faults.

My Sea-Me had stopped working, and both of the ships batteries were struggling to hold a charge, most of my navigation lights were out and both the AIS and GPS were repeatedly freezing up.

The 'Sea Me', was my electronic radar transponder. This began failing almost as soon as we set out. Since then I had spoken with eight passing ships and they all reported little or no radar return. It was now drawing precious power from my batteries and producing no benefit.

Lizzie had two batteries; No 1 was dedicated solely to starting the engine whilst No 2 supplied power for domestic and operational equipment. For some reason, both batteries were being drawn down simultaneously. They became flat and, for a time, I was unable to start the engine to recharge them. My only solution was to shut down every electrical device on board and sail the boat with the solar panel facing the sun until sufficient power was restored to turn over the engine. From now on, I would have to start the engine and boost the batteries more frequently than I would have otherwise chosen.

The only working Nav lights remaining were my red, port deck light and my white, top mast, anchor light.

All in all, I concluded that I could live without the Sea-Me and could manage the batteries. The lights were probably defective due to corrosion but they could be fixed when the warmer settled weather arrived.

This left the AIS and GPS.

The problem with these started on the eleventh day when my AIS unit bleeped out an alarm and a message, 'AIS frozen… No GPS signal'. I pressed the 'Unfreeze' button. Half an hour later, the same alarm and message returned. Sometimes it would happen every 15 minutes, other times the system would work fine for several hours before breaking down again. Sometimes I could get it back on-line, other times it refused to work for hours. It seemed to have a mind of its own.

The failure of my AIS, was the most worrying thing of all. Despite my ignorance of all things electrical, I had to try and fix it. Eventually, after days of deliberation, I opened up the switch panel and studied the installation instructions. The electrics looked like a multi-coloured nest of plastic spaghetti. 'Where the hell did all this stuff belong?'

To reduce the motion, I hove-to. Nervously, I investigated further and deeper until, quite by surprise and almost disbelievingly, I saw something which looked out of place. It was a little metal spade connector that had slipped out and a retaining screw which appeared to be loose. I checked the diagrams. It seemed to make sense that this was where it should be connected.

Against the jerking, snapping, rolling motion, I wedged myself tight against the board and, with the concentration of a footballer about to take a crucial penalty, I patiently, but firmly, pressed the spade connector home and screwed it in tight. It was done. I stepped back and looked at it, incredulously I thought.

'I've done it!'

I set about testing it. I took a deep breath and wrung my hands, 'Here we go.' My overwrought imagination had the better of me as I was reminded of Apollo 13, as she fired up her electrical systems, after her crippling sojourn through space. I adopted a check, double check manner, and called out the procedure as I worked our way back into operational mode.

I said aloud, 'Power on?' Then 'On.' I repeated.

'GPS on?'… 'On'. I said again.

'Key in waypoint Atlantic 001… Done.'. Waypoint Atlantic 001 came up.

'All looking good.' I said (with the authority of a NASA scientist).

I checked the cockpit repeater and then the VHF radio, everything was looking good.

Then I called out. 'Now for the Golden shot… AIS switch on… On'

And on it came with its customary bleep alarm test. The screen came up with its menu, 'Setup… Radar… List… Icons.'

I pressed 'Radar' and, within moments, the radar screen appeared as it should, with our position speed and course displayed and this corresponded precisely with the GPS.

'Yes… We have lift off…' I said quietly.

I looked at all the displays again, and I could barely contain my joy. With arms outstretched, I shouted to the heavens and earth with all my might,

'Yes… There is a God and He loves me… Oh yes He does.'

I clambered into the cockpit in the way that a man does when he comes from the darkest and deepest incarceration.... into the light. And in my mind's eye, I could see the clouds parting and a piercing light shining upon me, and the angels from heaven descending and singing, 'Alleluia, Alleluia, Aa.. llee..loo..yaa!'

But it was not to last. Cruel beyond cruel, within hours the AIS bleeped out its message, 'AIS frozen... No GPS signal'.

And we were back to square one.

I opened up the switch board again. This time I traced the signal wire that came from the GPS to four spur connections. They led to the radio, the cockpit repeater and the AIS, but I couldn't see where the fourth wire went. This was rather curious. They all seemed fine and securely connected.

I was mentally exhausted. I decided to sleep on it.

On the following afternoon, I fired everything up. The same problems remained. I pondered and started switching the items of equipment on and off in isolation. I found that the GPS could work provided the radio and AIS were switched off... But I had no idea why that should be?

As I looked behind the switchboard again, this time, I found a small electronic alarm which was connected to the AIS. It was a small cylindrical piece about the size of a £1 coin but maybe five times thicker. This sealed unit was covered in hard black plastic with a little hole in it, presumably to let the noise out. There were two very fine wires running into it, one red, and the other black.

As I investigated, I had this little device in my hand when *Lizzie* suddenly gave an unexpected lurch. I felt a slight tug and, to my horror, I saw that the red wire had pulled out of the sealed unit.

I cried out, 'Oh my God... No... No...No!'

But it was too late. This crucial life-saving piece that cost a few pounds to replace and pennies to make was broken. Even if the AIS was working and detecting a ship, the alarm could not sound. The unit was effectively… useless, and there was no possible way that I could fix it.

I sat miserably in the cabin with my head in my hands. How could I continue? How could I cross an ocean where half the time I would be sleeping or we would be running in darkness? Other times we would be in bad weather or in fog, and all the while, running a gauntlet through some of the biggest and fastest cargo ships in the world, all without an AIS ship warning system. I could find no answers. I was defeated.

For a few moments I thought I might actually cry. And in my misery I began to hear an inner, critical voice sneering, 'You useless sod…look at what you have done!'

It went on to wag an invisible finger and carried on delivering a whole lot of expletives which were probably well deserved.

This had happened on the evening of my 16th day at sea and now I was forced to face reality. I had no business being on the ocean with a boat in this condition. I needed to head for land which, turned out to be Terciera, an island that was familiar to me from two years earlier. I plotted a course and calculated that we should arrive at Praia da Vitoria at about 10:00 hours on the following morning. To this end, I slackened off the sails and turned *Lizzie* onto a beam reach, her fastest point of sail.

At last, she was comfortable and dry. I should have been happy with this but, in truth, I wasn't. I would rather have been close hauled, uncomfortable, wet and noisy, but most of all, still in the race, still making what little ground I could, to the West.

As the daylight ebbed away, I took to filling my gimballed oil lamp. I gave it an affectionate polish with a soft cloth. It was therapeutic to do something familiar and rewarding. To see the soft glow of brass brighten up and shine back at me. It made me feel better about myself. Sadly I said. 'There you go old pal, if only everything was as simple and reliable as you.' I put the lamp in the holder and lit it. True to form it brought warmth and soft light to my stark world. Then I wrote in my log those gut churning words.

'I think I'll let the Jester Challenge go this time...'

11

Morning came. I was really tired. With no AIS and an utterly useless Sea-me, I was back to watch keeping and 15 minutes cat naps. By 10:00 hours there was no sign of Terciera at all. The island should have been in plain view by now. With my binoculars, I scanned the horizon repeatedly. Nothing, absolutely nothing. I double checked the GPS against my handheld spare, both were producing the same readings and working fine.

Time passed, still no sign.

There was nothing for it but to check everything from top to bottom. I got out the charts and almanac and reworked all the coordinates, then checked the GPS. I found the problem. I had made an error in entering the waypoint into the unit and now I discovered that we had been going in the wrong direction all night. As I tried to clear my muddled mind, I realised that this waypoint had led me 30 miles off course, downwind of Praia da Vitoria. Worse still, the wind was strengthening to near gale force from the west, directly on our nose.

The full implications of my mistake began to sink in. If only we had remained close hauled throughout the night we would almost certainly have arrived by now and been safely ashore, warm and comfortable. As it was, we were in for a gruelling windward beat.

I closed my eyes and muttered, 'It's going to be a long day.'

Then I heard the 'Old Codger's' voice in my head, here he was, about to have another go. So easy to criticise, so easy to tell me how it ought to be done.

'Oh yes, you are so Mr Perfect, aren't you…?' I retaliated, in thought.

He was about to curse me for being so clumsy when I interrupted the thought and shouted,

'Aw shut your face… Who cares what you think you miserable old git… Okay so I made a mistake… Big deal… BIG FUCKING DEAL!'

The voice went silent and I realised I was shouting to no one. My pencil, protractor, chart and almanac had been scrunched up and thrown across the cabin and my head was in my hands. As I came to my senses, I realised what I had done.

'Good Lord.' I thought, '… Better watch this… I think I'm going mad.'

And then I found myself laughing and thought. 'Why be so hard on the Old Codger… He's only trying to help… After all, a bit of constructive criticism would do you no harm at all…'

This tickled my ribs further. Gasping for breath I struggled between fits of hysteria and said aloud,

'You poor old codger… You poor miserable old fuck.'

I could imagine him scowling at me, too disgusted to say anything and the thought of this made me laugh even more. This continued for some time. It felt wonderful. All the negativity and deadbeat stress were replaced with an acceptance of the situation and a perfect insight to that turn of phrase, 'Oh what the hell'.

Eventually, I calmed down and said, 'Okay let's get going *Lizzie*', and, with that, I reefed her down, altered course and beat … into misery.

It took 10 more hours to get to Praia da Vitoria and it was not without incident. During one of our many sail reefing exercises, I had gone forward to the mast when, from out of nowhere, a wave rose up. Slapping hard against the boat the wave sent a torrent of water all over me. I was drenched from head to toe. I held on and cursed until it passed. Clumsily, I made my way back to the cockpit. I was soaked through completely, as if I'd been dropped into the sea, stirred around, then hauled out again.

Mercifully the water was not too cold. However, by now, the only clothes I had left were already wet or very damp. Nothing dry remained.

Next, as we came within sight of the island, *Lizzie* crashed heavily into a breaking crest which sent a shockwave throughout the boat. The glass bulb flew off the brass gimballed oil lamp and shattered. My favourite lamp, 'old pal'.

Then, as evening wore on, I noticed a tear of about 6 inches on the headsail. All I could do was roll it up until the torn part was safely wrapped inside the furl.

As the afternoon passed and evening wore on, the wind began to slacken off leaving the sea sloppy and rough. At 18:30 hours we still had 10 miles to go. I decided to motor in. Even this however, would not be easy. In these conditions, the engine would struggle to make headway. I rolled the remainder of the headsail away and shook out the full mainsail and sheeted it 'hard a mid-ships'. I whacked on the engine and, for the first time since leaving Plymouth, I put her into gear. Slowly we motor-sailed in tacking zigzag motions towards the harbour entrance. It was too rough for the autohelm to cope and so, for four hours, I steered her by hand until we were safely in.

Lizzie and I entered the sheltered waters of the harbour at 22.30 hrs.

By now it was completely dark and I was stiff and sore. As I motored the last 30 or 40 metres towards the marina, I could see the outline of a man and woman walking along the outer pontoon. I presumed that they had had an evening ashore and were now retiring to their boat. The lady noticed me first. She stopped, tugged the man's arm and pointed to me. Together they quickened their pace towards the end of the pontoon.

The lady shouted, 'What nationality are you?'

I called back, 'I am British… Can you take my lines?'

She replied, 'Yes of course. Come here,' and pointed towards an empty berth.

I closed in and clumsily put *Lizzie* alongside. Cold, stiff, hungry and tired, I struggled to get up and throw my lines ashore. The lady instructed her partner, 'Otto… Quickly, hold her steady till we secure her alongside.'

There was no need for her to say this, for the man named 'Otto' knew exactly what to do.

With numb fingers, I fumbled around the ignition key and knocked off the engine. Unsteadily, I clamoured off the boat and onto the pontoon.

Our voyage had taken 17 days and 11 hours.

12

Meeting Otto and Esther would turn out to be one of the best strokes of luck that I would have throughout the whole voyage. They were Dutch. Otto was tall, slim and handsome. At a guess, I would say he looked about 60 years old. He wore gold-rimmed glasses, had short receding fair hair with a natural soft curl to it, a gentle manner and voice and was polite and unassuming. Esther was younger, perhaps 40 or maybe 45 years old. She was about 5'5' tall, purposeful, very attractive, with a fair complexion and blonde shoulder length hair. Both spoke English fluently and no sooner had I stepped off *Lizzie* than they asked a multitude of questions.

'What are you doing out there in this weather...? Have you lost your crew...? Has someone gone overboard...? Where have you come from...? Where are you going...? How long have you been at sea?'

I was overwhelmed with such a rush of human activity after almost 18 days of isolation. As soon as I began to answer these questions Esther interrupted me, 'Good God man you're freezing cold, you're shivering and your jacket is sodden.'

It was true. I must have looked a sight. Underneath my sailing jacket I was wearing, a pair of sandals a pair of shorts, underpants, a T-shirt and a jumper, all of which were soaking.

Esther immediately took charge of the situation. She said, 'Otto... You carry on with tying up the boat, I'm taking him below before he freezes to death.'

Otto nodded his agreement and without further ado, Esther grabbed me by the wrist and led me away.

Their boat was a 46-foot Beneteau, beautiful, sleek and modern. A cruising boat through and through. In the main saloon Esther stood in front of me, tutted, then helped me out of my jacket, pullover and T-shirt. All were thrown into a soggy heap in the corner. She put a tea towel on one of the seats and invited me to sit down. She disappeared and returned with one of Otto's woolly pullovers and a blanket. I put the pullover on and she threw the blanket over my shoulders and within moments I could feel the warmth, tingling back into my cool, blood- drawn white skin.

She opened a drinks cabinet and poured me a very large measure of whisky in a mug. I cupped both hands around it and took a draw which brought warmth and giddy pleasure to my sinuses, and a warm glow down my throat.

Otto arrived down the hatch and said, 'Your boat is tied up and secure... It took me a while, but I finally managed to switch off your navigation lights... Did you know that you only have one light working?'

I gave a short ironic laugh then said 'Yes Otto, I know about that, but believe me my friend, that is the very least of my problems!'

★

We sat up talking till 02:30 hrs. A mug of wine followed the mug of whisky then a mug of coffee followed the mug of wine. Ester made a bowl of spicy soup with noodles and with it came crusty slices of Azorean bread and butter. After I had relayed all the details of the voyage and the problems that had forced me to retire, Otto said, 'The weather here has been terrible. Nobody has left or entered the harbour for days. Many yachts are cooped up, waiting for things to settle before they can move on...'

I thought of the northern route and asked, 'What has the weather been like up North?'

He answered, 'It has been even worse. A very deep depression developed up there about six days ago and is still working its way to the east... All of your friends will be affected with this... I believe the pressure may be as low as 950 mbar... There will be no easterlies up there only headwinds and great seas.'

That answered the nagging doubt that I had held since our first gale, whether I was right to go South. Now I was at last satisfied that I had made the right decision.

13

There was much to do. That was the first thought that came into my head when I opened my eyes. It was past 10.00 hrs. The boat was warming up and bright sunlight was piercing through the chinks of space between my curtains. The weather had changed. The long spell of gales, cloud and rain had broken and now, at last, on this, my first morning in Praia da Vitoria, the world was filled with warmth and sunshine. Along with it came the clamouring of human activity. I could hear boat engines being started and movement around the pontoons. I climbed, blinking and shielding my eyes, into the cockpit.

My senses were assaulted by colour, shapes, light and movement, so different to the ocean that I'd struggled with and stared upon for the previous 18 days. I stretched and yawned and came to life. I was stiff and sore with a mild hangover.

I got together my money, ship's papers, passport and wash bag and reported to the marina office. Paolo was there, still in charge and working away exactly as I'd remembered him two years previously. He recognised me too. He said 'You are the one who came in last night. I see you have a new boat?'

Now I was really surprised, he even remembered my boat... after two years. We chatted away and I explained about the latest Jester Challenge and my need to make repairs.

Before I went for a shower, I went to the computer room and sent a brief email to Ewen.

'Retired to the Azores with multiple electrical problems and a torn sail, beyond this I am not sure what to do?

Den and Lizzie-G'

It felt good to be ashore, to have a break from the sea but still, it was deeply disappointing. In my heart of hearts, I knew that I wanted to go on.

After my ablutions I cleared customs and sent a text message to Mark. Soon afterwards I was pulling up all my damp cushions and suchlike onto the upper deck when my mobile phone went off. It was Ewen. I gave him an account of my voyage and asked how the others were getting on. He relayed all the news. He told me,

'The Russian boats have gone north, and everyone else has gone south. Duncan Lougee and *Vaquero* are somewhere in the Azores. He has retired with damaged rigging and will be returning to England once he's made repairs.' He went on, 'John Margarson is back home with *Fluffy*. He suffered a blown out headsail. Bill Churchouse fell overboard but managed to get back on board and sort himself out. He is now in Penzance...'

The list went on:

- Alan Rees, *Argos*, Retired due to gear failure, (no specific details).
- Scott Turner, *Altamira*. Retired due to losing his steering gear.
- David Graham, *Astro*. Retired. Due to gear failure, (no specific details).
- Chris Garbett, *Jasabe*. Retired. Steering gear damaged in a storm.
- Chris Jackson, *Sixpence*. Retired. Battery charging problems.
- Guy Waites, *Red Admiral*. Retired. Returning to the UK

with a damaged bulkhead.

- Nigel Stillman, *Grettal*. Retired. Due to slow progress and time restrictions.

It read like a casualty list. There was no news at all from Tim McCloy, Roger Taylor, Trevor Leek or Alexei Fedoruk but that did not surprise me since, like me, none of them carried any satellite communications.

Other competitors were still going strong. Tony Head, *Triple Venture*, was only 50 miles in front of me, to the south west of Terceira, whilst John Apps, *Glayva*, was about a hundred miles behind me. Behind him, Gus Davidson was battling along with his tiny 20-foot boat *'Just Right'*.

Roger Fitzgerald, *Ella Trout III* and Thomas Jucker, *Marta*, were battling it out somewhere in the north-west, somewhere along the direct, loxodromic route. While the two Russians Igor Zaretsky, *The Grand*, Michail Soldatov, *Gerda*, along with Andy Lane in *Amadeus* were even further to the North.

But the biggest surprise was Rory McDougall and *Cooking Fat*. He had passed through the Azores about five days earlier and was now 500 miles in front, to the West.

I remembered Rory's tiny engineless catamaran and wondered how on earth he had managed it. To come through those headwinds and seas and push ahead of us all? I was thrilled and delighted at this news.

Ewen asked, 'Do you plan to continue?'

I wanted to but I had used my engine and I had substantial repairs to make.

Ewen laughed and chastised me. 'You don't have to retire. If you wish to make repairs and carry on you're welcome to do so. It is entirely up to you. Under the rules you are entitled to enter any port you like in order to make repairs. You can stay there for as long as you wish. As for using your engine, it sounds to me as if you were exercising very good judgement.'

He went on. 'The rules make clear provision for using an engine in order to avoid collision or calamity and, in your case, you have done both, so you're quite within your rights to carry on.'

I was delighted and repeatedly asked, 'Are you sure... Are you sure?' to which he replied, 'Good God man, there are not many rules, you could at least have taken the trouble to read them.'

I must admit, that to this day, I still haven't.

14

My enthusiasm was now fully restored. Whilst my laundry was thrashing around the machines, I went into town and searched for an electronic shop where I might be able to purchase a replacement buzzer alarm. My shopping spree was a dismal failure. When shown the buzzer the typical responses were, 'I don't think you will find anything like that anywhere on the island,' or, 'I've never seen such a thing… I have no idea what it is.'

I went back to the marina and began 'knocking on hulls', asking if anyone could offer some help. None could, although an American single-handed yachtsman named Quentin, gave me a bag of spare electrical fittings and invited me to, 'Use whatever you need and give me back what's left.'

I decided to put the alarm to one side for now and set about repairing the navigation lights. Here I was much more successful and later, just as I was starting to tackle the headsail, Otto and Esther stopped by.

The torn sail, once off the roller foil, exposed a problem with the foil itself. It is made up of interlocking sections held in place by screws, which were coming undone. Fixing this was going to be a two-man job. I gladly accepted Otto's offer of help and arranged for him to come around on the following day. He and Esther invited me to dinner but I reluctantly declined. I had too much to do. They completely understood and were not offended.

I carried on with my jobs: resealing the locker lids, replacing the worn-out steering lines for the steering gear, laying out gear so that it could dry in the sun, returning my laundry, books, charts and notepads back into the dried out lockers and storage spaces.

During this time I received various phone calls and text messages. I had a long chat with Mark and I briefed him on my situation. As arranged, he, in turn, would pass on my news to everyone back home. It gave me great peace of mind to have Mark do all this for me and particularly for him to keep in touch with my kids. Encouraging text messages came in from other Jesters from our 2008 outing, Paul Feasey, George Jepps, and of course, Stan. This was prompted by the notice that Ewen had put on the Challenge website about my pulling in.

★

I worked on. As darkness fell, I strapped on my head torch and opened up the electrical panel. With a magnifying glass and a voltmeter, I began systematically identifying wires, doing voltage readings and resistance checks, and checking the tightness of each connection. Now that I had a stable boat and time to concentrate, I wanted to be thorough. Eventually I went back to the GPS wire that I had identified at sea. The feed cable with the four spurs coming from it.

One by one I carefully cut and remade the connections using new spurs from the bag that Quentin had given me. I switched on the GPS and when it had warmed up, I began to reattach the spurs. First the AIS. It immediately sprang into life. Then the repeater. This worked fine too. Then the radio. That too, was fine. As soon as I attached the fourth spur, which I could now see was connected to the electric auto helm, everything began to freeze. I disconnected it again and they all came back to life…. I had found the problem.

Reasoning that the auto helm would be able to work just as well without a GPS feed, I left it disconnected.

I was too tired for high-powered euphoria. It was half-past two in the morning. I had been working flat out all day. Leaving all the units switched on for the night, I closed the panel, climbed into my warm, dry, freshly laundered sleeping bag, and slept like a babe.

★

The next morning, everything was still working so, encouraged by my success, I turned my attention onto the broken alarm buzzer. If it couldn't be replaced, then it needed to be repaired. It was as simple as that. I took a hacksaw and gently cut around the circumference, close to the base where the thin red wire had pulled out until the plastic broke free. I prised it off. Inside there were two tiny solder points where the red and black wires came in. The black wire was still attached. The red one, of course, was broken off and the solder point much too small and delicate for any normal soldering iron to reach into.

During my earlier enquiries I'd been told of an electrical repair shop down at the far end of Praia da Vitoria. I collected up the broken pieces and hurried off down there. It was a clean, modern establishment with an opening in the back wall into which was set a serving counter. A man was at the opening talking in Portuguese to two customers. Behind him I could see a well-equipped workshop.

I waited until he had served the two people in front of me then I stepped forward and said,

'Good day, do you speak English?'

To my relief he smiled and nodded, 'Yes.'

I smiled back and showed him the pieces in my hand, the sawn-off plastic, the exposed electronic alarm and the detached red wire. I asked, 'Do you have a replacement for this?

He folded his arms, shook his head and said, quite simply…
'No.'

I went on, 'Could you get a replacement for me perhaps from the mainland?'

He pursed his lips and shook his head again while saying…
'No.'

I leaned forward as if to confide a great secret and said, 'I have come here on my sailing boat, and this little thing is very important to me. If I cannot buy a new one then I need to find a special man who can fix it. Can you fix it?'

He unfolded his arms and took the pieces from me. He examined them and said, 'I don't know, when do you want back?'

My answer was very direct, 'I want it back now or as quickly as I can.'

I was looking at him earnestly. He held my gaze for a moment, then put the pieces on the counter and went to one of the benches to pick up some solder and a very fine nibbed soldering iron. He returned, plugged in the iron and, whilst waiting for it to heat up, he picked up the buzzer to examine it more closely. I began to point out where the wire had come undone but he put up his hand to silence me with a, 'Shush shush…'

He proceeded to strip a piece of insulation off the little red wire and applied a thin coat of solder to the bare end. He laid the wire onto its solder point and with the greatest delicacy, touched it with the iron, with just enough force, and for just the right length of time, to fuse it all back together.

Throughout this whole operation, I stood watching, transfixed, holding my breath. The man stood back and put the soldering iron into its holder.

'It is done,' he said.

I smiled and asked, 'Are you sure. Will it work? Can we test it?'

He shrugged his shoulders and said, 'Yes, of course we can,' and with that, he located a small 9v battery and placed the wires on it. In an instant the little alarm screamed out its high-pitched, angry protest.

'That's fantastic,' I said. 'You are a very special man after all.'

He asked for 2 euros and I insisted that he took 5. I rushed back to the boat and wrapped insulation tape around the cut off plastic cylinder then plumbed it back into the wire box. It worked perfectly.

That afternoon, Otto hoisted me up the roller foil where I glued all the screws and segments of aluminium tubing back together. Once done, we moved on to the headsail, the two of us working on the stitching whilst Esther made sandwiches and coffee. Afterwards, I made a last trip to town to stock up fresh foodstuffs and, once everything was put away, I was able to stand back and truly say…

'Our Atlantic Challenge was back on the cards'.

That evening, I happily accepted Otto and Esther's invitation to dinner. They made me a three-course meal accompanied with copious amounts of beer, and wine, and followed by a whisky or two as a nightcap.

This gave me a well-deserved hangover and a 5-hour delay to my intended 05.00 departure.

15

I had spent three nights, two full days, and one late morning in Praia da Vitoria. As I left, I could not help but reflect on the wonderful people who, over the past couple of days, had done so much for a stranger in need of assistance. Not for the first time did I find myself indebted, and I resolved that if the opportunity ever came up, I would try and do the same for someone else.

I felt as if the first difficult 18 days of my voyage had never existed. We now had 2300 miles to go and we made excellent progress and enjoyed stunning vistas as we worked our way past the islands, Sao Jorge, Pico, Faial and finally, Flores. Ahead lay the open ocean. My plan was to go west in the direction of Bermuda until the strong constant south-westerly winds, that come up from the Caribbean, could be found. We would then turn north-west for a final run across the core of the Gulf Stream, straight to Newport USA.

Sounds easy! Except we were now in the 'horse latitudes', an area renowned for light and variable winds. But we were lucky; sometimes barely ghosting along and other times enjoying a stiff breeze, we managed to keep moving. The weather was bright, sunny and warm. Throughout the day, I would wear a T-shirt and underpants and a sun hat. When the sun went in, I would add my long, flock-lined, cycling trousers and a sweatshirt or woolly pullover. I would read for hours at a time and very much enjoyed Shirley Conran's book,

'Savages', which had sat unread on my bookshelf at home for over 10 years.

These were 'salad days', in every sense of the word. I enjoyed good food and had lettuce and tomatoes with everything. Sometimes it was corned beef with salad and steamed potatoes or a couple of boiled eggs with mayonnaise, paprika and salad. These were favourites. I ate sweet oranges and large slices of melon in the afternoon. I had crusty Azorean bread spread with butter and cheese and a generous mug of wine. The mug of wine became a daily ritual.

In the sunshine, the solar panel kept the batteries charged up nicely. In the evening, just after the light had gone, I would treat myself to an hour or two of music while sitting on my wash board seat. The intensity of sound together with the continuous motion of my rise and fall world was quite simply, sublime. It was like having chocolate running through my veins, rich and luxurious. I slept well, sometimes for 10 hours a day, getting up every hour to check things over and then back into my comfortable bunk.

I had cockpit baths. First I would wash myself from head to toe with Head & Shoulders shampoo, which gives off a rich lather in seawater. Once scrubbed, I poured buckets of seawater all over myself to rinse it away. I would then carefully measure out 2L of my precious freshwater and rinse my hair with it while catching the draining water back into a basin. I used some of that to sponge the salt off my body and the rest to rinse out my underpants and T-shirt. Nothing was ever wasted. During these salad days I never needed to use a towel to dry off. By the time I had hung out my laundry on the cockpit rail the sun had dried me completely.

We had a visitor, a huge whale, the first we'd seen since leaving Terciera. It was a giant colossal creature, the greatest I'd ever beheld, with a gigantic dorsal fin and tail. He was only 300m away, thrashing about on the surface, possibly trying to rid himself of parasites. I felt nervous until he disappeared. Soon after, we became surrounded by dolphins and sea birds. The excited squeals of the dolphins resounded through our hull - excited, lively and sharp, no doubt hunting and herding sardines.

The only downside I had during this happy period was a nagging back pain but I reasoned that it was better to have this now when life was easy. I also suffered quite badly from sunburn on my nose. I ended up protecting it by putting a couple of Elastoplast sticking plasters across it. I looked quite ridiculous but it was effective and besides there was no one to see it.

Gradually we left the high pressure area behind. At 13:30 hrs on the 24th day we arrived at our half way mark and, by coincidence, completed our best 24-hour run so far with a massive 160 miles. We were holding a near-perfect course of 268° and a cracking speed of 5.4 knots.

I wrote,

'I've just passed the halfway mark! Hurrah. Celebration. Stew and onions with mashed potatoes, custard and fruit and a mug of rum. 1680 miles left and counting down.'

But at sea nothing lasts. In the early hours of the 25th day the weather broke and we were back to reefing sails in the darkness. Sunrise found us racing along in a gale from the south south-west with the sails deep reefed and close hauled. We continued on a track of 275° at 6.2 kn with me hunkered down below. It got worse as the day continued and at 19:30 hours I had to heave to.

The seals around the cockpit locker lids were failing and I had water running through the boat again. I pumped out 3 gallons then turned in. At 22:00 hrs the AIS picked up the '*Terry Lee III*', a luxury motor yacht passing 10 miles to the north. I spoke to her English skipper and he kindly agreed to pass a progress report on to Mark. He also gave me a weather report which suggested more of the same to come.

We remained hove-to throughout the night, almost 12 hours in all, then the weather moderated and I was able to shake out the sails and get going again.

Eventually after another 12 hours or so, the wind dropped out and we were left wallowing uncomfortably in a big sloppy sea.

I dropped the mainsail, lashed the boom to the deck, rolled up the headsail and there we sat being thrown from beam end to beam end for nothing more than the pleasure of the sadistic gods of the sea. We wallowed like this all through another night for a total of 10 hours. I spent this entire time, wide awake, lying on the cabin sole between the bunks. It was too rough to prepare food, too sickly to read.

When at last at 07.00hrs the breeze sprang up, I reacted immediately. Its steadying pressure upon the sails created a much welcomed stability to our world again. The sloppy waves were still big, perhaps 2 or 3m but things were improving and by late morning the sun returned.

★

And so we continued. On plenty of occasions the sun came out to cheer us up as *Lizzie* sailed peacefully along. I had my mug of wine at 3 o'clock in the afternoon and most of the time I continued to wear nothing more than my pants, T-shirts and sandals. My cockpit bath and laundry schedule continued.

Things were going well and I should have kept to my plan and gone another 300 or 400 miles west, towards Bermuda, before turning northwest towards Newport. However, the thought of cutting the corner, and bringing the voyage to a quicker ending, became a temptation too great for me to pass up.

I altered course…. But I still wasn't sure.

Over the next two days I deliberated on whether I had

done the right thing or not. The arguments swung back and forth with the weather which ranged from near calm to gale, from sunshine to torrential rain. But, in the end, I decided to stay with my decision and keep on to the north-west. I wrote,

'It is too late to look for a softer option. We are back in the guts of things… Until the end, I only hope this discomfort gives us a good result.'

16

Day 30

03:15 hrs, misty fog, course 339° at 4.4 kn. Desired course 307°
Wind is shifting and pushing us too far north. SS 'Cape Bowden'
has shown up on AIS. Batteries are very low. I start the engine with
considerable difficulty.

My AIS was doing well through this misty fog which was just a
slight sea mist. It had detected the *SS Cape Bowden* long before
she had come into sight. I knew that further north I was very
likely to encounter deep, dense fog, and a working AIS would
be absolutely vital to me. Hence my concern for my batteries.
My AIS could not do the job without power.

Clearly, the charge from my solar panel was not enough,
so I needed to run the engine more frequently. However, the
engine was becoming increasingly more reluctant to start,
which was draining the batteries even further, which, in turn,
meant they needed even more charge - it was a vicious circle.

I now resolved that, during the daylight hours, I would
switch off all my electrical equipment in order to maximise
the charge from the solar panel. I reminded myself that in that
first race, back in 1960, Blondie and the other competitors
had managed all right with just a magnetic compass, so why
shouldn't I? It would just mean that I'd have to spend more
time keeping watch.

Actually I found that, at the end of the day, when the

sun had set and the solar panel was no longer producing any charge, I was reluctant to switch the instruments back on. Consequently, late in the evening and even into the early hours, I could be found sitting in the hatchway on my washboards seat, wearing a woolly hat and gloves, with a sheepskin rug across my knee and my feet cupped around the paraffin lamp that was fastened to the sink top table. And all the while, I was scrutinising every rising light, every star that came up on the horizon.

My mood swung up and down. A good wind and a promise of finishing made the world seem bright and rosy, while adverse winds and poor sailing angles had the opposite effect. More and more, I wanted to finish the voyage; I wanted comfort, I wanted to escape the constant effort, day and night, that was required of me.

As if to depress me further, on this 30th day I saw sharks. They were moving purposefully around the boat, ominously, with razor-like dorsal fins. There is delight to be had in having dolphins visiting you with playful manoeuvres and arcing flights on the ocean surface. You feel as if you could befriend the dolphin but not a shark... Never a shark.

★

My fresh fruit and vegetables were running low and I was long since out of bread. In this matter I had made some preparations. The galley on *Lizzie* did not have an oven, so whilst at home, I had experimented with making bread in the pressure cooker. My experiments worked well and produced a round loaf which, despite having no crust, was perfectly acceptable.

On our 32nd day, I attempted this at sea. The conditions were ideal: a warm day to help the yeast rise and a smooth sea to let it cook. Carefully, I mixed the flour, yeast, salt, sugar and water. As I did so, I could imagine my teeth sinking into soft white bread, spread with peanut butter and jam. I saw sandwiches with tuna, corned beef and pickle and cheese. I imagined it toasted, spread with butter and served with a fried egg…Mmmm.

I left the dough to rise for over two hours and it came up lovely. Time to cook. It sat in the pressure cooker for the allotted time on full-steam pressure. I was in 'food heaven anticipation' as I opened it up. Inside was what I described in my log later as, '…*A solid lump of pasta.*'

It was a bitter disappointment. I tried to think of some way to use it, as I hate wasting food, but in the end it was given a sailor's grave. But why had it failed? The only reason I could think of was that the movement of the boat might have agitated the air out of it.

Mother Nature, however, did try to brighten my mood when at 13:10 hrs –

'I am surrounded by two then three enormous whales… They are magnificent creatures and leave an enormous slick as they dive under the water. They seem placid. I am more curious than afraid.'

They were, I think, blue whales, which I believe are the largest creatures upon the face of the Earth. They cruised about 250 feet in front of us and two of them were at least 100 feet long, which was certainly the largest I had ever seen.

17

Throughout the evening and night of our 32nd day and into the early hours of the 33rd, we were running fast downwind. We raced and surfed along at 7 kn, rocking from side to side, gobbling up miles on a near-perfect course until, at 02:30 hrs, my nerve finally gave way. The wind was rising and I feared that we might tear the rig and sails apart. I reefed down to reduce our speed.

In the early hours of the 34th day, I raised a Japanese ship, '*Unjima*'. I asked him for a weather report which, perhaps because of the language difference, came across as:

'There is a low of 980 mbar in Halifax Nova Scotia which will travel east and the high in our area that will travel west…'

This did not make any sense to me at all. Did it mean good weather or bad?

However I soon found out.

By daybreak, the barometer was falling rapidly and by 06.00 hours we were in a near gale from the south-west. I tried to start the engine to boost the batteries but it refused to fire. After several attempts, the now flogged batteries refused to turn the engine over at all.

I shut down all the electrics.

The weather deteriorated further.

By 18:30 hours I wrote.

'*I heave-to and stow the steering gear. The seas are huge and breaking with very strong wind – Force 8(+). It is on a par with our first gale.*'

In fact it was worse, much worse.

★

The seascape that surrounded us was truly awesome and the power and violence that came with it was breathtaking. Fast-moving waves, taller than my mast, with breakers along their entire crests, stretched before and beyond as far as the eye could see. In the troughs, it was relatively quiet but as each wave lifted us back up, the howling wind screamed and shrieked as it made contact with the rigging.

'It's only wind and noise,' I would say. 'Don't let it intimidate you... It's just a bully with a big mouth.'

We were hove to and doing okay until the mainsheet, which is the name given to the rope that controls the mainsail, slipped through its jamming device. This in turn let the sail run out causing it to flog violently, threatening at any moment, to tear itself apart. In addition, *Lizzie* now turned sideways onto the waves. We were hit almost immediately by a breaker. It was like being struck by a freight train. Over we went but, like a game rooster, *Lizzie* rolled back up and carried on.

As she recovered, I scrambled out onto the deck and wrestled with the nest of thrapping, tangled rope, to haul it in and jam it off again. This rope had hardened with age and in these extreme conditions it wasn't very long before it slipped again. This time, just as I reached the cockpit, I saw a huge breaker coming onto us. I reacted instinctively. I hauled on the tiller and turned to run with it. *Lizzie* accelerated away and as she did, water broke over our stern and flooded all around me. The cockpit was pooped.

We charged on, with *Lizzie*'s nose surfing out of the water and the tiller, as light as a feather in my hand, as air and water raced under the boat. It was exhilarating and dangerous. In my rush to get topside I'd left the washboards out and my harness unclipped; now on the tiller, I could neither clip on, nor put the boards in. They were out of reach and I dared not leave my position, not for one second. If the next wave were to turn us we would be sure to capsize and I would be swept away. I needed to hold on and bring her through. Of this I had no doubt. As we hurtled on, I shouted, 'C'mon *Lizzie*, C'mon, C'mon!'

We crashed rather more gently than I expected, into the trough and, holding firmly, I steered her straight and true. The following wave lifted us and, with a sound like the witches from hell, the wind began to screech in the rigging, again I could hear the rush of breaking water, Thud, Roar, Hiss, and again we were pooped. Water flooded into the cockpit. I clung on.

'Good girl *Lizzie*, good girl, God bless you!' I called.

This cycle repeated itself, over and over. Another wave, another, Thud, Roar and Hiss, another rush of water over our stern.

I desperately needed to round up and heave-to. I saw a spot where the breaking surf had just settled and the dissipation had created a short-term calming slick. I steered into it. Rounding up, I quickly slipped the elasticated rope back over the tiller and with both hands working frantically, I hauled the mainsheet back in and jammed it off. This time I led it around the winch and tied it off securely to one of the cockpit cleats. 'Now stay there you bastard!' I shouted.

The next breaker struck us and, we rose safely and comfortably over it. I slumped down in the cockpit and breathed a huge sigh of relief.

The storm raged on into the night. There was lightning, racing across the sky; fearsome, wizard-like, random and electrifyingly dangerous. I saw it touch down on the ocean miles away. I imagined its destructive power and began to fear that our mast might attract its unwelcome finger of attention. Such a pulse of energy would blow every electrical device I had.

Realising the danger I quickly wrapped my spare, handheld GPS, into a Tupperware box and wrapped this in multiple layers of tinfoil, then put the box under the grill of my cooker. In this way I hoped to achieve a type of 'Faraday Oven' to protect it.

I stayed below as much as possible. The cockpit locker seals had failed again and water was running up and down the cabin sole. There was nothing much I could do except watch it, as I sat there, ready for action, with my sailing jacket and harness on over my clothes. Even with so little power left in the batteries, I elected to leave the masthead tricolour on and every hour or so, I switched on the GPS and AIS for a few minutes to see if any ships could be detected. Thankfully there were none.

Most of the time I was clammy, sticky and hot but in the darkest part of the night, just before dawn, I began to feel cold. I wrapped a blanket loosely around me then wedged myself up against the forward bulkhead of my little cabin. I was next to the brass gimballed oil lamp, 'Old Pal', which was lit. As we rocked and pitched, it flickered away with its soft, warm light. It was somehow comforting, pure and kind, and starkly in contrast to the sharpness of our surrounding world.

Sometimes I dozed off into a fitful slumber, then a judder or crash would wake me up. I nibbled on biscuits when hungry and sipped water when thirsty. I made occasional forays into the cockpit to make adjustments, then returned to thoughts of how to fix my engine, charge my batteries, seal my lockers and cope with my hardened mainsheet. I also thought of home and my children, recalling the words from Simon and Garfunkel's, 'Cathy's Song'.

'My mind's distracted and diffused,
my thoughts are many miles away,
they lie with you when you're asleep,
They kiss you when you start your day...'

Shortly after sunrise, the weather began to ease. We were still in a gale and hove-to, but the worst had passed. I opened up a tin of beef stew, a tin of beans and a tin of potatoes, then mixed them together in the same pot and heated it up. I ate the lot, straight from the pot, and having satisfied my hunger, I managed to sleep. By noon the wind had fallen away and the seas were settling. The storm had lasted 18 hours.

I went up top, *Lizzie*'s decks were glistening clean, the rig and sails had survived and the steering gear was still intact. I patted her coach roof affectionately and said.

'Thank you old girl… Thank you.'

She had done everything I had asked and here she was ready for more.

★

We had wind. Our position was 39° 41' North and 54° 19' West. We still had 792 miles to go. I shook out the sails, engaged the wind vane and whoosh, we were off.

I was itching from the salt on my scalp and skin. I took a much-needed cockpit bath then washed out my T-shirt and pants. I was hungry again. Two tins of minestrone soup were followed by crackers and cheese then a mug of coffee and a bar of chocolate. Now I was contented and felt that King Neptune and his wife were at last smiling upon us.

But the feeling was short-lived.

'16:00 hours; We have a Southwest gale pouring down on us. I hang laundry in the cabin, reef the sails and wham, bang, wallop we are in the middle of it again. Horrible! I daresay we will probably be hove-to again by nightfall. This voyage really is a pain. I really would like to get finished soon!'

20:00 hours; Holding a course of 314° at 3.7 kn. Comfortable motion. Wind has eased, seas are big with occasional breakers. What on earth will come next?'

18

During the night, I thought some more about the repairs that *Lizzie* needed. I could see that there were two things I should deal with as soon as possible. One was the water coming into the boat through the cockpit locker lids, which was doing neither of us any good, and the other was the engine. One day we might need the mechanical monster to get us out of trouble and it would be no good if it wouldn't start.

By morning the sea was reasonably calm. There was no time like the present and no time to lose. First, the cockpit lockers. The plan was simple; I would open each locker lid, dry the mating surfaces then smother them with Sikaflex, a marine compound sealant. Messy, but it would do the job. However, once the locker lids were fastened down and the Sikaflex had hardened, they would have to remain closed for the duration of the voyage. I moved everything out of the lockers that I might need, and stuffed it all into the fore ends.

On the starboard side, I refilled the main fuel tank from the spare cans then sealed the lid down. Inside the port locker I could see that the battery terminals were rusty and the top of each battery was wet, a consequence, no doubt, of the water ingress. Could this explain why they were not charging properly? I dried them off with a paper towel then using a dry, green scouring pad. I cleaned the terminals and retightened them. Lastly, I smeared a generous blob of Vaseline all over them. This locker lid was then sealed and the Sikaflex left to dry.

The engine was next. I took off both the fuel filters and replaced them with new ones. I bled the fuel line then tightened the alternator belt.

The solar panel had, by now, put some charge into the batteries, but would it be enough? I bit my lip, took a deep breath and after a generous amount of pre heat, turned the ignition key. She fired up. It was like music to my ears and now amps flooded into the batteries. Bit by bit, little by little, the charge indicator light turned from flickering red, to amber and from amber to green. I ran the engine for four hours and when I switched it off again, the little light stayed bright green. Fully charged!

We were back in business.

19

The following week was awful. On day 36, with a favourable wind, I constantly found *Lizzie* sailing at 45° off our magnetic compass reading. The Gulfstream was to blame.

The Gulfstream is a river within an ocean. It begins its life in the Caribbean, and makes its way northwards up the east coast of North America at speeds of up to 3 kn. At 30 to 40° North it starts to turn to the east and heads off on its own Atlantic crossing. We were in the 'core' of the mainstream, being carried north of our desired course. The more I tried to fight it, the slower our progress became.

On our 37th day we seemed to be sailing a good course at 4 kn yet, after nine hours, we had covered 14 miles. On another day our 24 hour distance was just 11 miles. Eleven miles!

As these miles crawled by, I couldn't help counting each and every one of them. If we couldn't escape from the Gulfstream, I began to fear that it would carry us all the way to Sable Island, an inhospitable place with no safe harbours. Over the years, it has been a graveyard for many ships and mariners and I started to imagine that another strong storm, on top of the effect of the Gulfstream, could put us on the beach.

I was being reminded yet again, that after the Azores, I should have stayed on my westerly course for longer.

During this period my log and journals showed some of the ups and downs.

On day 37 at 23:15 hours I wrote:

Time to turn in and forget my troubles. Lizzie has a charged battery and all the electrics are good. At least I can be assured of that tonight.

Dinner. A tin of creamed rice pudding.'

On the following night:

'We must break out of the Gulfstream! This time I will hold a northern course, (if I must), for at least 60 miles. Perhaps that will improve our condition.'

The following day, as if in a foot-stomping tantrum, I wrote.

'No more entries, into this log, until something sensible happens!!'

Then, later that evening,

'... Will keep going I expect... Till hell freezes over.'

It was all rather disheartening.

Lizzie and I had come a long way. It had taken a long time and now, I wanted it to end, I wanted to go for a walk, to pet a dog, to sit under a tree, to enjoy some company and drink some beer. When there was wind, I did everything I could to keep us moving in the right direction. When there wasn't, I fretted over the charts and forecasts. I agonised over every decision I had made, or was going to make. I knew full well that the ocean didn't know or care if I was there or not, but its constant indifference was, at times, hard to take.

I needed something to cheer me up. Then I remembered the envelope that Ewen had given to all of us at the skippers' briefing containing details about our hosts, the Newport Yacht Club. Just like the rules, I had never thought to look at this. Perhaps there would be something positive in there, something to encourage me, to lift my spirits.

Inside the envelope were two letters. The first, from the Commodore, Norm Bailey, outlined the facilities of the club, useful phone numbers and a little about the club's long history. It was a warm, kind and understanding letter written by a man who clearly understood what an ocean voyager might be looking forward to;

'We have showers with lots of hot water and laundry facilities. A discounted bar and restaurant which serves excellent food… You are welcome… to use these facilities for as long as you want…'

I thought about that. I closed my eyes and imagined myself clean and fresh with a large meal in front of me; T-bone steak, with a generous knob of garlic butter melting on top of it, a baked potato with coleslaw and sweetcorn, onion rings, mushrooms, grilled tomato and a pitcher of beer! I pictured this man, Norm Bailey, and his friends and the Jester lads who had made it, all around me. We would all be telling tall tales… And women…!

Denis…! America has some of the most beautiful women in the world. Perhaps one of them would fall in love with my Scots accent and… well… who knows where that could go…?

'This is ultra-positive!' I shouted out, 'Bring on another storm… Get me to America!'

Greatly cheered, I read the next letter. Its tone was much more resolute and deliberate.

'If there is anything you need, if you need transport to buy food, fuel or equipment, or if you're in any kind of trouble, call me. I will be available 24 hours per day, seven days per week…'

A number was enclosed and the name, George Pike, was at the bottom.

'Well if I end up in jail I know who to call,' I thought cheerfully.

Then I re-read the name, George Pike, and I realised that this was the same man who had helped our Russian friend, Alexei Fedoruk, when his crippled yacht, *Fason*, had limped into Newport two years earlier. I thought,

'I'm looking forward to meeting you, George Pike.'

★

The two letters had brightened my mood and, to cheer me further, the following morning brought good wind and, an improved course. We were at last out of the Core. The Gulf Stream was losing its strength.

We sailed briskly under a foreboding dark sky. It felt good to be moving so purposefully and, as the morning wore on, the sky began to lose its grumpy look. I decided that we were in salad days again… without the salad! The sailing was excellent and my mood was bright. It felt good to be alive.

When the sun finally broke through, I arranged my wet books around the cockpit and let it do its radiant work. During the previous night, I had started this drying process by tying the hurricane lamp to the top of the cooker and arranging the books closely around it, with the open pages spread across the gimbals. Surprisingly, this worked well and as each book dried out, I moved it into my now empty vegetable locker, which was one of the driest places on the boat. This was immensely satisfying.

I decided to have another go at making bread. This time I cooked the dough in a frying pan rather like a large deep pancake. As it began to rise and brown, the smell of comfort and warmth spread across the cabin. I breathed it in deeply. It was sublime. This produced a loaf 9" round and 3" deep. There was sufficient dough left over to make a pizza which I cooked in the frying pan then flipped over. I topped it off with mashed sardines in sunflower oil, seasoned with lots of black pepper. I carried it through to the cockpit and ate it with a mug of white wine. Hot bread, sardines, wine, the sway of a purposeful boat, and a view to die for.

I savoured every moment of it.

I promised myself that I would make the loaf last for two or three days but in the end, the temptation was too great, my earlier privations too unkind. By evening, I had smothered the loaf in jam, and ate the lot!

★

Friday, 2 July. It was our 41st day out from Plymouth. At daybreak, our excellent winds deserted us and our speed through the water slowed to a crawl. I noticed that the servo blade from the steering gear was disengaged. The locking catch was damaged and the blade, instead of being vertical and deep in the water, was now horizontal and skimming along the surface. It was a simple repair. I took the blade off, drilled out the hole, put in a fresh rawlplug, screwed in the locking catch and reassembled it. By the time this was done, we were... becalmed.

I decided to make the most of it and, before too long, my bedding was hanging in the rigging being aired out, the last of my books were drying in the cockpit and I was as naked as the day I was born, having a cockpit bath. This time however, I washed myself and my laundry entirely with freshwater. I allowed myself this luxury as we now had only 400 miles to go to Newport, and 90 litres of water spread throughout the boat. Plenty by any standards.

Relaxing and sleeping, relaxing and reading, relaxing and eating, what else is there to do when there is no wind?

The next day was equally beautiful but I was starting to tire of it. What I really wanted was wind. I made another loaf, this time with molasses as I had no sugar left. The combination worked well and this cheered me for a while.

I considered running the engine but Newport was well beyond my fuel range and anyway I really wanted to complete the challenge under sail. No... I gritted my teeth and carried on...waiting. It was hard.

I wrote;

'I decided that this last third part of the voyage is as spiteful and as awkward as the first! A least we are not hove-to in a storm... Making equally little progress.'

That night, I brought out my CD of Billy Connolly. I put the disc into the portable player, slipped on the headphones and closed my eyes. I listened. I laughed and, as I did, I recalled the good old days and the great Glasgow people that I grew up with. I thought of Dad and Gran and Uncle Eddie and all the rest. Good times, so many good times.

As the CD ended. I sat for a while with my eyes closed... Missing them all.

'Come on! Time to switch on the Nav lights.'

I took off the headphones and as I opened my eyes, I found, that both my cheeks were wet.

20

The next day was 4 July. Whilst America was waking up to celebrations and parties, I began my day with a tin of mandarin oranges and a tin of custard. A welcome change from porridge. We were in light winds, so light that *Lizzie* ghosted along at an agonisingly slow pace. I tied out the sails with poles and preventers, and moved gingerly around the boat to keep her in balance. We kept moving…but only just! With every crawling mile being coaxed and manipulated, we were slowly getting closer.

The next morning at 08:30 hours, we wallowed to a halt, but this time, no amount of manipulation could drive *Lizzie* any further. We sat and waited.

Being becalmed was as hard on the soul as pounding to windward, or riding out a gale. After so many days of fickle light breezes, this new, total loss of wind, and movement, left me feeling cheated. But no amount of complaining made the slightest bit of difference. Mother Nature does not listen… does not care.

Sadly I wrote;

'I deliberately came north to be in the wind… But none to be found…'

I tried to keep a positive outlook and decided to have a shave and a cockpit bath. Then I tried fishing. No luck. I am the worst fisherman in the world. It was no use. We were becalmed and I was bored. I stared out at the ocean.

Then I saw a ship coming over the horizon, the mighty *Maersk Georgia*. She passed within half a mile, going west. I requested a weather forecast. She told me to expect fog and wind from the north later. Half an hour later another ship passed in the opposite direction, going east. I looked at the AIS and found another four ships displayed in my area but not yet in sight. It was starting to get busy.

Then it dawned on me. I had drifted smack bang into the middle of the New York to Europe shipping lane. Remembering the forecast given by *Maersk Georgia,* my last doubts about using the engine were removed. Without apology or delay, I reached for the keys and motored due west for two hours until we were well clear. But I was glad to switch it off again. The noise was giving me a headache. We returned to wallowing.

There were, however, two significant things I witnessed during our 10-mile drive. Three insects showed up. A butterfly, a wasp and a fly. Could they have come from the land?

The second thing of note was the water. For many weeks the sea had been a lovely sapphire blue. It was now a cool duck pond green. This must mean that I was finally out of the warm Gulfstream and into the cold Newfoundland current that comes down from the Arctic. This is where fog is formed, and here it is notorious for being deep and constant.

It wasn't long in coming and when it did, it hung heavily, like a damp shroud. Its colour ranged from bright white to every imaginable shade of grey. The heavy moisture content turned into tiny water beads on my clothes and worked its way through, soaking everything. Waterproofs had to be worn…in fog?

Although my AIS was on and working, I was painfully aware that only ships of 300 tonnes and more are required by law to transmit AIS signals. This leaves any number of smaller vessels, including fishing boats, that don't. I resolved to keep my eyes, ears and nose fully open.

In the days that followed, I spent hour after hour staring into the fog's cold empty soul, listening for the faint sound of an engine, or a throb or vibration that was mechanically made, sniffing the air to detect hot fragrant pollutants, the smell of exhaust fumes, anything that was different from the, by now, very familiar sights, sounds and smells of the seascape.

I had a foghorn which gave a good 'blood and guts' type of roar. It was loud when you were standing next to it, but would it be heard on the enclosed bridge of another vessel? I had my doubts. Nevertheless I kept it ever ready.

I wore a lifejacket constantly and kept my small panic bag strapped across my shoulder. My life raft was in the cockpit, untied and ready to go. My dinghy was part-inflated and tied loosely on the foredeck.

I heard somewhere that the Vikings believed that fog had mythical qualities, 'dragon's breath' or some such thing. When the fog came down, they put themselves into the hands of the gods and accepted their fate, death or glory. All very well for them, but those were real ships out there...somewhere. But, for all that, I was as well prepared as I could be. All I could do now was to keep watch. And trust in the gods.

21

My head and body craved sleep. I'd been napping whenever I dared; up and down every 20 minutes or so; keeping a lookout, staying prepared for whatever might happen. I couldn't afford to relax.

As we came past midnight and entered our 46th day, the fog lifted. From horizon to horizon it was clear and at last, I had an uninterrupted view of the stars and heavens above. We were under full sail and the wind vane was steering us nicely. The sea was calm with an oily swell and the gentle breeze was giving us 2 to 3 kn of speed, in the right direction.

I began to unwind mentally. It seemed like the right time to catch up on some rest, so after taking a good look around, I set the alarm on the AIS and turned in. My eyes closed and straightaway I fell into a deep, mind-and body-restoring sleep.

At 02.00 hours I was awakened by the angry little … Beep… Beep…. Beep… Beep… Beep of the AIS alarm. It was assuredly persistent.

I got up, stiff and slow, lumbered over to the control panel and switched off the alarm. I put on my glasses and looked blearily at the screen. 'What have we got here…?'

There was a ship at our 4-mile perimeter. I pressed the data button. It normally took a few moments for the data information to come through, so I climbed into the cockpit to have a look. No fog, it was still clear. To our left, coming up from the south-west, I could see the ship's Nav lights clearly.

She looked big. I looked around and another set of lights were on the horizon to my right. This was a much smaller vessel, maybe a fisherman or even another yacht… 'Maybe a Jester,' I mused.

I returned below. The data had come through. The ship was *'Sealand Racer.'* She was doing 19 kn and was smack bang on a collision course with us. I gave off a hearty yawn then got on the radio, '*Sealand Racer, Sealand Racer, Sealand Racer,* this is sailing yacht *Lizzie-G, Lizzie-G, Lizzie-G*…over.'

Sealand Racer replied and I went on, 'I have picked you up on AIS. We are on a collision course. I am directly in front of you four miles out. I am limited in my ability to manoeuvre. Can you please take avoiding action? Over.'

The reassuring reply came back, 'Roger that *Lizzie-G,* we have you in sight and on radar and will pass you to port.'

'Thank you *Sealand Racer,* I shall stand by on channel one six… *Lizzie-G* out.'

Lizzie and I had gone through this routine many times before. Ordinarily I would watch and wait until the ship had safely passed by but I was dog-tired and desperately needed to rest. It was a clear night. *Sealand Racer* had spoken to me, seen my lights, had me on radar and had agreed to alter course. The situation was under control.

I set the egg timer to 15 minutes and lay on the bunk. I put my head onto the warm pillow and draped the still warm sleeping bag over me. It was so comfortable. My little oil lamp was creating its warm restful glow and my eyes were heavy, so heavy. I began my downward spiral to the land of rest and relaxation, thinking, 'In 15 minutes I'll get up and reset the AIS alarm. *Sealand Racer* will be long gone by then… I must get up in 15 minutes…'

Then another thought - like a razor of lightning, flashed through my mind! What if it was not me on their radar screen…What if they were looking at the other vessel instead?

The one to my right. *Sealand Racer* will be racing towards me, right now!

My eyes opened wide, I threw off the sleeping bag and scrambled across to the AIS screen. There she was, less than a mile away, heading straight for us at 19 kn! I grabbed the mike, and this time all semblance of calm and order gone.

'*Sealand Racer, Sealand Racer*, this is *Lizzie G*. I am under your bows. We are about to collide. I am 0.8 of a mile directly in front of you. Please alter hard to starboard... Hard to starboard!'

I threw the mike down, grabbed the ignition keys and clambered into the cockpit. There was no time to lift the servo blade. If it got wrecked from our propeller wash then so be it. As I fumbled with the key I looked to my left. There she was, square on, looming large, with all three lights showing, red, white and green. I heard the radio comeback.

'Roger that *Lizzie G*. We are altering to starboard.'

I was too busy to reply. I put the ignition key into the switch. My hands were trembling. The thought ran through my mind. 'No time to pre-heat... I don't have 15 seconds to piss about with... Let's just rev up and fuck off as quickly as we can...'

I should have used the pre-heat.

'Chug... Chug... Chug, chug, chug.' The engine refused to fire. It was no use. It was too late anyway... I just stood there, staring helplessly as the great ship bore down on me. It was up to her now. The liferaft was at my feet. I wrapped the trigger cord firmly around my hand and resolved to hold tightly onto it whatever happened. If by some miracle we missed the propellers, there might still be a chance... Maybe.

I looked up again. I could see the red port light, but the green starboard light had disappeared. She was turning, but it was going to be close, much too close. I could hear her engines; smell the burning oil; feel vibrations through the air and water and see the great white foaming wash break off her bow.

It missed us but, as she raced by her turning action was sweeping her stern towards us.

The push of water from the side of the ship helped to fend us off. We pitched and tossed violently as the wall of steel careened past, blackening out the horizon.

As the stern quarter shot past we found ourselves, miraculously, in the wash of her mighty propellers, rolling on a calming slick, a sea of phosphorescence. We had survived.

The radio cracked into life and an anxious voice called out, '*Lizzie G, Lizzie G*, are you there…?' Then again - 'This is *Sealand Racer* calling *Lizzie G*… Are you there?' I clambered below, took a moment to wipe the disbelief from my face, and then picked up the mike, '*Sealand Racer* this is *Lizzie G*. Thank you for your avoiding action. We have successfully passed your port side… It was close but we are fine. No damage…Over.'

There were two or more persons on the bridge and there was a fair amount of alarm and consternation at our near collision. I had been right. It was the other vessel that had shown up on their radar screen, not me. From their bridge, with their great length and high bow, they had failed to see my tiny sailing vessel.

Someone's prompt action upon hearing my request for them to turn 'hard to starboard,' had undoubtedly saved my life, and themselves a lot of trouble.

I just know that on that night, I came as close as I ever have, to losing everything.

★

Within half an hour of *Sealand Racer* passing, the fog returned. I became a Viking again and so, with dragon's breath all around, I returned to my bunk. As I slept in that still, fog-drenched ocean with *Lizzie* eating up the miles at, 'Oh so slowly knots per hour...' I let the gods decide on glory or oblivion, with just one or two caveats. I left all my instruments switched on, with the noisy little alarm buzzer primed and ready to go, whilst above us the masthead Nav light shone out its hopelessly diffused red, white and green halo. I was extremely thankful that I still had a stout ship under me, and a good mast and rig above.

22

As the sun came up on our 46th day, the world turned from a dark mist to one of whiteness and the halo at the top of the mast became lighter and weaker.

I checked our position. We had 170 miles to go.

When preparing for the voyage, I had been asked many times about how long it would take. This was a difficult question to answer but when pressed, I settled on the idea that 40 days would be reasonable. Including the three days spent at the Azores, I was now, theoretically, three days overdue. Bearing in mind that I was alone, with nothing more to do than fret and worry about such foolish predictions, my thoughts now turned to my son, Mathie. In two days' time, 9 July, it would be his birthday. I could imagine him waking up, day after day and asking. 'Has Dad arrived in America yet?' Going off to school, coming home with his friends, always wondering… 'How much longer?'

The thought of him waking up on his 14th birthday with still no news, horrified me. Wouldn't it be wonderful if I could phone him on his birthday? What a joint celebration that would be. With these thoughts, 'The Jester Challenge' started to become 'The Matthew Challenge'. I had two days to cover 170 miles. Not impossible but…

★

At 10:00 hrs I picked up the *Queen Mary II*. She was passing a few miles to the south and her deck officer, in perfectly clear-toned English, gave me a precise weather report.

'Overcast, cool with fog clearing at times, flat sea with cats paws from the South bringing 2 to 5 kn of breeze, becoming variable.'

Sure enough the wind continued to drop and by noon we were making just 2 kn. We crawled on until late in the afternoon, and found ourselves smack bang in the middle of another shipping lane.

At 19:00 hours I wrote;

'I decided the only sensible thing to do is to motor through the shipping lane and head to the south-west edge of the Nantucket Shoals; there I will switch off the engine until wind comes to the rescue. If it is tidal and no wind, I'll put my anchor down.'

Then at 20:15 hours;

Engine off... We will sail... Suck it and see... No easy choices today and I will almost certainly miss the deadline for Mathie! I'm so disappointed.

But only 20 minutes later the fog started to lift and a light breeze came up from the East. I spread the full mainsail and head sail out in goose wing fashion and our speed gradually increased to 3 kn as, rocking gently from side to side, we headed west. We were on our way again.

As we moved into the early hours of Thursday, 8 July, our 47th day, we approached the relative safety of Nantucket Shoals, where big ships do not go. As we did so, I noticed that we were picking up more and more radio traffic. Distorted and broken at first, it steadily became clearer the further west we went, talking, shouting, laughing and cursing at each other. 'You son of a bitch... You're crossing my bows... Get to hell out of my way...!'

Who were they, and what were they up to... Why all this banter?

As we emerged from the fog, I found the answer. They

were fishing boats. I looked around and counted 13 sets of lights, some of them quite near. I put on the engine and motored briskly out of the way as one of them cut across my path. I rolled away the headsail to give me a clearer view. They were like dodgem cars in a fairground coming much too close and much too quick. All were trawling their nets, with wire cables strung on gantries, high and wide from each side of the vessel. Colliding with them would be fatal. *Lizzie* would be sliced straight through.

I got on the radio to announce my position but was completely ignored. This fishing fleet had their own language, rules over radio use, methods of manoeuvre and rules of the road - apparently, no rules at all. It was a free-for-all and we were stuck in the middle of it.

I put on all my Nav lights, tricolour, anchor light, steaming light, deck level lights… everything I had. The fog came down again and our vision shortened to 500 yards, then shorter still. The radio babble continued. I scurried below and turned the radio down. I needed to concentrate and their noise was off-putting. I grabbed my lifejacket, a signal lamp and a packet of biscuits, then returned quickly to the helm.

We motored along at 3½ kn, not too fast to run into trouble and not too slow as to be a sitting duck. Thankfully, the fog cleared a little and the breeze picked up. Ever mindful of our limited fuel supply, I rolled out the headsail and cut the engine. An hour or so later the fog came down a little closer… and closer still. The breeze held. I mumbled something that resembled a prayer and sailed on… 4 kn … Good speed.

After another hour, the fog cleared completely and I could see a bright sky full of stars, a clear horizon and - a fleet of fishing boats. I now counted 36 of them and they were closing in. I rolled away the headsail and started the engine again.

Red, white and green, I lost count of how many times I saw this combination coming straight at us, with those cheese wires on either side? As they approached, I would illuminate the mainsail. Sometimes they would turn and sweep away with comfortable ease, but mostly it was left to me to swerve and dodge to avoid the collision… only to find another set of lights coming my way. We worked on like this throughout the night, weaving our way through, always returning to our westerly course whenever we could.

At 06.00 hrs we finally broke through, and put them behind us. We were now in even shallower water, so shallow in fact that we came across one of their boats with her bow stuck high and fast on a sandbank. I could see one of the crewmen on deck. We were too small to offer any help and there was no indication of danger to the crew, but nevertheless I motored close, to about 20 m. The crewman looked up. We must have looked a curious sight out there, sailing along with our little red Ensign fluttering in the breeze. In the mayhem of everything that had gone on in the night, I had put up the 'red duster' as an act of defiance.

The man, incredulous at what he saw, pointed at me and shouted to his mate. 'What the hell… Do you see this guy?' At first I felt too aloof to bother to answer but then, the feeling came over me that I had achieved some sort of victory over this wild fishing fleet. Pointing at his upturned bow, I called over. 'You're not supposed to do that!' The crewman laughed and gave me the thumbs up. I responded by picking up a biscuit, showing it to him, then sticking it in my mouth.

★

Soon the fog returned, murderously thick, menacing and unwanted, but no matter, its ability to cause us harm had significantly reduced. I checked the radio. All I could hear was an occasional faint chunter. I studied the chart and double-checked our position. No obstructions or rocks lay in our path and the depth of 60 feet or so was too shallow for big ships or most commercial fishing vessels. The breeze was good too. I spread out the sails, cut the engine and on we went, sailing true and straight at 4 kn.

I wanted to stay up and keep watch but I had not slept for 20 hours and had been on my feet all night. Fatigue was biting hard and rest was an absolute priority. With a muddled mind, I checked and rechecked everything, I had to turn in!

We were Vikings again.

23

I slept for an hour at a time, got up, did my checks, and then turned in again. Tirelessly, *Lizzie* just kept on going. Six hours later I was much refreshed and we were 30 miles on. We had come through into bright, clear sunshine. The wind was still with us and *Lizzie* was bowling along like a racehorse at the head of the field.

Things were looking up. We were now 76 miles from Newport and it seemed that there might yet be a chance that we could get in on the following day, 9 July, Mathie's birthday. I yearned to pick up a phone and simply say. 'Happy birthday son.' The Matthew Challenge was definitely on. After eight days of variable light wind and four days of deep, fog-bound entrapment, it seemed that the broad Atlantic was finally opening up for us.

A fishing vessel came into view, the FV *Norseman*. I asked about the fishing activity at Nantucket Shoals. He explained that the grounds opened up on 1st July for just two weeks, and each boat with a licence, was allowed two visits. He explained that every boat from the East coast of America was converging there. I couldn't have picked a worse time to take my boat through.

★

As darkness fell, we were passing Martha's Vineyard. The shortest route was via an inshore passage between the main island and a small island outcrop called 'Noman's Land', but I didn't have a detailed chart. Further south lay deep water and a red navigational light to guide us past. We turned south, and aimed to pass as close as possible to that light.

As we pulled away, I could see distant fireworks going off. They were fantastic. It seemed strange because it was the last thing I was expecting to see at this point in my voyage. I treated myself to a glass of rum and, with a ringside seat in my very own cockpit, I sat down to enjoy the show. It felt good to be there. The fishing boat that had run aground and now these fireworks were physical proof that land was near.

Our long, slow voyage was coming to an end and, as I sat there, I found myself thinking way back to my early childhood - our deranged mother, Smilum, visits to Gran and Uncle Eddie. And then I remembered the day, when Dad and I were standing, holding hands at the bus stop. The day that I was saved, when my life began again, when Lizzie Gorman was allowed to be my mum. And I found myself asking, why had he looked so sober, so absorbed in his thoughts? Had it been foreboding, at the enormity of the task he had before him? The raising of three children on his own? Or was it bitterness towards his wife who had let him down so badly, or self-pity? If so, who could blame him?

However, none of these options seemed to fit. None of them rang true to the nature of the John Gorman I knew and loved. Then a new possibility occurred to me; perhaps, just as I was now, he had been thinking about his Dad ...and missing him.

Long after the fireworks had ended, I remained there, in the stillness.

I needed to lighten the mood. I switched on the radio in the hope that I could pick up an American station and sure enough there they all were. The first was 'Jesus 24/7 FM radio,' or some such thing. I enjoyed this, but after a few minutes I re-tuned. This time I picked up a suave, comfortable, confident and latently aggressive political channel. There were regular 'sponsorship interruptions', selling anything from powdered milk and diapers to cars and houses. The main agenda for the evening was New York's Mayor Bloomberg. After a while I laughed at the absurdity of it and turned it off.

We passed the red light at the southern edge of Noman's Land, so close I could touch it with a boat hook. In the distance, I could see the dark outline of the island, the first land I'd seen since we had left the Azores 30 days earlier.

★

We sailed briskly on throughout the night still under full sail. Sometimes goose-winging, other times broad reaching, constantly working to gain every bit of speed. In the early morning light, the wind began to slacken off. Slowly, as each hour passed our speed dropped off a little further until, at the very entrance to Narragansett Bay, it fell away completely.

We lay totally becalmed, in bright sunlight, still air and a mirror-flat sea. The impressive Newport Suspension Bridge was clearly visible. Just three miles ahead of us I could see the tiny white building known as Castle Hill, which marked the finish line. I looked at it for a few moments through the binoculars, then scanned the buoys that marked out the dangerous Brenton reef.

It was 12 noon on 9 July, Mathie's birthday. It would be 5 pm in England. I needed to get a move on and the only way I could do that, was to start the engine. But within the rules, I had no legitimate reason for doing so. I was in no danger. There was no emergency. Using the engine this time would be purely for my convenience. Had I come so far only to default within sight of the finish line? I reflected for a few moments. Then, smiling at the irony of it, I gave the engine 15 seconds of pre-heat and sparked her into life.

It was my son's birthday. That was reason enough for me.

Finisher Results

1st. Russian
Igor Zaretskiy, **The Grand,** *a Peterson 25, arrived on 26 June after passage of 34 days.*

Igor, an established yacht racing champion, took the northern route with the single-minded intention of winning and this he did in style. There was a true and funny story that when the Newport Yacht Club launch came out to meet him, the first thing he asked for was some tobacco. They had none and, so, as the launch crew put on a line to tow him in, he sprinkled some tea leaves into a piece of newspaper, rolled it up and smoked it. The Americans were horrified.

When I went on board Igor's boat for a tour, I asked him to show me his victuals, at which he opened a bunk locker and revealed an endless amount of identical tins with no labels. I asked Igor, 'What is in the tins?'

He replied in broken English, 'Cows and pigs.'

I then asked, 'Which one is cow and which one is pig?'

To which he explained, 'Both in same tin…'

Now I was horrified.

Ever quick to pick up the mood, this wonderfully devilish man went on to ask, 'You want some, I give you some now… You eat?' to which I insisted, 'Hell no, I would rather eat my arse.'

We both laughed. Igor had a great sense of humour. I gave him one of my spare hurricane lamps as a gift.

Igor. The man is made from girders.

2nd. British.

Rory McDougall, **Cooking Fat,** *a Wharram 21-foot Tiki catamaran, arrived on the same day as Igor and just two hours behind him.*

Rory took the southern route, a little to the south of the Azores. His frail, tiny boat turned out to be lightning quick. He beat the headwinds by regularly dropping his sails and deploying his parachute sea anchor to stop being blown downwind. In this way he never lost ground. When the depressions blew through, he would haul in his parachute then start sailing again, quickly, always quickly. Light wind posed no trouble to him at all as his unballasted little boat could progress in all but the faintest of breezes.

His boat was limited in its ability to offer shelter or carry weight; so, he virtually lived in his dry suit throughout the whole voyage and topped up his freshwater supply from rainwater he caught along the way. When he passed Castle Hill he had only 3L of water remaining. Rory knew his boat intimately. He had built her himself and spent six years sailing her around the world, albeit in more southerly Trade Wind climates. This tough Atlantic Challenge would be one of the hardest voyages of his sailing career.

He was due to depart on the day following my arrival. I pleaded with him to stay in harbour for another 24 hours. I wanted to know everything about his voyage but, alas, he was committed to go. We spent his last evening having a drink or two at the Newport Yacht Club bar. In the morning he took me on board and showed me his method of deploying his parachute. It would turn out to be an invaluable lesson. Rory took just 23 days to return home. Rory is happily married to Michelle and has two children, Josh and Sophie. They live in a modest house overlooking the River Exe where they still enjoy sailing *Cooking Fat.*

3rd. British

Roger Fitzgerald, **Ella Trout III,** *a Dehler 29, arrived on 27 June with a passage time of 35 days.*

Roger, at the charming age of 72, was the undisputed grandfather of the fleet. He spared himself no comfort and pushed *Ella Trout III* hard all the way across the pond only to be met with disaster at the very gates of Newport.

Roger had arrived at the entrance to the harbour in thick fog when suddenly, and for no apparent reason, all the electrical equipment shut down. This would turn out to be a minor electrical glitch but it happened at a critical time. Roger went on to tell me, 'I took my eye off the ball for just a minute. I thought we were holding a course to clear the Brenton reef when I went below to sort out my electrics... but, of course, *Ella Trout III* began to go off course and pick up speed. I had just got the electrics going again when.... Bang! We struck the reef and I was thrown right across the cabin.'

Ella Trout III was seriously damaged. Every moment on a reef is critical and Roger knew he had to act fast if there was any chance to save her. He immediately dumped the sails and started the engine in an attempt to reverse off but it was no good. He was about to get on the radio and call for help when a powerboat came close by and offered to put a line on him, which he immediately accepted. *Ella Trout III* was pulled off.

He went on to say, 'She bumped and scraped as she came off the reef. It was terrible. I felt so stupid. I felt as though I'd let her down...'

A call was placed to the Newport Yacht Club and their launch was immediately sent out to meet him. After such a remarkable voyage with such a talented and competitive skipper, *Ella Trout III* suffered the iniquity of being towed across the finish line. Ella Trout III was returned to England on the deck of a cargo ship where she was repaired and restored to full glory. In the fullness of time, Roger and *Ella Trout III* would go on to sail in other great races and challenges.

4th. British
Tony Head,* Triple Venture, *a 28-foot Twister, arrived on 4 July. A passage of 42 days.

Tony is a retired Royal Navy captain. He is modest, courteous, sincere, extremely knowledgeable and helpful. Everything he does, he seems to do with a competent degree of forethought. Tony had built *Triple Venture* with his two brothers years earlier. As time went by, the partnership reduced until Tony became the sole owner.

He was already a highly experienced offshore yachtsman when this Challenge came up and he tackled it with enviable relaxation, hosting regular blogs about his fine dining arrangements and daily sail plan. He would typically write.

'Today, chicken in white sauce with sweetcorn and pasta and a fine bottle of Sancerre… Wind is light from the North giving us a fine beam reach, a relaxing day and excellent progress.'

Norm Bailey, the Commodore of the Newport Yacht Club would later say to me, 'That guy Tony head is an impressive fellow. You know something… I read his blog every day and when he came into Newport, I swear I knew more about his voyage than he did!'

Whilst in Newport I had many social occasions with Tony and we each threw dinner parties on our boats. He is an excellent cook.

In 2014 I visited Tony at his home in Plymouth. I noticed on the landing wall a display piece commemorating his 2010 Atlantic Challenge. There are photographs of our friends at Newport Rhode Island and the wooden wind vane that had steered him both ways across the Atlantic. It was then I realised that Tony's voyage was every bit as hard as mine; he simply chose to play it down.

Tony still sails with *Triple Venture* and is a member of the Cargreen Yacht Club.

5th. Swiss.
Thomas Jucker, **Marta 28-foot (modern) Bristol Channel cutter. A passage of 42 days.**
(Thomas arrived soon after Tony, on the same day).

Thomas was probably the most experienced deep sea yachtsman among all of the Jesters in 2010. He was, by profession, a newspaper editor who had taken many breaks in his career to go sailing. He is polite, unassuming and generous.

As I got to know him, I began to understand the scope of his sailing ventures. He survived two hurricanes in the Pacific. He had run a sailing school in the Caribbean. He had also designed and built his own yacht, which he and his wife Irene had cruised extensively for many years. He had already crossed the Atlantic seven times before entering the JC.

Irene flew to America to join us. She worked for Greenpeace and I enjoyed learning all about the activities and issues that the organisation was involved in. She was so popular that, at the end of our many social occasions, we would gather around her and sing a rendition of the song, 'Irene'.

'*Good night Irene, good night Irene... I'll hold you in my dreams...*'

Having completed the task, Thomas sold *Marta* in America.

6th. Russian.
Michail Soldatov. **Gerda, a 27-ft Albin Vega (sister ship to Lizzie-G). Arrived on 6 July, a passage time of 44 days.**
I only met Mikhail briefly in Plymouth before the start of the challenge. He and his wife came on board *Lizzie*-G and I was about to show them around and offer them a drink, when I

was called to the companionway to answer some enquiries. Seeing that I was busy, Mikhail shook my hand, wished me a safe voyage and politely left.

It was a regret to me that I never got the chance to get to know him better. What I can say is that, like Tony Head, he was a retired captain, but from the Russian Navy. He took *Gerda* on the northern route. Upon arrival, he had her hauled out then flew home, most likely due to time constraints. It would appear that *Gerda* got him through the northern route without any damage. I was told that his intentions were to return in the following year to take her back to Russia.

7th. British.
Den Gorman, Lizzie-G 27-ft. *Albin Vega (sister ship to Gerda)*. *Arrived 9th July, passage time 48 days.*

Upon my arrival I immediately explained about the usage of my engine to get out of the great Eastern shipping lane, to clear the fishing fleet at Nantucket Shoals and to enter Newport. Nobody seemed to mind or make any kind of fuss over it.

Lizzie-G had not weathered the Atlantic gales well. Soon after my arrival, while my children were visiting, we cruised to a well-known holiday location, Block Island, a mere 20 miles away. On our return voyage the unfurled headsail split wide open. The roller foil, that we repaired in the Azores, had now disintegrated and needed to be replaced. There were other deficiencies. The main sheet, jamming block, headsail sheets and batteries were all shot and needed replacing. The cockpit lockers needed resealing. Then, by mistake, I blew the diodes on my alternator.

By the time my kids went home, time was running out. The hurricane season was coming close. Assuming I could clear this, there still remained the threat of strong and prolonged autumnal gales that frequent the Western approaches of the English Channel.

It was Thomas Jucker who calmly offered a wise solution, to leave the boat in America and do the return voyage the following year. I took his advice and Irene helped me to book my flight tickets. I stayed in Newport for five weeks.

In April 2011 I returned and stayed another five weeks before commencing my return voyage. Of all the JCs I believe I was the only one to have remained in the area for such a long time and to have cruised extensively around the Newport area, but I was not always alone.

In 2011 John Margarson flew out and joined me for two weeks and we cruised to New Bristol, Jamestown, Martha's Vineyard (namely Nemenska pond and Lake Tashmoo) and onto Nantucket. We also took a bus trip up to the once renowned whaling town of New Bedford and Fairhaven, where Joshua Slocum set out with *Spray* on his epic round the world voyage.

In many ways, my return voyage was as hard as my outbound journey. This time, I took a direct and more northern trajectory. I wanted to do the crossing without stopping and without using my engine at all. The most notable difference was that it was much colder. I never had the cockpit baths and it was too cold to make bread. The 15 kg of flour that I carried was never used until I returned home.

In this trip, with 400 miles remaining to Falmouth, I found myself in a position where *Lizzie-G* became unmanageable and I was forced to deploy a parachute sea anchor. The lesson that Rory McDougal had taught me in Newport became invaluable.

My return took 35 days.

8th. Australian.
John Apps. Glayva. UFO 27. Arrived 11th July.
John Apps is easy-going and affable with a friendly comfortable style, which is so typical of the Australians. John had competed

in the first 2006 outing and had been beaten back by severe weather and damage to his rig. However, in 2009 he undertook the voyage and successfully made the crossing.

Now in Newport for a second time, he was invited to the Lady Mayor's office and was given not one, but two medals of merit on behalf of the city of Newport. He responded by handing her a small cuddly toy of a koala bear, which she graciously accepted.

9th. Russian.
Alexei Fedoruk. Fason. *A 29-foot modified Olympic Class Dragon.*

Alexei showed up unexpectedly on 17 July. He had missed the start of the race because of the ice that had kept him bound up in Russia. He had previously come to Newport two years earlier and steered *Fason* into the harbour with a jury rig and jury steering. It was the generosity and kindness of George Pike and the patrons of the Newport Yacht Club that had saved Alexei from calamity.

George had managed to get free winter storage and a replacement mast for the boat for a mere $200. He organised a whip round and raised sufficient money to allow Alexei to fly home. Alexei returned the following year to complete his repairs and take Fason back to Russia.

In Russia the story had caught the public imagination and many articles were written about his voyage. Alexei had joined the 2010 JC for no other reason than to see George Pike again. He wanted to present him with a copy of a magazine in which he described George as 'My American Angel'.

Shortly after Alexei arrived, journalists from the Russian yachting fraternity appeared and took photographs and interviews of this meeting and presentation. There was no doubt that Alexei had a great fondness for George Pike and George, in turn, would have done anything to help Alexei.

Sadly, Alexei's voyage would end in tragedy. On the approaches to St Petersburg. Alexei had fallen asleep. *Fason* wandered off course and ran onto the rocks. His yacht was mortally wounded and Alexei was taken off. When he returned the following day to see if he could salvage her, there was nothing remaining.

However, Alexei would go on to fight another day and at the time of writing he is currently working on his next boat.

10. British.
Guy Waites. **Red Admiral,** *26-foot Contessa.*

Guy had been beaten back on our 2010 Challenge with storm damage that had caused his main bulkhead to split.

In 2011, in typically modest fashion, he had set off again and made it to Newport Rhode Island in a time of 43 days. He arrived with damage to his steering gear, a ruptured main water tank and strained rigging. *Red Admiral* was in dire need of repairs. However, a serious problem arose when he discovered that he did not have an American visa. He had simply overlooked this.

It was Norman Bailey who came to the rescue and, speaking to the customs official, he explained the situation. The customs man told Norm,

'I have a pile of paperwork on my desk and I shall put this file to the bottom of it, but in seven days' time it will be at the top, and it will be dealt with. Make sure your friend is away by then.'

Seven days was enough. Norm took Guy everywhere and anywhere to get whatever was needed and to get things done. They remain great friends to this day.

The Remaining Challengers

Andy Lane. *Amadeus*, a 21-ft Coco Class.

After a voyage of 24 days on 16 June, *Amadeus* was overtaken by a Force eight gale as he closed to within 52 miles of where the *Titanic* had sunk. It was approximately 3 o'clock in the afternoon when his mast came crashing down and one of the spreaders punctured the hull. *Amadeus* was mortally wounded and taking in water. Andy set off his EPIRB and prepared to abandon ship. Seven hours later the 600ft American ship, 'MV *Courage*', came into view and took him off. *Amadeus* soon foundered. Andy was landed in Antwerp, Holland.

Gus Davidson. *Just Right*. A 20-ft Gaff Rigger.

Arrived in Ponta Del Garda and retired due to the time taken.

Roger Taylor. *Mingming*. A modified 21-ft Corribee.

Although Roger had come across the start line with us, it was never his intention to sail to Newport Rhode Island. He had another mission in mind. He wanted to take *Mingming* on an observational tour of the north-west Atlantic between Greenland and Baffin Island. It was whilst in this area that he was knocked down by a rogue wave. Having been thrown across his cabin and having landed heavily, he found that he had broken a rib. In great pain and discomfort, he turned

Mingming around and successfully brought his boat back to Plymouth. His voyage was one of the inspirations that led to his third book, '*Mingming and the Tonic of Wildness.*'

Tim McCloy. *China Blue*. (Sister ship to *Jester*).
Tim had an ambition to sail across the northern route and make a hasty arrival at Newport Rhode Island. This would never come to pass. The weather in the Atlantic of 2010 was regarded as being quite severe by normal standards. Like me, Tim was forced to go south and here, he came up with an alternative plan. He would go the long way.

Tim sailed right down to the Canary Islands where he waited, then picked up the trade winds and went all the way to the Caribbean. From here he cruised north until he got to Bermuda. Having realised that he needed an American visa and that his had expired, he gave up on Newport and headed for home via the Azores. His Atlantic circuit took almost a year to complete!

Trevor Leek. *Jester*, a 25-ft modified Folk Boat.
Trevor took *Jester* north. He got as far as 360 miles to the north east of the Flemish Cap, looking for the Easterlies that would take him to America. Instead, he found himself confronted with strong headwinds and flat calms. In one four-week period he covered just 192 miles. He had to take into consideration that, with a crossing of 60 to 70 days, he had neither the time nor sufficient water supplies to continue. Reluctantly, Trevor turned *Jester* around and headed for home.

There is, however, another aspect to the story that I only found out after the event had wound down. It transpired that prior to our departure, Kia Easton came to QAB Marina and gave a package to Trevor. It was the ashes of Mike Richey. She asked if he could scatter them somewhere near to where the original *Jester* had foundered. Trevor, of course, obliged. He would go on to tell me, 'It was very emotional. It was a still calm day and I hove-to. I scattered Mike's ashes and then opened a bottle of wine. I poured a glass into the sea for Mike and another for King Neptune. The rest I sat and drank myself. A light wind came up but we stayed there for the whole night. As dawn broke the following day, I turned *Jester* around and headed for home.'

It was a fitting farewell to a great sailor.

★

Some accounts from our first gale

Rory McDougall and *Cooking Fat* (*Cookie*).

Rory and *Cookie* were, quite probably, the most audacious of all the entrants for the JC. His voyage was the most incredible.

His tiny catamaran is very light and has very shallow keels. Ordinarily, this type of boat would be blown downwind very quickly. They are known to have poor windward performance and cannot be righted when capsized. So what did Rory and *Cookie* do when the gales and big waves struck, and how did they cope?

Cookie avoided being blown downwind, avoided capsize and avoided the discomfort of attempting to fight the gales, by pounding to windward. She avoided this because Rory did something that was distinctly passive and well proven to him already.

Using her inherent hull form stability, sleek superstructure and hull shape, he would simply hove-to and let the wind and sea blow through and wash over his boat. If conditions deteriorated further, his next action was to drop *Cookie*'s sails and deploy his 8-foot parachute sea anchor with 200 feet of line off her bows. The seas might rise and tumble and break all around him but, as they did, his hulls easily sliced them, his decks easily drained them, the beams and the hulls easily flexed against them. The wind blew harmlessly over the small streamlined superstructure and through the modest rig.

Put simply, the sea never got a chance to get hold of the boat.

In the case of our first gale, Rory found that heaving-to was sufficient. Not wanting to complicate matters further, he proceeded to make himself a flask of cocoa. Once done, he then snuggled down into his warm dry bunk and read his book!

Roger Fitzgerald and *Ella Trout III*

Roger Fitzgerald, at the impressive age of 72, was the oldest and arguably the most competitive yachtsman amongst us. His boat was a rakish German Dehler 29 which vaunted a vertical bow line and wide flat bottomed transom. *Ella Trout III* was built for speed. She oozed with German efficiency. She was modern and clean, with smooth white mouldings and a light airy interior.

In a way, you would think that Roger and *Ella* were a mismatch. You might expect a white-haired bespectacled London-accented Yorkshireman to smoke a pipe, complain about the youth of today, and have an older, more traditional type boat. Something with a wooden hull, gaff rig and heavy spars. Something heavy and laborious, slow but dependable. However, what you find with Roger was quite the opposite. He was by nature more akin to Francis Chichester than to Denny De Souter. He loved the thrill of fast sailing and big challenges. He had a motivation that would put to shame many a man half his age.

Roger was always cheerful and friendly and sociable. He liked to laugh. He was labelled 'The Grandfather of the fleet', not only by merit of his age, but also because of his doting family. Roger had a wife and three daughters and numerous grandchildren. When in harbour, he could be seen with his brooding family fussing around him, and he, in turn making time for each of them. It was obvious that they would worry about him but Roger never seemed to worry about anything. To me, he seemed completely relaxed about crossing the Atlantic.

As expected, *Ella Trout III* got off to a good start, however things were not all going Roger's way. Two days into the voyage, he began to feel the effects of flu, which he thought may have come on board from one of his many visitors. Soon after, the full-blown effects became apparent; Roger began to suffer headaches, nausea, aches and pains and a severe loss of appetite. By the time the gale struck, Roger described himself as feeling, 'Bloody awful!'

He said, 'As the gale was getting up I prepared to go on deck and reef down when I was thrown across the cabin... I smacked my head onto the bulkhead and ended up cutting my head and had a nosebleed at the same time. My glasses broke too, there was blood everywhere and I couldn't see what I was doing...'

Typically, Roger cleaned himself up then reefed *Ella Trout* down. Unlike most of us, he never thought there was a need to heave-to and never considered retirement. He just kept going.

Scott Turner and *Altamira*

Scott was approximately 50 miles behind me and had experienced the same conditions as *Lizzie-G*. As conditions deteriorated around him, *Altamira* was broached and his wind vane self-steering gear was ripped off the transom. Without this gear engaged and working effectively, *Altamira* was crippled and became wildly out of control and at risk of capsize. Scott kept his cool and successfully brought *Altamira* under control and hove-to.

With water constantly breaking over his cockpit and his bilges flooded, he braved the elements and worked at trying to retrieve his steering gear which was still attached to the boat by steering lines. It was no use. In those conditions, it was much too heavy to pull back on board and, besides, it would be nigh on impossible to reattach it to the transom when the gale passed.

There was another pressing problem. The loose gear had protruding steel rods and these were now banging against his hull. It was only a matter of time before they smashed through. Scott knew that if he cut his steering gear away, his Atlantic crossing would be over and his return to England would be very difficult. He was by now over 300 miles offshore but, in reality, he had no choice. He cut the lines and let his wind vane fall away.

When the gale passed, Scott turned *Altamira* back towards Plymouth. His return voyage took six days, steering by hand, day and night, with only short periods of snatched sleep until he brought her safely into port. Scott's Atlantic Challenge was over but he had made a very good account of himself. When I think of Scott Turner, I think he had the heart and spirit of a champion and, when the time came, his courage was intact and his seamanship was sound.

A very good lad.

Bill and *Belgean*

Bill Churchouse was 200 miles west of the Scilly Isles. Initially, the gale did not present any significant problems to him. He and *Belgean* had been through many before and Bill knew exactly what to do. However, calamity struck when he was on the upper deck at the fore ends. In the process of reefing in his jib, a sudden combination of movements threw him off balance as a wave broke over the deck.

He was washed off the boat.

Bill was attached by his harness and a 9-foot lifeline. Some might scoff at the idea that a lifeline should be so long as the current belief is that a lifeline should be short enough to hold you onto the deck of the boat if you are knocked over. However, Bill had a method to his madness. Bill knew his boat. Every curve, angle and shape was as familiar as a maiden to the hand of her lover. Like a mountain goat on a familiar path, he could work his way around her decks in daylight or darkness with equal aplomb.

He had gone as far as to experiment with his son on the helm as he deliberately went over the side in Poole harbour. He conducted this experiment with the traditional short line and then with his preferred longline which was a 3 strand rope with a 1" diameter. This allowed him to lock the rope off around the stays and deck cleats as he worked forward and aft, along the deck.

With a long line he found that, once overboard, he could twist and turn sufficiently to gain a bodyboard attitude as he was pulled through the water. Coupled with this, the thickness of the rope, and its 3 strands, gave him what he called a 'grabbable diameter', to haul upon. In calm sheltered waters, this practice worked fine but here, in the wild Atlantic his contingency plan was put to the test.

He told me, 'When I went over the side, the first thing that hit me was the shock of it all, then the coldness of the water. Incredibly, my glasses stayed stuck to my face as the force of water pressed them on. I began to swallow lots of water and I felt myself being pulled under and pressed up against *Belgean*'s hull...' He went on,' ... I could feel myself beginning to panic, I thought to myself, I'm going to die.'

Bill resisted panicking and managed to pull himself to the

surface. By now, he was choking and spluttering, blinded with the press of salt water on his eyes. He felt too weak to pull himself back on board and, for several minutes, he held onto the rope.

He was hanging off the port side, his harness rope was locked around a deck cleat which had tethered him to a point just forward of the mast and the main superstructure of the cabin. This put him in an ideal position at the lowest part of the freeboard just aft of *Belgean*'s pug-nosed bow. There he waited until *Belgean* lent him a helping hand. As they lay beam on to the sea, she crested and tumbled off the top of a large wave. Here *Belgean* listed heavily to port, dipping her sides down low enough for Bill to reach in and grab a handhold. As she righted herself, Bill held fast and was pulled halfway onto the boat. With one last frantic effort, he managed to clamber aboard. Now gasping for breath and quivering with cold and shock, he worked his way back to the cockpit, whereupon he tumbled in, and vomited.

Bill had survived but it had been a close call. He owed his life to his equipment, his training and his cool thinking. Bill, too would, retire from the Atlantic. Eight days later, he dropped his anchor at Penzance. Bill was weak and sick but in the following weeks he went on to make a full physical recovery. What took longer was his mental state. In his dreams the shock, cold, gushing pressure, retching and sickness and gut-wrenching fear would revisit him. In the year that followed, Bill had many abrupt awakenings and sleepless nights as in his slumbering mind he was transported back to the day when he was washed off *Belgean*, back to those few minutes when he hung between life and death on the end of a rope.

The damage however, was not permanent and Bill and *Belgean* recovered. At the time of writing, they are preparing for another crack at the Atlantic.

Guy Waites and *Red Admiral*

Guy was an enigma to me. I'd seen his name on the entry list and found a very professional web page about him and the refitting of his yacht *Red Admiral,* a Contessa 26.

I had wanted to meet him but, due to various delays, Guy had failed to reach Plymouth in time to attend the briefings and skippers' dinner. He arrived at QAB Marina a day after we had set off across the start line.

It must have been a great disappointment to him but he wasted no time in lamenting over it. *Red Admiral* had a number of deficiencies to be put right and so he spent the next couple of days working on the boat and resupplying her with food, fuel and water. Within 48 hours of his arrival, he had slipped his lines and was underway.

Guy is a tall, lanky and unassuming fellow. Polite and gentle and predominantly vegetarian. He is a lover of yoga and can spend hours in meditation examining the peaceful sanctuaries of his existence. Those who do not know him could be forgiven for not recognising the true inner mettle of the man. He certainly does not display it and he is a man without any boastful or self-praising qualities at all.

At the time of our first gale, he had made good his delay and was 150 nautical miles to the west of the Scilly Isles when the first part of a two-part calamity struck. Whilst beating to windward, *Red Admiral* fell off a particularly large wave. As she raced down she ploughed her bow deep into the back of the next wave. The effect of this caused a massive punishing compression along the length of the hull as Red Admiral was arrested to a dead stop in the water. The following wave then rolled over the length of the boat and compressed the deck.

Something had to give. Guy described, 'I felt the pressure run over and through the boat and then a loud horrible cracking and splintering noise from down below, and I knew, that was not good!'

The noise was the splitting of the main bulkhead, leaving the deck beam bending and flexing with every twist and compression of the hull. Guy hove-to and set to work making repairs.

The only available strong timber he had was the bilge locker lid, which he hammered into place between the main bulkhead and the forward bulkhead, thus creating a bridging piece. This would keep the main bulkhead directly under the deck beam where it would support the deck and mast.

The repair looked good and Guy continued with the voyage. Six days later, whilst pushing to windward at an impressive 4½ kn with three reefs in the mainsail and up against another gale, *Red Admiral* smashed catastrophically into another wave in a near identical incident. This time, there would be no repair or question about continuing on. The main bulkhead, which was made from half-inch mahogany marine plywood, split right across the width of the boat and collapsed. Without this support, the deck above was flexing and the mast which stood on it was in danger of falling off the boat.

Guy had no choice but to retire. In his own words he described it as, 'Game over.' At the time, he had reached 24° west, 900 miles into the Atlantic. Nursing his boat, it would take Guy 14 days, with a favourable Gulf Stream and following winds, to reach the safety of a British port.

He would live to fight another day.

John Margarson and *Fluffy*. – Thomas Jucker and *Marta*
Right from the start, I had John Margarson pegged as a potential winner. His boat was an out-and out racing machine and, together with John's experience and robustness, it seemed like a winning formula.

As we came to the start line, it was John and *Fluffy* that stretched out in front, making seemingly effortless progress while the rest of us wallowed and struggled to make any advance in the fickle breezes. John's knowledge and experience of sailing was unquestioned. Another Beneteau Figaro, a sister ship to *Fluffy*, had been sailed across the Atlantic successfully by Eric Andlaur in the 2006 JC, one of only two yachts to complete the voyage from a total of nine entrants that year.

A racing yacht, such as *Fluffy*, would, without question, require more careful, thoughtful handling than a steadfast, heavy, long keel traditional type yacht. Even so, Eric had proven that she could go up against Atlantic weather and still make a safe, fast passage to Newport. Or so one would think.

The first gale struck our little fleet on Friday, 20 May, our sixth day out from Plymouth. By this time, John was on target to win having covered 800 nautical miles. He was ahead of the fleet by a good margin, with almost a third of the distance covered. So far everything had gone in his favour and all to his advantage. *Fluffy* was in her element producing her best qualities when the winds were light. Now, however, the Atlantic was showing another side to its personality. Being so far out, John found himself in the epicentre of our gale.

Thomas Jucker, 200 miles behind, described it as, 'Among the worst weather that I have ever seen, with constant breaking waves everywhere...'

For Thomas and his hardy, heavy, long-keeled Bristol Cutter, it presented no significant problems. He simply reduced sail, battened down, then hove-to. He spent the gale snug and warm in his bunk whilst *Marta* cradled him safely as she wore the day and night out.

John had no such luck. As soon as the wind began to rise sharply, *Fluffy* began to run out of control and at the critical moment, as John tried to pull in the roller furler, to reduce his headsail, the rope jammed within the drum. Try as he might, this would not budge and *Fluffy* sped off at hair raising speed of 14knots plus... in the direction of Greenland!

John was in a desperate situation and needed to get *Fluffy* under control. He went forward to attempt to free off the drum and struggled for almost an hour while the sea repeatedly washed over him. All the while, the headsail was flogging itself and threatening to pull the rig apart.

Eventually, he managed to pull out enough rope to unlock the jam and no doubt thought he might yet get it wound in, when, another disaster struck! The headsail, by now, had taken a huge amount of punishment and, at its midriff, split right open from end-to-end. John wound the tattered sail in. With just a deep-reefed mainsail remaining, his attempts to bring *Fluffy* under control failed. She would not slow down or heave-to.

He resorted to another tactic, letting her 'run-off'. It was a hair-raising white knuckle ride and in his journal he recorded '… regular dangerous lurches in excess of 35 to 60°'.

John was, by now, out of options. He was cold, wet and exhausted and suffering from hypothermia. He knew his race was over but worse, as night fell, the gale reached Storm Force proportions. John knew that he might not survive. He dumped his mainsail onto the deck and 'lay-a-hull'.

Shivering cold and with a numbed mind, John went down below and fastened down the hatch. Fluffy had over 10 inches of water slopping around the floor. With her rounded hull and flat bottom she had no bilge for water to drain into and this made it impossible to pump out. The water sloshed from side to side always evading the sucking end of the bilge pump, which was at the midsection. *Fluffy*'s cabin was stark, cold, wet, noisy and lurching. She was in constant danger of inversion.

John wrapped his arm around the inner chain plates and held on. Incredibly, in amongst this cacophony of noise, disorientation and misery, he had had the presence of mind to write some notes in his journal. His last thoughts of the day were to Isabella his wife of some 30 years.

He wrote:

My Darling Isabella my love,

You have been a very good wife and have made me very happy. Thank you for being my lovely wife. You must go on now.

All my love John.

Hypothermia is as insidious as it is deadly. As Navy divers, we were taught to look out for it and recognise its symptoms. The body tries to warm itself by shivering then, as the body core becomes cold, the shivering stops and the mind of the victim begins to wander. Logical thinking and the ability to act rationally quickly diminish.

John put his notes and letter to Isabella in a Tupperware box. That was probably his last rational act. Thereafter he stripped off all his clothes until he was completely naked, and climbed into his bunk. He had no sleeping bag or blanket. And so, with the world around him going to hell in a basket, John did the one thing that a victim of hypothermia must never do. He closed his eyes and fell asleep.

John survived the storm and the cold and made it through the night. The following day he turned *Fluffy* around and headed for home.